THE COMPLETE IDIOT'S GUIDE® TO

Guitar

WITHDRAWN

by David Hodge

ALPHA

A member of Penguin Group (USA) Inc.

Making music is about sharing one's life and emotions. Teaching music is perhaps even more so. This book is dedicated to my brother, Tom Hodge; my best friends, Laura Pager and Greg Nease; and especially to my "partner in everything," Karen Berger. All have shared more with me than I can ever hope to do in my lifetime, and all continually make me a better teacher, musician, writer, and human being.

ALPHA BOOKS

Published by the Penguin Group

Penguin Group (USA) Inc., 375 Hudson Street, New York, New York 10014, USA

Penguin Group (Canada), 90 Eglinton Avenue East, Suite 700, Toronto, Ontario M4P 2Y3, Canada (a division of Pearson Penguin Canada Inc.)

Penguin Books Ltd., 80 Strand, London WC2R 0RL, England

Penguin Ireland, 25 St. Stephen's Green, Dublin 2, Ireland (a division of Penguin Books Ltd.)

Penguin Group (Australia), 250 Camberwell Road, Camberwell, Victoria 3124, Australia (a division of Pearson Australia Group Pty. Ltd.)

Penguin Books India Pvt. Ltd., 11 Community Centre, Panchsheel Park, New Delhi—110 017, India

Penguin Group (NZ), 67 Apollo Drive, Rosedale, North Shore, Auckland 1311, New Zealand (a division of Pearson New Zealand Ltd.)

Penguin Books (South Africa) (Pty.) Ltd., 24 Sturdee Avenue, Rosebank, Johannesburg 2196, South Africa

Penguin Books Ltd., Registered Offices: 80 Strand, London WC2R 0RL, England

Copyright © 2010 by David Hodge

International Standard Book Number: 978-1-61564-021-8
Library of Congress Catalog Card Number: 2010903640

12   11   10   8   7   6   5   4   3   2   1

Interpretation of the printing code: The rightmost number of the first series of numbers is the year of the book's printing; the rightmost number of the second series of numbers is the number of the book's printing. For example, a printing code of 10-1 shows that the first printing occurred in 2010.

Printed in the United States of America

Note: This publication contains the opinions and ideas of its author. It is intended to provide helpful and informative material on the subject matter covered. It is sold with the understanding that the author and publisher are not engaged in rendering professional services in the book. If the reader requires personal assistance or advice, a competent professional should be consulted.

The author and publisher specifically disclaim any responsibility for any liability, loss, or risk, personal or otherwise, which is incurred as a consequence, directly or indirectly, of the use and application of any of the contents of this book.

Most Alpha books are available at special quantity discounts for bulk purchases for sales promotions, premiums, fund-raising, or educational use. Special books, or book excerpts, can also be created to fit specific needs.

For details, write: Special Markets, Alpha Books, 375 Hudson Street, New York, NY 10014.

Publisher: *Marie Butler-Knight*
Associate Publisher: *Mike Sanders*
Senior Managing Editor: *Billy Fields*
Acquisitions Editors: *Karyn Gerhard, Tom Stevens*
Senior Development Editor: *Phil Kitchel*
Production Editor: *Kayla Dugger*
Copy Editor: *Krista Hansing Editorial Services, Inc.*
Cover Designer: *Kurt Owens*
Book Designers: *William Thomas, Rebecca Batchelor*
Indexer: *Julie Bess*
Layout: *Brian Massey*
Proofreader: *John Etchison*

Contents

Part 1:   The First Steps of the Journey 1

1   Getting Acquainted and Getting In Tune 3
Your Instrument of Choice...3
   A Quick Show of Hands...4
   The Three Guitar Families.......................................4
   A Brief Introduction to Guitar Anatomy 5
Getting In Tune...7
   Naming Notes..7
   String Names 8
   Using a Guitar Tuner 8
   Tuning to a Keyboard or Piano................................10
   Tuning to Yourself 11
Practice, Practice..11

2   Warming Up One Note at a Time 13
Posture and Position 13
   Sitting 13
   Standing 14
Right Hand 15
   Using Thumb and Fingers 15
   Picking a Pick 15
   Proper Picking 16
The Left Hand 16
   Thumb Position and (Not) Gripping........................17
   Fretting Notes..18
A Quick Look at Guitar Tablature 18
   Warming Up 19
Practice, Practice..20

3   And Now, a Few Chords 21
Chords and Chord Charts 21
   Translating Grids into Chords..................................22
   Your Very First Chord 23
The Simplest Chord Change..23
   A Chord of a Different Color 23
   Smoothing Out the Changes....................................24
   What Not to Practice 25
A Few More Chords 25
   A Minor 25
   A Major 26
Your First "Official" Song 26
Practice, Practice..27
   Making Chord Changes 28
   Moving Your Fingers as a Unit.................................28

4   Learning to Read Rhythms............................ 29

Finding Your Pulse..29

The Big Problem with Tablature 30

Music Notation 31

From the Staff to Your Frets.................................32

Accidentals 33

Rhythmic Values of Notes..33

Chords in Notation and Tablature.............................34

Tying Notes Together..34

Rhythmic Notation..35

Adding Some Pizzazz 36

Root Notes and the "Boom-Chuck".......................36

Alternating Bass Notes..38

One Last Visit with Tom 39

Practice, Practice 40

5   Learning to Play Rhythms 41

The Sock-Puppet Approach...41

Counting by Four..42

Strumming by Eight..43

Skipping Along 43

Missing Downs 44

Practicing Rhythms...45

The Myth of "Strumming Patterns" 47

Working the Banana Boat 47

New Chord—B7...49

Practice, Practice 49

Part 2:   Making Great Progress!...........................51

6   Swinging with the Blues 53

Triple Time..53

Playing Triplets 54

Swing Eighths..55

Shuffling Along 55

Double Stops 56

Blues Shuffles and Rock Shuffles............................57

Some More Seventh Chords 58

The D and D7 Chords 59

The Complete Idiot's Blues (Take 1) 60

Stretching Out the Shuffle 61

The Complete Idiot's Blues (Take 2) 61

Some Quick Changes and a New Voicing 63

Practice, Practice 63

7   Stretching Out with Three New Chords............. 65

Stretching Out...65

The C Chord..66

C Chord Alternating Strums and the C7 Chord 67

The G Chord 68
    More G Options 69
    G and the Alternating Bass 69
Changing G to C 70
    Let Your Fingers Do the Walking 70
    Adding the D or D7 72
    Handsome Molly 72
One Tough Chord 74
    Working the Half Barre 74
    Viable Options 75
    Walking C to F and Back 76
Rowing the Boat Ashore 76
Practice, Practice 78

8   Making Your Guitar Sing with Slurs **79**
Introducing Slurs 79
The Mighty Hammer-On 80
    Saving Grace 82
    Fret-to-Fret and Multiple Hammers 83
Pull-Offs 84
    Multiple Pull-Offs 85
    Combining Hammer-Ons and Pull-Offs 85
Slides 86
Bends 88
Putting It All Together 89
    Wayfaring Stranger 91
Practice, Practice 94

9   Strumming by the Measure or by the Note **95**
Three's a Crowd 95
    Dots 95
    Basic 3/4 Strumming 96
    Adding an Alternate 97
    "The Streets of Laredo" 98
Charting the Pulse 99
    Six Eight 99
    Changing on the Fly 100
Arpeggios 100
    "The House of the Rising Sun" 101
    Mixing Things Together 103
Practice, Practice 104

10   Stop and Go **105**
Further Subdivision 105
Making a Rest 107
Rests as Rhythm 108
    Left-Hand Muting 108
    Palm Muting 109
    Percussive Stroke 110
"The Gallows Pole" 111
Practice, Practice 114

11   Finger Picking in Style **115**

Pick a Finger 115

Revisiting Arpeggios *117*

Pinches and Pedals *118*

Basic Travis Picking 119

Being Contrary and Picking Parallel........................ *120*

Pinching Mr. Travis *124*

"The Cruel War" *126*

Practice, Practice 127

Part 3: Learning a Little Local Lore **129**

12   A Major Step Forward **131**

The Steps (and Half-Steps) to Building Scales.........................131

The Major Scale *133*

Scales by the Dozen *133*

Open and Closed Scales 134

Closing Positions *134*

Moving Around the Fingerboard................................ *135*

Root 5 Major Scales *136*

Walking in Steps 137

Putting Scales into Chords *138*

"Oh! Susanna" *139*

Practice, Practice 142

13   Building Chords from Scratch **143**

An Interval on Degrees..143

Triads 144

Building Four Basic Chords with Thirds *145*

Chords Without Thirds.. *146*

Sixths, Sevenths, and Beyond 148

Five Sevenths... *148*

Beyond the Octave *149*

Slash Chords 150

Practice, Practice... 151

14   Barre Tending **153**

Getting Ready to Barre.. 153

Half a Barre.. *153*

Four, Five and Six Strings... *154*

Full Barre 154

Name That Chord! *155*

"Down by the Riverside"..*155*

Cheaper by the Dozen 158

"Motherless Children"... *158*

Turning Barres into Slashes and 5s *160*

"Jesse James" *160*

Practice, Practice... 162

15 Using Your Intelligence **163**

The Key to Keys 163

Twelve Major Keys.. 163

Pallet of Chords.. 164

Minor 166

Harmonic Minors 166

Melodic Minors 167

Starting to Put Pieces Together 167

Connecting the Dots 167

Chord Embellishment and Substitution 169

"John Barleycorn" 169

Partial Barres 172

Thumb Wrap 172

Practice, Practice 172

Part 4: Exploring Even Further **173**

16 Clipping on a Capo **175**

Transposing 175

Secret Decoder Ring... 176

Concentrate on the Roots 177

Playing with a Capo 177

Raising the Chords 179

Applying the Math 179

Doublespeak 179

Capo Considerations 180

"Make Me a Pallet" 180

Making a Second "Pallet" 182

Practice, Practice... 184

17 Beyond Standard Tuning **185**

Standards Within Standard 185

Lowering One's Standards 186

Heavy Flopping 186

Drop D 187

"Tanz" 188

Rock On 189

Open Season 189

Finding Oneself in Uncharted Territory 190

The Keith Richards Sound 190

But Wait! There's More!.. 191

Alternate Reality 192

"The Lakes of Pontchartrain" 192

Practice, Practice 197

18 Filling In the Blanks.. **199**

Fills and Riffs 199

Gather 'Round the Chord... 200

Anticipation 200

Playing Around Some More 201

Where to Fill and What to Use 201
   The Pentatonic Scale *201*
   The "Easy Fill" Solution *202*
   Fitting In *204*
Revisiting the Blues..204
Moving Minors About 206
   Blue Notes and the Blues *206*
   "Midnight Special" *207*
Practice, Practice 210

19   Bringing Melody and Chords Together **213**
Anatomy of a Song 213
A "Twinkle" in One's Eye 214
   The Basic Model *215*
   Second Time Around *216*
Harmony in Pairs 217
"Beautiful Dreamer" 218
Practice, Practice 220

20   Making a Solo **221**
The Creation Process 221
Phrases and Phrasing 222
   Rhythmic Templates *223*
   Adding the Guitar's Voice *224*
   A New Addition to Bends *225*
Scaling the Fingerboard 226
   Taking a Position *226*
   Getting Shifty *229*
   Third and Fourth Phrases *230*
Thinking and Feeling 233
Practice, Practice 234

21   Picking Up Speed **235**
Flat-Out Flatpicking 235
   More Finger Picking *236*
   Alternate Picking *237*
   "The Temperance Reel" *238*
Picking Up Clues from Tablature 239
Crosspicking 241
Hybrid Picking 242
Picking with Fingerpicks 243
Practice, Practice 243

Part 5:   Cool Places to Visit **245**

22   A Little Country **247**
"Four Nights Drunk" 247
   Sustaining Interest *250*
   A Long Walk *251*

A Little Western with Your Country...................................251

A7 to D in Harmony Pairs 252

"Home on the Range" 253

23   Rock Solid **257**

Driving a Song 257

Giving Punch to Power Chords 258

"Whiskey in the Jar" 259

24   Blues in the Night **267**

Typical Blues Song Structure 267

Blue Notes, Blues Scales 269

"Complete Idiot's Blues" (Take 4) 270

"Saint James Infirmary" 271

25   The Classical Touch **275**

Studying the Studies 275

"Study by Giuliani" 277

Bach in a "Minuet" 278

26   Some Folks Say **281**

"Greenland Whale Fisheries" 283

"Scarborough Fair" 286

27   The Wearing of the Green **291**

"Paddy Whack" 291

Hammering Out a Celtic Mood..292

"The Irish Washerwoman" 293

28   Jazzin' It Up **297**

Going Comping 300

"Take Me Out to the Ballgame" 300

29   Pop **303**

"Piano Style" Guitar Playing..303

"The Water Is Wide" 304

"Julia and John" 306

Appendixes

A   Directory of CD Tracks **311**

B   Chord Charts..**313**

C   For Further Study **317**

D   Glossary **319**

Index **325**

Introduction

You don't know it yet, but you are about to totally change your life. If you've never played a musical instrument, you're about to discover the joy and satisfaction of making music, and to learn that playing guitar is easier than you might have imagined.

The guitar is an incredible instrument, capable of playing soft, quiet lullabies as well as rocking and rowdy sing-alongs. It can be strummed, providing rhythm and chords to accompany a singer. Whether you're in the mood for something by Bach or the Beatles, Johnny Cash or Johnny Rotten, the Kingston Trio or the Killers, the guitar will be able to make the music you want to play.

It can also be a one-man band, providing melody, basslines, and harmony for any song. Just because you don't (or don't want to) sing, that doesn't mean you can't let your guitar sing for you. The musical repertoire of the guitar goes back almost 500 years and includes classical works, traditional folk music, flamenco, blues, rock, and more.

And there's no end to the musical arrangements you can create for the single guitar. You'll hear ancient Irish dances and Appalachian fiddle tunes played with dazzling speed by bluegrass guitarists, while jazz players can make an old pop standard sound absolutely magical on a single guitar.

The joy of playing the guitar, of creating music and sharing music with your family and friends or with total strangers, is one of the most amazing and satisfying feelings you will ever experience. And it becomes more satisfying as you learn more about your instrument and as you develop into a better musician.

Why This Book Is for You

The Complete Idiot's Guide to Guitar is a step-by-step guide designed to get you started playing. It is a book for a total beginner; even if you've never held a guitar in your life, you will be able to read this book and jump right into playing music.

"Step-by-step" is slightly misleading. Learning any musical instrument—almost anything, for that matter—is rarely done in linear fashion. Given that a book is, by its nature, totally linear and the pathways between each aspect of learning the guitar are tightly interwoven, it's impossible for any one single book to cover everything.

What *The Complete Idiot's Guide to Guitar* does is get you *playing* songs. If you've read any of my previous books or lessons (both online and in magazines), you know that my core philosophy is that music is meant to be played and shared. For instance, playing the arrangement of "Oh! Susanna" in Chapter 12 of this book teaches you about the practical uses and implications of the major scale instead of just lecturing you about why it's important for guitarists to know.

Learning chords and strumming and various guitar techniques, and then playing songs you know that incorporate what you've learned, is probably the most effective method to start playing guitar. And that's what *The Complete Idiot's Guide to Guitar* offers you.

What You'll Find in This Book

The Complete Idiot's Guide to Guitar is set out in 29 lessons—chapters, if you prefer—that are arranged in five general parts.

Part 1, The First Steps of the Journey, starts you on your lifelong musical adventure. You will learn how to tune your guitar; learn how to read chord charts, guitar tablature, and basic rhythm notation; and start playing songs immediately. You will also pick up some very simple guitar techniques, like the alternate bassline, to make your strumming sound great right from the start.

Part 2, Making Great Progress!, builds on your initial steps by teaching you blues and rock rhythms, as well as teaching you how to use guitar techniques like hammer-ons, pull-offs, slides, and bends to add more flair to your strumming. Plus, you'll get chapters covering arpeggios and basic finger-picking technique.

Part 3, Learning a Little Local Lore, gives you an easy introduction to music theory and also shows you why it's important through practical applications like forming barre chords. In this part, you'll pick up the basics you need to start creating your own song arrangements, as well as the techniques needed to play solos and chord-melody-style guitar.

Part 4, Exploring Even Further, does just that by introducing you to transposing and using a capo to create more interesting chords and finger-style guitar. You also get to visit some of the many possibilities of alternate tuning and learn about creating fills, solos, and single-guitar chord-melodies. Add a chapter on bluegrass-style crosspicking, and you'll find that you've covered a lot of ground.

Part 5, Cool Places to Visit, looks at specific musical genres, as well as the typical guitar techniques you're likely to encounter playing these styles. You'll get a hearty sampling of country, rock, blues, classical, folk, Celtic, and jazz music, and you'll even dabble a bit in pop.

At the end of the book, you will find four helpful appendixes: a track listing for the CD that accompanies this book, charts for chords, a list of books and other tutorial material that you'll probably find useful as you continue to grow as a guitarist, and a glossary of guitar and music terms.

Practice, Practice

You'll also find a section in each chapter in the first four parts labeled "Practice, Practice." Here you'll get practice tips to help you make the most of that particular chapter's lessons, as well as general practice advice that you can use anytime.

Sidebar Icons

You also find even more advice and useful information in the numerous sidebars found throughout *The Complete Idiot's Guide to Guitar*. Four types of sidebars occur in this book:

DEFINITION

These provide definitions and details about various musical terms and specific guitar-playing techniques.

SOUND ADVICE

These give you advice on various topics, from playing chords, to practicing, to working out rhythm, and many other subjects and techniques you read about.

KEEP SHARP!

These offer guidance to keep you from developing any bad habits that will hinder your playing abilities in the future.

 LISTENING LIBRARY

These direct you to songs and artists worthy of your attention, particularly when it comes to a specific style or technique.

Using the CD

Throughout this book, you'll find an icon that looks like this:

This indicates that the example is on the compact disc included with this book. The first track is a tuning track, and you'll find audio examples for most of the exercises in this book. Many of the exercises and examples in the book are on the CD as well. Much of the CD is devoted to the various songs that you use as examples in the chapters of the book.

In keeping with the "beginner philosophy" of this book, we've gone out of our way to keep these tracks simple and clean. The guitar (Lowden O Series) is recorded clean, using microphones instead of an internal pickup.

Many thanks go to Todd Mack and Will Curtiss of Off The Beat-n-Track Studio in Sheffield, Massachusetts, for their invaluable assistance in putting together, mixing, and mastering the CD. This is the third book I've done with Will and Todd, and each time they surpass their previous efforts. It's an honor to have their talents and assistance, and I can't thank them enough for their work in helping produce the music for this book.

Some Notes About the Songs

Owing to copyrights, all the songs you'll find in *The Complete Idiot's Guide to Guitar* are traditional songs in the public domain. But that doesn't mean you're going to find them dull and ordinary! These songs were selected because most of them have been covered by some of the great guitarists and performers of our time, artists as diverse as Paul Simon; Eric Clapton; Neil Young; Bruce Springsteen; James Taylor; Led Zeppelin; Nirvana; Metallica; Johnny Cash and his daughter, Rosanne Cash; Leadbelly; the Grateful Dead; Mick Jagger; Tori Amos; David Bromberg; Eva Cassidy; Steve Winwood and Traffic; the Animals; Peter, Paul and Mary; the Kingston Trio; Harry Belafonte; and more.

The songs have been arranged to teach specific guitar techniques and styles—so when you listen to "Jesse James" in Chapter 14, for example, you'll hear a bit of Springsteen's version, but you'll also get a bit of how a group like the Band might play it as well.

I'd like to give a special acknowledgment of thanks to Leslie Ann Maxwell, who spent a great deal of time and effort assisting me with both the selection and the researching of these songs. Thanks go out as well to the many members of the Guitar Noise community who made numerous song suggestions, many of which were ultimately used here.

Since the guitar often accompanies a singer, many of the song examples were sung. All but one of those (my own piece, "Julia and John," in Chapter 29) were performed by my good friend Nick Torres, who deserves more praise than I can possibly give him. As these songs were arranged in specific keys to teach specific techniques and ideas, Nick's task was to make them work whether they were in his vocal range or not. Both his singing and his creative interpretive abilities far exceeded my expectations, and I hope you enjoy his talents as much as I do.

One last note about these songs: as of the time I write this, Alpha Books is in the process of creating a comprehensive, interactive website where you can find even more practicing ideas and suggestions and more details on various guitar techniques, as well as tips on buying guitars, changing strings, and other great information on the care and upkeep of your instrument. Go to www.idiotsguides.com and click on "Book Extras" at the top of the page.

I'll post all news about the book as it becomes available. You can also leave messages about both *The Complete Idiot's Guide to Playing Rock Guitar* and *The Complete Idiot's Guide to Playing Bass Guitar.*

Let Me Know What You Think

You can use my website to contact me directly with any questions you may have about this book. You can also e-mail me anytime at dhodgeguitar@aol.com. I try to answer every e-mail, but sometimes with my teaching schedule, I fall a bit behind. Rest assured that every e-mail gets read, and each one is appreciated. I will do my best to reply to you as soon as possible. I look forward to hearing from you and to hearing how things are going with your guitar playing! As a teacher and a writer, your thoughts and opinions are not only appreciated, but usually quite helpful.

I hope you find playing the guitar and making music as much fun as I do. I also hope that one day I have the honor of hearing you play!

Peace.

Acknowledgments

First and foremost, I want to thank my agent, Marilyn Allen, as well as Karyn Gerhard of Alpha Books, for making this book a reality and for choosing me to write it. Special thanks also go to Alpha's Tom Stevens, Phil Kitchel, and Kayla Dugger for all the time and energy (not to mention enthusiasm) that went into this project. And to all the rest of the team at Alpha, including Marie Butler-Knight, Mike Sanders, Billy Fields, William Thomas, and Rebecca Batchelor, whom I can't thank enough for their collective efforts in creating this book.

A big tip of the hat must also go to Paul Hackett, the creator of Guitar Noise (www.guitarnoise.com), who took me on as a writer back in 1999 and who has been one of my biggest supporters ever since. Through Guitar Noise, Paul introduced my writing and teaching to the world, and it still blows my mind to think that people in places like Singapore, Peru, Turkey, and hundreds of other countries have learned guitar in part from my lessons.

Any guitarist learns much about playing from playing with others, and from the very start I have been honored to know and become friends with hundreds of people through playing music. I can't begin to list them all, and I'm sure I couldn't do so without making omissions! But I'd like to thank Glen Russell, Bill Hendrickson, Chris Stephens, Paul Contos, Roy Wogelius, Kyle Roth, Bill Supplitt, Randy Skigen, John Matsuura, Rod Del'Andrea, John Patterson, Randy Farr, Dan and Laura Lasley, Mike Sexton, Anne O'Neil, Jeff Brownstein, Pete Mazzeri, Paul McKenna, Tony and Joe Nuccio, Rich Schroeder, Kathy and John Reichert, Mike Roberto, Chuck Yoder, Helena Bouchez, Jamie Andreas,

Tom Serb, Tom Hess, Michele Wells, Andrew DuBrock, Nicole Solis, Phil Catalfo, Dan Gabel, Fred Schane, Claudia and Sean Barry, Joel Schick, Sammy Brown, Phylene Farrell, Cathy Dargi, Patti White, Tracy Wilson, Sandy Moderski, Kathy Manship, Pam Foster, Josh O'Gorman, Darrin Koltow, Alan Green, Tim Bennett, Graham Merry, Marilyn Miller, Glen Polson, Lisa Paris, Shaun Buckler, and Todd Lange for everything they've done to make me a better teacher and writer.

Finally, I'd like to especially thank the four people to whom this book is dedicated for the strength, guidance, and friendship each has given me throughout my life. To my youngest brother, Tom, who put up with a lot of loud practicing and musical get-togethers; to Laura Pager, whose encouragement and friendship kept me going through every tough time I ever faced; and to Greg Nease, who also serves as technical editor on *The Complete Idiot's Guide to Guitar* and has been a continuous musical companion for two thirds of my life, I offer thanks and more.

And to Karen Berger—my "partner in everything," my home and my center—where do I even start? None of this happens without you, and none of it matters without you.

This list of acknowledgments doesn't even begin to cover the people I've met and the friendships I've made through music. I could easily spend a whole book just writing about that.

Special Thanks to the Technical Reviewer

The Complete Idiot's Guide to Guitar was reviewed by an expert who double-checked the accuracy of what you'll learn here, to help us ensure that this book gives you everything you need to know about playing guitar. Special thanks are extended to Greg Nease.

Trademarks

All terms mentioned in this book that are known to be or are suspected of being trademarks or service marks have been appropriately capitalized. Alpha Books and Penguin Group (USA) Inc. cannot attest to the accuracy of this information. Use of a term in this book should not be regarded as affecting the validity of any trademark or service mark.

The First Steps of the Journey

It all begins right here. First you learn how to get your guitar in tune, then you learn how to properly hold it, and then you start playing!

After getting your fingers limbered up with some warm-up exercises, you'll learn to play your very first chord (and also how to read chord charts!)—and before you know it, you'll be playing some songs.

You'll also learn how to strum chords with good rhythm and discover how a few easy techniques, like the alternating bassline, along with some simple strums, can make you sound like you've been playing guitar a lot longer than you have.

Getting Acquainted and Getting In Tune

In This Chapter

- Guitar anatomy
- How a guitar makes notes
- The names of musical notes
- Standard tuning
- How to tune with a tuner
- Other methods of tuning

You couldn't have made a better choice! Few things in life compare to the joy of making music, and the guitar is an ideal instrument to make music with, whatever your musical dreams may be. Would you like to play some down-and-dirty Delta blues? How about a bouncy Celtic jig or a bluegrass tune that will get everyone's toes tapping and hands clapping? Maybe a breathtakingly beautiful romantic melody is more your style? Some swinging jazzy number, perhaps? Even just sitting around a campfire and singing old favorites with your friends is a lot more fun if you're strumming a guitar.

Playing the guitar is an adventure that will last a lifetime, not to mention seemingly endless musical roads to travel and explore. And it all starts right here!

Your Instrument of Choice

The guitar has a long history. Its lineage can be traced back from its current incarnation to the Spanish *vihuela* of the 1500s, to the various *guitarra* (around 1200), to the European *lutes*, to the *ouds* of the Moors, and even back to the *cithara* of Ancient Rome.

You might think that, with all this history and evolution, the guitar would have settled into a rut, but it is still the primary instrument for many genres and styles of music, from classical, blues, folk, country, and pop to jazz, flamenco, rock, heavy metal, punk, reggae, and so much more. One of the coolest things about learning to play the guitar is that you will never run out of new things to learn!

LISTENING LIBRARY

You can learn a lot about the guitar's history even in this digital age. Start with lute music on CDs, such as *The Golden Age of English Lute Music,* an excellent collection of recordings by Julian Bream, one of the greatest classical guitarists of our time. You'll find plenty of oud music as well, such as *Oud Masterpieces: from Armenia, Turkey and the Middle East,* by Alan Shavarsh Badrezbanian.

Right now, though, you want to get started with the basics. And regardless of the type of music you want to play or the type of guitar you have, learning the guitar starts at the same place. You want to learn about the various parts of your instrument so that you have a frame of reference when you start on technique. And then you want to tune your guitar correctly.

A Quick Show of Hands

It also helps to know *how* you want to play guitar—right-handed or left-handed. Generally, if you're right-handed, you play guitar right-handed as well, meaning that you strum with your right hand while your left hand frets notes on the neck of the guitar. You may think your dominant hand should do the fancy playing on the neck, but the truth is that your dominant hand should do the very important job of keeping rhythm.

Playing left-handed, it's the other way around. Your left hand strums, handling the vital rhythm duties, and your right hand works on the neck.

If you're not sure which way you want to play, give yourself a simple test: pick up a broom or anything close at hand, without thinking, and pretend to play. You can even just play air guitar—the point is to do so without thinking and see what your natural inclination is. If you're strumming with your right hand, play right-handed. Play left-handed if you automatically start strumming with the left hand.

To keep things simple, this book assumes that you, like most people, are and will play right-handed. The strumming hand will be referred to as the right hand and the fretting hand as the left hand. Those of you who are left-handed have been left-handed long enough to be able to deal with this!

The Three Guitar Families

Most guitars can be put into three distinct categories—classical guitars, *acoustic* guitars, and electric guitars. *Classical guitars* are the grand patriarch of the guitar family, direct descendants from the first six-string guitars, which began to appear at the very end of the 1700s. They have nylon strings instead of steel strings. Their tops and sides are often of the same woods (or laminates) as many acoustics, but the classical guitar is typically slightly smaller than the average acoustic guitar (particularly the dreadnought style).

> **DEFINITION**
>
> Technically, the term **acoustic** applies to any guitar that is not an electric guitar. However, the convention nowadays is to use the term *acoustic* to refer *only* to steel-string flat-top guitars, thus separating the acoustic guitar from both the classical and the archtop (used primarily for jazz).

Classical guitars also have a wider fingerboard than the normal acoustic, allowing for easy spacing of fingers on the frets, and slightly shorter necks; the fingerboard joins the body at the twelfth fret instead at the fourteenth, as most acoustics do.

SOUND ADVICE

The top of a guitar is the side that faces the audience when you play it. That's where the sound hole (or pickups on an electric guitar) usually are. The back of the guitar faces your abdomen. The guitar's sides connect the top and bottom.

Acoustic or *steel-string guitars* are far and away the most popular guitars, and there isn't a musical genre in which you won't hear someone playing one. Whereas classical guitars are almost all identical in appearance and shape, acoustic guitars come in many subcategories.

The top and back of typical acoustic guitars and classical guitars are flat. But there are archtop guitars whose tops and backs are arced like the bodies of violins. They also have "f" shaped sound holes (again, like a violin) instead of the round sound holes of the standard acoustic or classical guitar.

SOUND ADVICE

Most guitarists prefer to have solid wood tops instead of wood laminates (a top made of thin sheets of wood pressed together). The tops of most acoustic guitars are spruce, although the specific types of spruce can vary. Cedar is also used quite a bit for the tops of guitar bodies, particularly on classical guitars and acoustic guitars marketed to finger-picking players. Cedar is softer than spruce and scratches very easily.

Electric guitars are the brash kids of the family. They come in two main types—solid body and hollow (or semi-hollow) body. It's impossible to think of music today without electric guitars. You'll hear them in rock, blues, jazz, country, and just about any type of music you can think of. Electric guitars also usually have very narrow fingerboards, and the strings are much lighter than those of an acoustic.

Some acoustic guitars are fitted with pickups so that they can be plugged in to an amplifier or directly into a PA system without the need of a microphone. These are called "electric/acoustic" or (surprise!) "acoustic/electric" guitars.

You can play almost any kind of music on any kind of guitar—you just have to know that the music is going to sound different depending on the guitar you play. Traditionally, nylon-string guitars are used for classical music or flamenco music (there are flamenco guitars, too, which are smaller, lighter versions of the classical), but you'll hear them in jazz, Latin music, and pop as well.

A Brief Introduction to Guitar Anatomy

Some guitars look wildly different, but they usually have the same basic components. The following illustration details the vital parts of your guitar, whether it is an acoustic or electric model.

Most guitars can be divided into three main sections. The headstock is the "top" of the guitar, if you will. This is where you'll usually find the tuning pegs and tuning mechanisms of your guitar. One end of each string is attached to the guitar at this end.

The neck is the area between the headstock and the body. Here the guitar's strings run the length of the fingerboard (sometimes called the fretboard because it's where the frets of your guitar are). This is where your left hand is most of the time.

The body is the bulky part of the guitar, where you'll find the bridge and saddle (where the strings are attached at this end of the guitar). The body of an acoustic guitar is essentially a hollow resonating chamber that projects the sound of the vibrating strings directly from its top, as well as out through the sound hole. The body of an electric guitar houses the pickups and other electronic hardware that converts the string vibration into an electric signal that is sent out to the amplifier via a cable connected to the guitar's output jack. The body is the section of the guitar over which you'll be picking or strumming the strings.

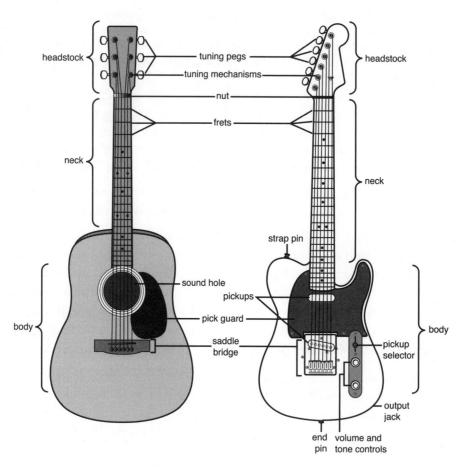

The essential parts of your guitar.

That picking or strumming of the strings gives the guitar its voice. A number of strings (usually six) stretch from the bridge/saddle area of the body to the tuning mechanisms in the headstock. Essentially, you pick a string, the string vibrates, and the sound comes out of the guitar—through the sound hole on an acoustic guitar and through the amplifier if it's an electric.

Of course, there's more to it than that. A string's length and mass (typically expressed as its "gauge") and how tightly it is stretched (tuning "tension") determines a string's specific note, which is sounded when you pick, strum, or pluck the string. You change the note produced by a string by placing a finger along the fingerboard and pressing that string down against a fret. That changes the vibrating length of the string and thus its pitch (note). The shorter the vibrating length of the string, the higher its pitch.

Getting In Tune

You can also change the note of any given string by how you tune it. Turning the tuning button so that it tightens the string raises the pitch of the string. Turning it in the other direction loosens the string, which lowers the pitch.

You can tune your strings to almost any note you'd like; however, to learn the basics of guitar, you want each string to be tuned to the same notes most other guitars are tuned to. This is called *standard tuning*. When your guitar is in standard tuning, you have a point of reference for everything from reading music to making chords to playing the cool riffs from your favorite songs.

Of course, to tune your strings to the correct notes, it might help to know a little more about the names of notes and how they relate to each other. You'll delve deeper into this subject in Part 3, but for now, here are some basics so that you can start making music.

Naming Notes

Notes in music are given names of the first seven letters of the alphabet, going from A to G as you go higher in tone. When you reach G, the note names cycle around again, so A is the note after G, but that A is at a pitch (vibration frequency) one octave higher than the A that started the sequence:

A   B   C   D   E   F   G   A   B   …

You can begin counting off notes anywhere as long as you keep them in order. For instance, you could begin with C, like this:

C   D   E   F   G   A   B   C

So far, so good, but, of course, there is a slight catch! Five additional notes fall "between" some of the others. These are called *accidentals* and are labeled as sharps (♯) or flats (♭). Each accidental shares a name with another. The accidental between C and D, for instance, can be called either C♯ or D♭.

DEFINITION

Notes are musical sounds or tones, as well as the symbols used to indicate such tones. In Western music (meaning music of the Western Hemisphere), there are 12 different musical notes.

Adding these five to the original seven, they are arranged, from low notes to high notes, like this:

C	C♯/	D	D♯/	E	F	F♯/	G	G♯/	A	A♯/	B	C
	D♭		E♭			G♭		A♭		B♭		

String Names

Your guitar has six strings. That seems simple enough, but naming and numbering the strings often causes initial confusion. You may think you should count from the top, but the "first" string is the thinnest one, on the bottom, and the "sixth" string is the thickest. It's easier for most people to think of strings in terms of pitch. When you hold the guitar, the low string, meaning the sixth (thickest) one, is the one closest to you when you look down at your guitar. The high string, the first (thinnest) one, is closest to the floor.

SOUND ADVICE

It's important to know your string names, so take a moment to learn them. Some people use mnemonic phrases, like "**E**at **A** **D**arn **G**ood **B**reakfast **E**veryday," to remember which notes to tune to. "**E**ddie **A**te **D**ynamite **G**ood **B**ye **E**ddie" is a phrase that everyone seems to remember!

As a beginner, you want to have your guitar in *standard tuning*. That means that the notes you want to tune to, from the lowest (the sixth or thickest) string to the highest (the first or thinnest) one, are E, A, D, G, B, and E. Notice that the first and sixth strings share note names. When you strike them together (after they are properly tuned!) they sound somewhat similar, although the first string sounds higher than the sixth.

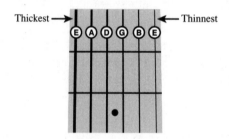

Notes of your guitar strings in standard tuning.

Using a Guitar Tuner

If you have a guitar tuner, getting in tune is very easy. You just turn on your tuner, strike a string, see how that string compares to the note you want to tune to, and then tighten or loosen that string's peg. Some guitar tuners are set specifically to each string of the guitar and, when you play each string, indicate whether its pitch is sharp (higher) or flat (lower) in relation to the note you want. Your tuner probably displays this by means of a virtual meter (where you normally want the pitch indicator—the meter's needle—to line up in the middle of the range on the screen) or by colored lights that show when your string is in tune. Some tuners use both types of displays. There are even tuners that will beep to indicate that you've gotten the string in tune.

SOUND ADVICE

Buying a guitar tuner along with your first guitar is a very smart investment—probably the best $20 or so you'll ever spend. With a little care and occasional batteries, it will last a lifetime and make tuning your guitar a snap. You'll find many different brands and makes of tuners out there, so it's good to know exactly how yours works. Have your friendly music-store person demonstrate its operation on your guitar before you leave.

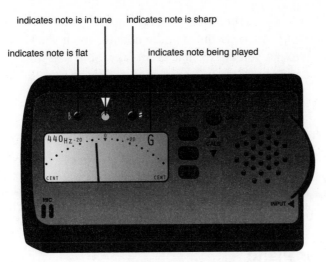

A typical chromatic guitar tuner.

Place the tuner close to the guitar (on your knee works nicely), turn it on, and then strike the sixth, or low-E, string (the thick string closest to you) with either a pick or your thumb. Be sure to strike just the one target string.

Many tuners are chromatic tuners, meaning that when you strike a string, the display screen shows you the name of the note you're playing and then you adjust accordingly. So if you're trying to tune the sixth string to E and the screen says you're on D♯ or E♭, then you are flat, or too low, and you should turn the tuning peg so that you're tightening the string and raising the note. If your tuner reads "F," "F♯," or even "G," then your string is sharp, or too high, and you want to loosen the string.

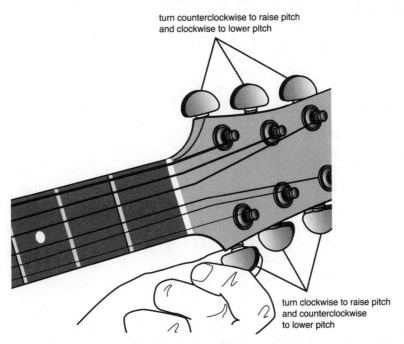

Turning the tuning pegs.

When you tune your strings, it's best to tune them *up* to the proper note. If you tune down to get a note, the natural tendency of the string and, consequently, the note to which you've tuned, is to continue to loosen—not a lot, but enough to put you out of tune eventually. So if you find that a string is higher than it should be, loosen the string to *below* the note and then tighten it to the proper note. This helps the string stay in tune.

 Track 01

For your convenience, the first track of the CD that came with your book is a "tuning track." You'll hear each string, from the lowest to the highest, played one at a time, so you can make sure you're in tune.

But you probably do want to get a tuner. Carrying around the CD all the time, not to mention something to play it on, isn't the best thing to do at your first gig or open mic!

Tuning to a Keyboard or Piano

If you have a piano or keyboard at home (or are playing someplace that has one), you can tune your guitar to it—provided you know where the notes on the piano are!

This method of tuning isn't always as accurate as using a tuner (not all pianos are in tune!), but if you're playing with a keyboardist, you should tune up to them. Fortunately, it's fast and simple. To help, here's an illustration showing how the notes of the open strings of your guitar correspond to those of the piano:

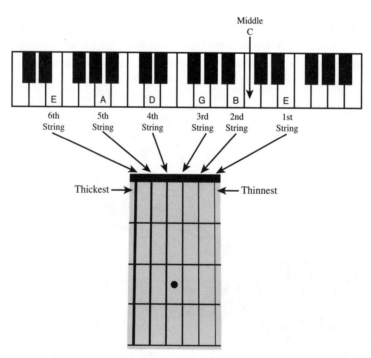

Notes of your guitar strings in relation to those on a keyboard.

 KEEP SHARP!

Some people use pitch pipes as a tuning aid, primarily because they're cheaper than electronic tuners. This is fine, but be sure to have the pitch pipes tested first at the music store against an electronic tuner. Occasionally you might buy a set of pitch pipes that aren't in tune to start with!

Tuning to Yourself

If you know that one of your strings is in tune, you can tune the others by means of *relative tuning*. You can find each note of your guitar in multiple places on the neck, except for some of the highest notes on your first (thinnest) string and those played on the first four frets of the lowest (thickest) one.

Remember the chart of all 12 notes?

C   C#/   D   D#/   E   F   F#/   G   G#/   A   A#/   B   C
        D♭   E♭   G♭   A♭   B♭

Each of these notes is a musical half-step away from its neighbor, and each fret of your guitar is a half-step. So when you place a finger on the first fret of your low-E (sixth or thickest) string, you change the note from E to F. The note at the second fret is F# (or G♭, if you prefer), and so on. Here is a fretboard map to show you all the notes along the neck of your guitar, from the open strings to the fifth fret.

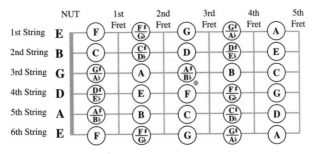

Notes up to the fifth fret.

This means that the note at the fifth fret of your low-E string is A, which is the note of your open fifth string—the A string.

So once you've gotten your sixth string in tune, you can match the tone of the A note at the fifth fret to that of the open string and adjust it accordingly. Likewise, the note at the fifth fret of the A string is D, and the note at the fifth fret of the D string is G.

B, however, is just four half-steps higher than G, so you match the open B string to the note at the fourth fret of the G string. Finally, you match the open high-E (first) string to the note at the fifth fret of the B string to finish getting your guitar in tune.

Practice, Practice

Your ears are possibly the greatest asset you can have as both a musician and a guitarist. And simply listening to your guitar as you tune is a great start. Use the relative tuning method, even when you're tuning with a tuner, to test your ears. Can you hear when a note is sharp or flat? Can you hear when two notes are in tune with each other?

As you'll learn in the next chapter, it's easy to accidentally put a note out of tune by fingering the fret incorrectly. So listening to what you're doing right from the start is a good way to give your ears some practice.

The Least You Need to Know

- The basics of learning guitar are the same for both acoustic and electric guitars.
- The three main parts of a guitar are the headstock, neck, and body.
- Being in tune is the key to sounding good.
- In standard tuning, your strings, from low to high, are tuned to the notes E, A, D, G, B, and E.
- A chromatic tuner is a very helpful device and should last for a long, long time.

Warming Up One Note at a Time

In This Chapter

- The importance of posture
- Holding your guitar while sitting or standing
- Positioning the right and left hands
- Playing single notes
- Understanding guitar tablature
- Warming up

Once you're in tune, you're ready to start playing your guitar. But even though all you want to do is to grab the neck with your left hand and bang the strings with the other, there's more to this than just using your hands. Your whole body goes into playing guitar. That may seem obvious, but it's very important to remember.

Posture and Position

Start by getting loose. Roll your shoulders and shake out your arms and hands. Even though you're trying something totally new, you want to be as tension free as possible. Being relaxed means sitting or standing in the best possible position for playing. It makes all the difference in getting good, clean notes. Posture plays a big part in this. Whether sitting or standing, keep your back straight so that your arms and hands are loose and free.

Sitting

Your fretting hand should be about chest high so that it can move freely along the neck.

When you're sitting, the guitar usually rests on your right leg (unless, of course, you're left-handed). Be sure to keep the neck of the guitar elevated; your left wrist should be able to stay relatively straight.

KEEP SHARP!

Don't use your left leg as a "wrist rest" and hold the neck of your guitar as if it were a TV remote. This makes it difficult to place your fingertips cleanly on the strings. Wearing a guitar strap, even when you're sitting, helps you keep the neck of the guitar up where your hand can best finger the frets.

If you have a classical or folk-style acoustic, you might try using the classical position, resting your guitar on your left leg and using a small footstool to elevate your left foot. Having the neck raised at a sharper angle puts your fretting hand in better position than the regular sitting position.

The "regular" and "classical" sitting positions.

Standing

When playing standing up, you still want to give your fretting hand the best possible position for playing the strings, so don't hold your guitar so low on your body that your wrist is doing contortions just to fret a note.

Holding the guitar higher may not look as cool, but if you're playing the notes you want, you shouldn't worry about how you look! When you get better at playing, you'll be able to play with your guitar slightly lower on your body. If you can play well, people won't care how you hold your guitar.

guitar too low   optimal guitar position

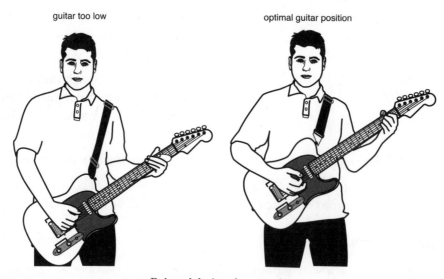

Do's and don'ts when standing.

Right Hand

Your right hand is responsible for picking or strumming the strings and for keeping the rhythm, so you want your arm free and loose. Your right hand should naturally find itself just over the sound hole of your acoustic or classical guitar. Depending on the style of electric guitar you play, it will be around the middle but slightly to the neck side of the body of the guitar.

You can strum or pick the strings with your thumb and fingers, or use a pick. Both methods are fine and each produces its own sound. Some players never use picks and some rarely use their fingers, and you may develop a preference for one or the other. Still, it's best to try both and to explore the different sounds and feels of each. We cover techniques for both styles later, so don't begin by limiting your choices.

Using Thumb and Fingers

Generally, you use the side of your thumb for downstrokes when strumming. You can angle your thumb so that you use the tip, but that becomes fairly awkward when you're playing even a simple rhythm.

LISTENING LIBRARY

Many guitarists never, or rarely, use a pick, even when playing electric guitar. Two with whom you might be familiar are Mark Knopfler (of Dire Straits) and Lindsey Buckingham (from Fleetwood Mac). Part of their unique guitar sounds come from their "fingers only" playing styles. Jeff Beck is another excellent example of someone who uses his fingers to explore the many sounds his guitar can create.

You can also play upstrokes with the thumb, but the nail tends to sound harsh against the strings. Making the stroke by brushing the fingers in an upward motion gives you a smoother, cleaner sound. You can use just one finger (most people use the index) or go with two, three, or four. Each slightly changes the volume and tone, so experiment and listen and decide what you like.

Picking a Pick

Picks, or plectrums, are small, usually triangular pieces of plastic (although they can be made of almost anything) that guitarists often use to strike the strings. Calling them "triangular" can be misleading because they come in all sorts of shapes and sizes. Plus, their edges are a bit too rounded to look exactly like triangles.

Picks also come in different thicknesses, which is what you want to get a feel for first. Generally, the thinnest and thickest picks are harder for beginners to control, as they have not yet developed enough finesse (and confidence) to feel comfortable picking. Most guitarists will tell you to start with a medium pick and then experiment with other thicknesses as you get more accustomed to using one.

The term *flexibility* might be more apt than thickness. Picks are made from all kinds of materials and a "medium" pick made of nylon listed as 0.75mm thick may well have less flexibility than a "heavy" plastic pick listed at a thickness of 1mm. This is why you want to try out as many different types as you can and get a feel for what works best for you.

Proper Picking

You can hold a pick in many ways, but most people use this method:

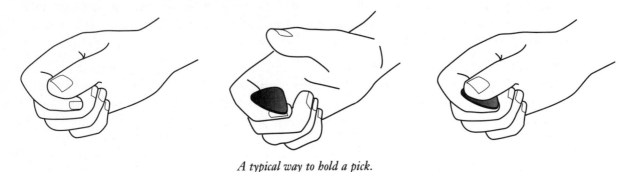

A typical way to hold a pick.

First, hold your right hand as if you were holding a key. Your thumb should rest right along the edge of your index finger. Lift your thumb and place the pick so that it's pointing in the direction your index finger would be pointing if the finger were straight and not slightly curled. The tip of the pick should extend just slightly, not even as much as a quarter-inch beyond the tip of your index finger. Place your thumb on the pick with just enough pressure to keep it in place. Look directly at your thumb and imagine it pointing to 12 o'clock; the pick should be pointing between 8 and 9 o'clock. If it is, then you're good to go!

KEEP SHARP!

You have to control your pick—don't let the pick control you. Don't grip it too lightly or too tightly. A firm but flexible hold does the trick. Also, try to choke up on the pick so that only a quarter-inch or so sticks out beyond your finger. Leaving too much of the pick exposed gives you less control over it, and it can get caught up and tangled in the strings.

Try to keep the pick perpendicular to the string when striking, and use as little motion as possible. Small pick movement leads to greater pick speed as you progress and get confident with your abilities. If you dig into the guitar with the pick or let it sweep outward from the body of the guitar, you'll get a twangy tone that you might like, but you'll be a long way from the string for your next pick strike.

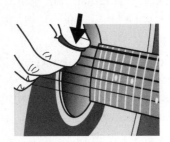

Playing with a pick.

The Left Hand

While your right hand is busy picking the strings, your left hand's job is to fret the strings along the neck of the guitar. Place the tips of your fingers (between your nail and the whorl of the fingerprint) on the strings. Think of your fingertips as ballerinas *en pointe*, if you will.

You can get away with slightly angling your fingers if you're playing only a single note. But soon you'll be playing more than one note at a time, so your fingers have to be fairly arched and on their tips, to ensure that you're not blunting or muting adjacent strings.

SOUND ADVICE

It's a good idea to wear a guitar strap even when sitting. The strap will help you adjust the neck angle, helping you position your fretting hand about chest high and giving it free and easy movement along the neck of the guitar.

Thumb Position and (Not) Gripping

Do yourself a favor and put down your guitar for a moment. Pick up a glass or, better yet, an empty half-liter bottle of water or soda. Without even thinking about it grip it as if you're going to take a drink. Don't squeeze it too tightly, because that would push the water (or soda) all over you!

Now look at how your thumb and fingers are positioned on the bottle. Your thumb is probably directly opposite the fingertips, and probably lined up between your index and middle fingers. Try grabbing more with your thumb, and you'll see that your fingers can't help but move in the opposite direction.

SOUND ADVICE

If you can feel the lower edge of the neck of your guitar along your palm, you are pulling your fingers down and keeping them from getting optimal placement. An excellent trick to help you avoid holding the guitar incorrectly is to slip a pencil (or a chopstick or something about the same diameter) between your hand and the neck of the guitar, to keep you aware that you don't want to grip the neck too tightly.

Grabbing the neck of your guitar with the thumb does the same thing. The more you grab, the less likely you'll be able to get the tips of your fingers on the strings because you're pulling them away. Even with very long fingers, you'll find it difficult to cleanly fret the notes. So relax and let your thumb rest against the back of the neck of the guitar in a natural, nongripping way. Ideally, only the pad of your thumb should be in contact with the neck most of the time you play.

Placing your left hand on the neck.

Your fingers have the important job of fretting the notes cleanly. Get them into position first and then let the neck of the guitar rest against the thumb. Your fingers will (and should) decide where your thumb will be; your thumb shouldn't dictate where your fingers go.

Keep the neck angled so that your fretting hand is about chest high, and have an easy, relaxed hold on the neck. This puts your fingers in an optimal position to cleanly fret the notes, while keeping them arched and on their tips.

Fretting Notes

Knowing what part of the finger to use in fretting notes is just the first step. You also want to find the optimal place on your guitar's neck to place your fingertip.

When you put your finger "on a fret," that means your finger is *between* the two frets, slightly closer to the body side of the guitar, as shown in the previous illustration.

You don't need to apply nearly as much pressure as you might think: just enough to press the string so it rests solidly upon the fret closer to the guitar's body. Using your fingertips helps ensure that you push the string straight onto the neck of the guitar. If you push the string too much to one side, you're likely to deaden the note or, worse, cause the string to bend slightly, giving you a note that's out of tune.

A Quick Look at Guitar Tablature

We've now reached the point where you need a bit more musical information to guide you, and *guitar tablature* fills the bill nicely. Tablature, or just "tab," is one of the two main ways of reading guitar music. In tablature, the notes are written out as a series of numbers (usually from 0 to 22) on a staff of six lines, like this:

DEFINITION

Guitar tablature is a system for reading musical notes on guitars and other stringed instruments. Six horizontal lines represent the strings of the guitar (low E, the sixth string, being the bottom line). Numbers on those lines indicate upon which fret to place your finger on any particular string.

Track 02 (0:00)

The six lines represent the six strings of your guitar. The line at the top of the staff is your first string, the high E. The lowest line is the low-E, or sixth, string. The numbers tell you which fret to place your finger on. 1 is the first fret, 2 the second, and so on. 0 means to play that string open, without any fingers on it.

Chapter 2, Example 1.

You read tablature from left to right, regardless of what string a number appears on. Here, you start by placing a finger of your left hand on the third fret of the A string, and then you pick that string with your right hand. Then you play the open D string. Then you place a finger on the second fret of the D string and play it again. Then you place a finger on the third fret of the same string and play it one more time.

Continuing on, you would play the open G string, then the note at the second fret of the G string, and then the open B string. Finally, you would place a finger on the first fret of the B string to finish this exercise. Speed isn't the issue here (you'll learn about timing and rhythm soon enough). Just focus on making clean, clear notes.

KEEP SHARP!

The tablature numbers indicate which fret to play. They *don't* dictate which finger to use to fret a string.

Once you get over the initial jitters, try it again, and you should hear yourself playing the C major scale, which some of you will recognize as "Do Re Mi" from *The Sound of Music.*

Warming Up

Now that you can read a little bit of guitar tablature, you can start with what many guitarists refer to as the "one finger, one fret" warm-up exercise:

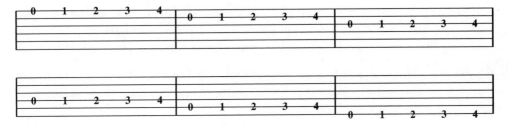

Chapter 2, Example 2.

Track 02 (0:17)

Start by striking the open high-E string. Then place your index finger on the first fret of that string (labeled 1 on the tablature) and play the new note (which, incidentally, you know is F because of your earlier reading!). Then move on to the middle finger at the second fret (labeled 2), the ring finger at the third fret (3), and the pinky at the fourth fret (4). Move on and repeat this process with the remaining five strings.

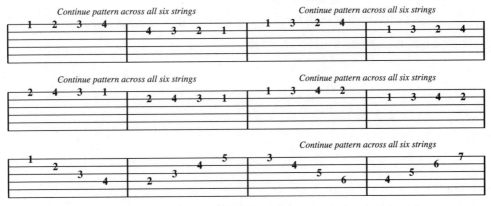

Additional warm-up exercises.

Again, the object isn't speed. You're merely trying to produce clean, clear notes. If you get a buzzing note, you're probably too close to (if not on top of) a wire fret. If you hear a half-hearted, muted note (I call this a "tunk"), then you're not using your fingertips, or you're pressing the string sideways along the fingerboard rather than applying firm, gentle pressure to the strings.

When you get comfortable with this last exercise and have confidence that you can make clear and clean notes on your guitar, try some of these variations. Be sure to use each finger of your fretting hand as indicated.

These exercises are all great ways to start any practice session. They allow you to warm up and gradually stretch your hands and fingers. You should also feel free to experiment and come up with your own variations.

Practice, Practice

You don't just toss on some sweats and run a marathon. You have to prep in advance, and it's the same when it comes to playing the guitar. You want to warm up first and get your body and your mind ready.

Getting yourself into a relaxed state, both physically and mentally, is an important part of playing well. You will often find that, especially as you get going with chords in the next chapter, when you're having trouble fingering notes on the neck, just taking care of your posture helps solve the problem.

Use these basic warm-up exercises to start your practice, and be sure to use *all* your fingers when warming up. There's no rest for the pinky! You're going to need all four of those fingers at some point, so get them up and involved right from the start.

And remember, warm-up exercises are just for warming up! Don't make them so hard that you use up all your practice energy in the first 10 minutes!

The Least You Need to Know

- Being relaxed and sitting or standing with good posture makes playing your guitar easier.
- Keep your fretting hand about chest high.
- Don't grip the neck like a baseball bat!
- Guitar tablature is a way of reading guitar music that uses numbers instead of notes.
- Warming up first is an essential part of practice.

And Now, a Few Chords

In This Chapter

- An introduction to chords
- Playing the Em chord
- Making a simple chord change
- Learning the E, Am, and A chords
- Playing your first song
- Practicing chord changes

As a beginning guitar player, it's easy to psych yourself out about learning chords. There seem to be so many of them—and a lot of them, like C#m7(♭9), just to pick an example, seem to be written in some kind of strange code. But the reality is that you can learn them at your own pace, and even though there *are* a lot of chords, you don't need all that many to start playing songs. Some songs, in fact, have only two chords. And if I told you how many songs use only three chords (at last count, I think there were something like 118,263, give or take a dozen), you'd never believe me.

Chords and Chord Charts

In the simplest terms, a *chord* is what you get when you play three or more different notes at the same time. Different combinations of specific notes create specific chords.

Take your guitar and strike the open high-E (thinnest) string. *Open* means that you don't put any finger of your fretting hand on it. Assuming that your guitar is in tune, you have just played the note E. Now take your thumb or a pick and strike both the high-E string and the B string simultaneously. You have just played two notes at once, B and E. This is called an *interval*.

DEFINITION

An **interval** is the musical distance, in terms of steps and half-steps, between two different notes. A **chord** is the combination of two or more intervals. In other words, you need two different notes to create an interval and three or more different notes to create a chord.

Now strum the three thinnest strings of your guitar—the high-E, -B, and -G strings—at the same time. You've just played an E minor chord. That certainly wasn't all that hard!

You'll be learning a lot more about chords—where they come from and why some of them have such outlandish names—later in Chapter 13. Right now, you just want to start playing some, and the best way to do that is to understand how to read a *chord chart*, a graphic representation of where to put your fingers on the fingerboard of your guitar. A typical chord chart looks like this:

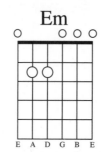

The E minor (Em) chord.

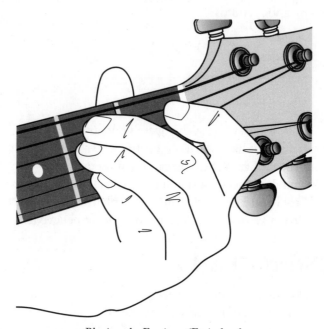

Playing the E minor (Em) chord.

Translating Grids into Chords

Think of a chord chart as a map. The thick line at the top represents the nut of the guitar. The six vertical lines are your six strings, the low E (thickest) on the left edge and the high E (thinnest) on the right. The horizontal lines are your frets.

When you see a string with an "O" above the nut, that means you don't put a finger on that string. You just play it open. An "X" above any string (and you'll see some later in this chapter) indicates that you're not to play that string. Depending on which string is not to be played, you may actually have to mute the string, which you'll learn about with one version of the G chord in Chapter 7. Any circles on the strings themselves represent your fingers and indicate the string and fret where you should place them.

KEEP SHARP!

Sometimes chord charts have numbers in the "finger circles," which are meant to indicate which finger to use on which string. "Suggested fingerings" are good for learning the shape of a chord, but when you're changing from chord to chord in a song, you often find yourself using fingerings different from the suggested ones. Because most songs have more than one or two chords, it's good to know that there are other possible fingerings than just the suggested ones.

Occasionally, a number may be placed beside one of the fret grids, usually at the first fret grid and to the right of the high-E string. This number indicates that you want to be on a specific fret higher up on the neck. You'll come across a number of these sorts of chords later in the book.

Your Very First Chord

The name of the chord in the chord chart is written above the chart. In this case, it is "Em," which is short for E minor. This Em chord uses all six strings and not just three, like the one you played earlier.

To play the Em chord, place one finger on the A string at the second fret and one finger on the D string, also at the second fret. You can use whichever fingers you'd like, but I recommend trying your middle finger on the A string and your ring finger on the D string.

Once your fingers are in place, strum with either your thumb or a pick across all six strings. It's very important that you keep your fingers on their tips. If your fingers collapse slightly, they will muffle the strings that are supposed to be played open and you'll have a sorry-sounding chord.

This may come quickly to some of you, but it does involve both coordination and patience, not to mention making certain that your fingers are in the right place. And, believe it or not, you could unintentionally be making it harder for yourself! It's second nature to tip the guitar top and neck slightly toward you so that you can see where you're putting your fingers along the neck. But tipping the guitar this way puts your fretting hand (especially the wrist) at a difficult angle to cleanly fret the notes. So once you have a good idea where your fingers are, tip the guitar back so that it sits perpendicular on your knee. That will help you make a better-sounding chord.

The Simplest Chord Change

Keeping the Em chord in place, strum it several times at an even pace. Try counting to four aloud, slowly and evenly, as you strum, strumming the strings downward with each count. Notice that you probably aren't hitting the strings at all as your hand comes back in place to make the next strum.

Now try strumming it while counting in sets of four, saying "One, two, three, four; one, two, three, four; one, two, three, four" over and over again. Be sure to keep your counting even. Tap your foot while you're counting. Your toe will hit the floor as you say each number and rise between the numbers. It will almost be like there's an invisible string running from your thumb (or pick) to your toe. You make the downstroke as you count and as your toe hits the floor, and both toe and thumb rise in between the numbers. So far, so good!

A Chord of a Different Color

It's time to learn a new chord, which we're going to call "Chord #2" for the moment. I don't want to freak you out with its real name! This new chord is actually very easy to play, as you can see in the following chart.

Chord #2

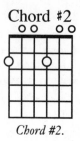

Chord #2.

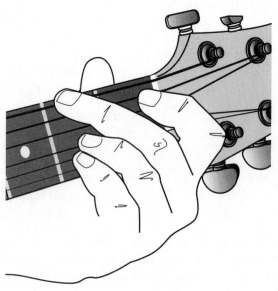

Playing Chord #2.

Start by fingering your Em chord. Now move your middle finger from the second fret of the A string to the second fret of the low-E (thickest) string. Then move your ring finger from the second fret of the D string to the second fret of the G string. Think of it as doing "jumping jacks" with your fingers on the strings. Your fingers will be on the same frets but will end up with two strings between them instead of being on adjacent strings. When you're set, strum the chord. It should sound kind of mysterious, as you'll hear in a moment.

Smoothing Out the Changes

Track 03

It's time to work on changing between these two chords. Listen to Track #3 of the CD that came with your book. You'll hear me counting to four and then you'll hear me play the Em chord four times, then "Chord #2" four times, and then the Em chord again, followed by four more strums of "Chord #2" and one final strum of Em.

LISTENING LIBRARY

If playing these two chords over and over again starts to sound familiar, give yourself a pat on the back: They are the two chords used in the song "Horse with No Name" by the band America.

The original recording has more than one guitar playing at the same time, and they use much more complicated strumming, but the song is essentially these two chords played over and over again.

You want to do this slowly at first. Use the space between beats 4 and 1 to make your chord change. It shouldn't take you long to be able to change between these two chords without thinking about it.

What *Not* to Practice

When you're practicing switching between chords, you'll probably find that you can keep the rhythm steady but that your left hand isn't keeping up with the chord changes. This is normal!

What you don't want to do is strum on the count of "one, two, three, four," then stop while you make the change, and then resume counting and strumming again. This won't help you practice changing chords—it'll help you practice bad timing! Simply slow the counting to a point that you can make the change relatively smoothly. Your fingers will develop muscle memory and will get better and better the more you practice.

A Few More Chords

Since you're off to such a good start, how about taking on a few more chords? Start again with Em, remembering to use your middle finger on the second fret of the A string and your ring finger on the second fret of the D string. Now place your index finger on the first fret of the G string, as shown in the following chord chart.

This chord is E major, or simply E. Once you're comfortable with the fingering, try first strumming the Em and then adding your index finger to play E. Can you hear the difference between the two? Some people say that the Em chord sounds sadder or that the E chord sounds happier. The main thing is that you *do* hear a difference. If you can't, it's possible that your ring finger is muting the G string and you aren't getting a good note there. That note on the G string makes all the difference between the two chords.

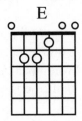

The E major (E) chord.

A Minor

If you take your E chord and move each finger to the next string closer to the floor, you have the A minor (Am) chord.

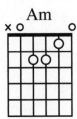

The A minor (Am) chord.

Notice the X above the low-E (thickest) string on the chart. This means that you don't want to strum this string when you play the chord. You want to start on the A string, strumming the five strings closest to the floor instead of all six strings.

LISTENING LIBRARY

The song "Life During Wartime" by Talking Heads uses two chords: Am during the verses and E for the chorus (the "… this ain't no party, this ain't no disco …" part).

Strumming five strings instead of six initially requires some effort on your part, but it is important. You will run into many situations when you don't want to play all six strings of your guitar. In fact, if you play electric guitar, striking all six strings is a rare occurrence! Make a point of doing so as you practice, and before too long, you'll find yourself strumming the Am chord from the fifth string down without even realizing it.

A Major

Okay, one more chord! This time, you want to place a finger on the second fret of the B, G, and D strings, like this:

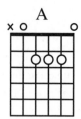

The A major (A) chord.

The A chord can be a bit tricky. Most people first go with using the ring finger on the B string, the middle finger on the G string, and the index finger on the D string. If you're comfortable in that position, that's fine. But some people find it a bit cramped. You might find that switching your index and middle fingers (index on the G string and middle on the D) gives you a more comfortable, and probably cleaner-sounding, chord.

If you've got big fingers, you might be able to cover the D and G strings with one finger (usually the index, which you'll have to flatten slightly to fret the two strings) and then add the middle finger to the B string. Many classical guitarists use this fingering.

Your First "Official" Song

Take some time to get comfortable and confident with these new chords. When you're ready, you'll use the A and E chords to play the traditional song "Tom Dooley." You start with the A chord and strum it for three sets of 4 beats (a total of 12). Then you change to E and strum that for four sets of 4 (16) beats before you change back to A for the final 4 beats. You can follow along with Track 4 on the CD.

Track 04

A

One	two		three	four	one	two	three	four
Hang down		*your*	*head*	*Tom*	*Doo*	*ley*		

A   **E**

One	two		three	four	one	two	three	four
Hang down		*your*	*head*	*and*	*cry*			

E

One	two		three	four	one	two	three	four
Hang down		*your*	*head*	*Tom*	*Doo*	*ley*		

E   **A**

One	two		three	four	one	two	three	four
You know		*you're*	*going*	*to*	*die*			

This may not be as simple as it seems the first few times you try it! You may start out great, but then switching from the A to the E chord may throw you off. You want to make the change, but you don't want to lose the timing, so what do you do?

You cheat! Well, it's not really cheating—it's more a way of keeping up while you're learning. The first line should pose no problem for you, as it's just eight beats of A. The next line starts with four beats of A and then changes to four beats of E. If you know you're having trouble switching to E, just strum the first beat of A in the second line and then use the next three beats to change your fingers to the E chord. Likewise, if you're having trouble switching from E to A in the fourth line, just play the E chord on the first beat of that line and make your chord change on the next three beats. The main thing is to be ready and on time for the first beat of the new chord.

Think of this as part of the learning curve you're facing. As you practice making the changes between these two chords, you'll soon find yourself taking only two beats to make the shift instead of three. Then you'll need only one beat. And even though it may seem like forever while you're practicing, before you know it, you'll be switching chords right on time.

Practice, Practice

You cannot practice forming and changing chords enough. Getting better at knowing and playing chords is going to be your primary focus as a beginning guitar player.

Every time you learn a new chord, you want to first memorize how to finger it—which frets need to be pressed in order to play the chord. Try it with different fingers to see what works best for you and to see if there are other ways to play it. There almost always are, and you will almost always find a reason to finger a chord in a different way at some point in your guitar adventures.

 SOUND ADVICE

You want to memorize chords as soon as you possibly can. Once you learn a chord, work on being able to move your fingers to play it when it turns up in a song. Memorizing chords also frees you to enjoy playing a song without constantly looking at your chord chart!

Making Chord Changes

Once you know a new chord, you want to practice changing from that new chord to every other chord you know. So right now you want to be able to switch quickly and cleanly between any of the following chords: Em, E, Am, and A. Don't worry about Chord #2 except as a warm-up exercise. You're not likely to run into it again soon.

When you're first working on changing between two chords, don't worry about timing and keeping the beat. Just work on getting your fingers from one place to another. Some chord changes won't be all that involved. Changing from Em to E, for example, means simply adding your index finger to the first fret of the G string.

KEEP SHARP!

Most beginners start each chord by totally removing their fingers from the fingerboard. Try to avoid this; you can make faster chord changes if your fingers don't have to travel too far. Look for similarities between chords—fingers being in the same relative position to each other or being on the right string but perhaps a different fret. The less you have to move, the faster you'll get.

Some chord changes are moderately difficult. To move from Em to Am, you need to pick up both your ring and middle fingers and move them from the second fret of the A and D strings to the second fret of the D and G strings, and add your index finger to the first fret of the B string. Notice that your ring and middle fingers maintain their basic position in relation to each other.

Moving Your Fingers as a Unit

Ultimately, you want your fingers to move from one chord to another as a unit, and two simple exercises can help you get started in that direction. First, form a chord you're working on—say, E. When you have your fingers in place, relax them but don't lose contact with the strings. Now press your fingers hard onto the strings simultaneously, harder than you normally would to play the chord. You're likely to hear the notes of the E chord as you press the strings onto the neck of the guitar. After you press hard, relax again but still keep in contact with the strings. Don't lose the chord! Repeat this 10 to 12 times.

The companion exercise is pretty much the same, but you want to start by having your fingers on the strings as if you were playing the chord. Then relax and raise your fingers, as a unit, just off the strings. Keep them close enough that you can put them back on the strings at the same time.

The object of these exercises is to get your fingers acclimated to working together on the chord. Eventually, they will learn to leave one chord and arrive at another as a team.

The Least You Need to Know

- Chords are created when you play three or more notes.
- Chord charts are little maps that show you where to place your fingers on the fingerboard to make chords.
- It's easier to form chords cleanly if you don't tip the face of the guitar toward you to see your fingers.
- Memorizing chords means you don't have to look them up every time you want to play one.
- You want to practice making chord changes whenever you can.

Learning to Read Rhythms

In This Chapter

- The importance of rhythm to the guitarist
- Time signatures
- Why guitar tablature isn't always helpful
- An introduction to music notation
- Rhythm notation
- The "boom-chuck" and alternate bass style of strumming

Songs are made up of three essential parts: the melody (the part that is sung or played with single notes), the harmony (the chords), and the rhythm. Your left hand is handling the harmony when it plays the chords, and your right hand takes care of the rhythm. They have to work together, and it's a huge mistake to think that one is more important than the other. You spent the last two chapters concentrating on the left hand, so now it's time to work a bit on the right.

Finding Your Pulse

When you strummed the chords to "Tom Dooley" in the last chapter, you counted in sets of four to keep track of how many strums you made. That wasn't by chance. Most songs—most of the music that you know, in fact—is counted out in sets of four.

And that's only part of the picture. Depending on the feel of the song, certain beats may have more emphasis than others. If a particular song is counted in sets of four, the stronger beats may fall on the one and three. They could also fall on the two and four or any one of those beats. This emphasis is called the pulse of the song.

You'll be exploring more about pulse and timing as you progress through this book. Right now, you want to know how to tell how many beats you're dealing with in a particular song.

This is where *time signatures* come in. A time signature is a pair of numbers stacked atop each other, much like a fraction. You'll find one at the beginning of any piece of music. Here are some examples.

Various time signatures.

The number on the top indicates how many beats a song gets in each measure. Don't worry about the lower number for the moment, as you'll be learning about that in just a little while. Understand that time signatures do *not* indicate at what *tempo* (how fast or slowly) a song is played.

DEFINITION

Time signatures tell you how many beats per measure a song should get. **Tempo** determines how quickly those beats should be played. Typically, tempo is measured in beats per minute (BPM) markings. Metronomes are devices that set the BPM to an audible or visual signal (sometimes both) so that you can play or practice at a specific desired tempo.

As mentioned earlier, four is the most common number of beats a measure gets. Quite a few songs have 3 beats per measure, and you'll also find some with 2, 6, and 12.

Any number is possible, but four beats is far and away the most common. In fact, it's so common that there is a "shorthand" symbol for 4/4 timing that looks like this:

This "C" means common time. It is often used in place of the 4/4 symbol.

A *measure* is a small bit of music that lasts for a specified period of beats. It is represented by a vertical line that crosses through the horizontal lines of both guitar tablature and music notation.

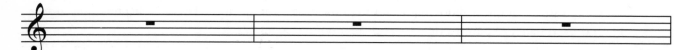

Measures as shown in music notation and tablature.

The Big Problem with Tablature

Most guitar players insist that they don't need to read music. They have guitar tablature, and that's enough for them. Tab can show you where on the fingerboard to place your fingers whether you're playing single notes or chords. The truth is, though, that while tablature does have its good points, it also has some glaring problems. Remember the first bit of tablature you played back in Chapter 2? It was just a simple C major scale, like "Do Re Mi" from *The Sound of Music*. Here it is again, only this time backward:

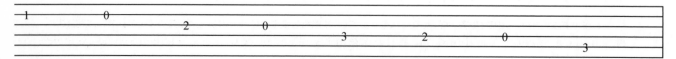

Chapter 4, Example 1.

 Track 05 (0:00)
I play it for you twice on the first half of Track 5 on the CD. The first time, it sounds like I'm playing a scale backward. The second time, it sounds like the first line of the Christmas carol "Joy to the World." They're both obviously very different. Which is correct?

According to the tablature, they're *both* correct. Guitar tablature doesn't give you any clue about rhythm or the timing of the notes of a song. And as you've just heard, the timing can be the only thing that distinguishes a generic group of notes from a song that everyone knows.

For all its helpfulness, guitar tablature is concerned with just part of your playing—the left hand part. And as you've already read, you need both hands to be a guitarist.

Music Notation

Fortunately, you have more than just guitar tablature at your disposal. There's also standard music notation, which you might have learned a bit about back in grammar school.

In music notation, notes are written as dotlike symbols on a staff of five lines. At the beginning of the line is a clef, which tells where the notes are going to be. Usually guitar music is written on a staff with a G clef (also called the *treble clef*) and looks like this:

The staff and G clef in music notation.

Notes are placed on the staff either on a line or in one of the spaces between the lines. Where those notes are placed on the staff determines what the note is. Notes on the lines, from low to high, are E, G, B, D, and F. You might remember learning **E**very **G**ood **B**oy **D**eserves **F**avor at some point. This is where that comes from.

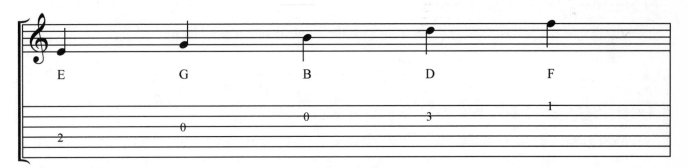

E, G, B, D, and F locations on the G clef.

Lines in the spaces, again from low to high, are F, A, C, and E (remembering that "face" rhymes with "space" may help).

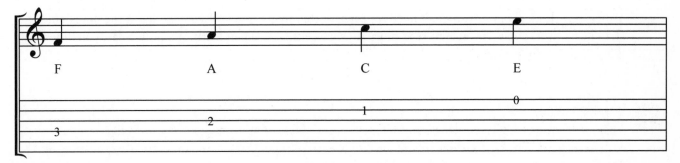

F, A, C, and E locations on the G clef.

Notes can be added above and below the staff by means of *ledger lines,* which extend the range of the staff in both directions, like this:

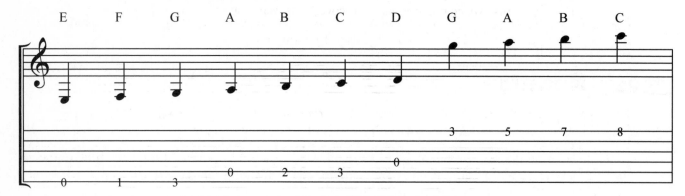

Notes on ledger lines.

F is the note on the top line of the staff. G is the next note higher than F, and it goes in the space immediately above the staff. A, the next note higher than G, goes on the ledger line immediately above the space where G is. B is placed in the space above A's ledger line, and C is on a second ledger line, immediately above B's space.

Since E is the note on the bottom line of the staff, D has to be in the space below the staff. C, the note before D, is drawn on a ledger line below the space that D occupies. B is below C, A is on the line below B, and so on.

From the Staff to Your Frets

Here's how the notes on the staff match up with the numbers in guitar tablature:

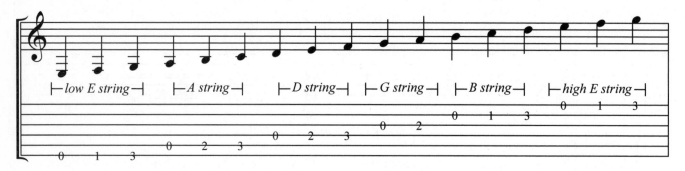

Notes in music notation and guitar tablature.

When you think about it, you don't need to learn all that many notes. If you can learn the notes on one string each week, you'll be able to read music in six weeks. If you can learn one note a day, you'll be reading music in less than a month!

Accidentals

You might remember from Chapter 1 that there are accidentals, notes that are marked with either sharp (♯) or flat (♭) signs. Music notation has that covered as well. You'll see a ♯ or ♭ placed immediately before the note in question, like this:

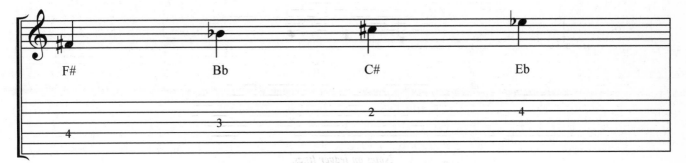

Accidental notes in music notation and guitar tablature.

Any symbol for an accidental lasts for an entire measure. So if you were to see an F♯ at the start of a measure and then an F later in that same measure, you would play that as F♯ as well.

Accidentals also play an important role in knowing what key a song is in, not to mention giving you clues as to which chords a song likely has. This is covered in Chapters 15 and 16.

Rhythmic Values of Notes

The beauty of music notation is that each note performs two functions. The placement of the note tells you what note to play, while the configuration of the note tells you the beat value the note has.

Notes have a body, which is either hollow or solid. Notes other than the whole note also have stems attached to one side of the body. The stems can point up or down, but that doesn't matter when it comes to telling what the note is or what beat value the note has.

<table>
<tr><td>whole note
(4 beats)</td><td>half notes
(2 beats)</td><td>quarter notes
(1 beat)</td><td>eighth notes
(1/2 beat)</td></tr>
</table>

Whole notes, half notes, quarter notes, and eighth notes.

Whole notes are hollow and have no stems. These notes are held for four beats (a whole measure). Half notes look like whole notes, but with a stem added. These are held for two beats (half a measure). Quarter notes look like half notes, but the body of the note is solid. They are one beat each, or four to a measure. And eighth notes look like quarter notes, except that there is a flag attached to their stem; they're often connected by a single bar at the top of their stems. Eighth notes are half a beat each; there are eight to a four-beat measure.

Chords in Notation and Tablature

When you see a group of single notes stacked atop each other, this is a chord. The four chords you learned in the last chapter look like this:

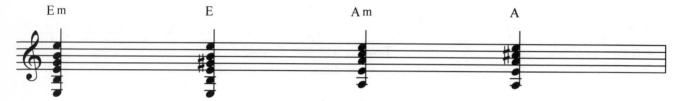

Em, E, Am, and A written out in music notation.

Chords in guitar tablature are also shown as stacks of single notes. Here are the four chords (not counting Chord #2 from the last chapter) you already know:

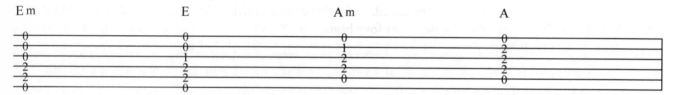

Em, E, Am, and A written out in guitar tablature.

In guitar tablature, when you see two or more numbers written on top of one another, you play those strings at the same time. Any 0, remember, means an open string. So the tablature for the Em chord, as you see here, says to place a finger on the second fret of the A string (the 2 on the second line up from the bottom) and one on the second fret of the D string (the 2 on the third line up from the bottom), and to play the other strings open. That matches perfectly with the chord chart you saw in Chapter 3.

Being able to recognize chord forms in either notation or tablature will be a big help to you. If you want to play classical pieces, you'll be able to see the basic chords in the notation even when written as single notes. And knowing chord shapes in tablature makes playing riffs and fills and even some lead guitar a breeze. You'll read more about all of this in Chapters 18 and 20.

Tying Notes Together

Sometimes notes last longer than four beats, and sometimes notes start in one measure and have enough beats to end in the following measure. *Ties* are musical symbols that literally tie the rhythmic value of two (or more) notes together. They are curved, arched lines that can appear either above or below the note heads, as shown in the following example:

Example 1

Two tied whole notes = 4 beats + 4 beats = 8 beats

Example 2

Eighth note tied to half note = 1/2 beat + 2 beats = 2 1/2 beats

Example 3

Two tied eighth notes = 1/2 beat + 1/2 beat = 1 beat   Two tied eighth notes = 1/2 beat + 1/2 beat = 1 beat

Tied notes in music notation.

In the first two measures of Example 1, you first see two whole notes tied together. When you see a tied note, you play the first one (in this case, the G of the open G string) and then let it last for the duration of *both* of the tied notes combined. So in this case, you strike the G string and let it ring for eight beats. You don't strike it again after four beats.

Ties can connect notes in two different measures, even notes of different rhythmic values, as shown in Example 2, where the G note is played on the last half of the fourth beat and then is held for the first two beats of the following measure as well. Since the initial eighth note is half a beat and the half note in the next measure is two beats, the total rhythmic value of the two notes is two-and-a-half beats.

More often than not in guitar music, you will find two eighth notes tied together, as in Example 3. Tying two eighth notes together creates a note that lasts for one beat, the same value as a quarter note. Many music notation programs break all the beats of any measure into "packets" so that all the notes of one given beat can be linked together. This can help you visualize the time, especially with strums, where you miss a stroke on the beat, as you'll see in Chapter 5, and also when working with complicated rhythms like the ones you'll be encountering in Chapter 10.

Rhythmic Notation

Reading chords, whether in notation or in tablature, can be tricky, and it takes some practice to recognize what chords they are. This is why most guitar players prefer chord charts or even just the name of the chord written somewhere in the music.

If you're just strumming along, you really don't need to know what notes you're playing. But you do need to know the rhythm. At first glance, rhythm notation looks a lot like regular music notation, but it actually shows only the rhythm component.

whole note   half notes   quarter notes   eighth notes

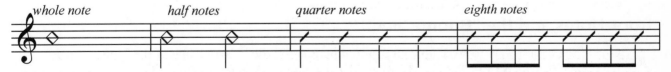

Various note values shown in rhythm notation.

You'll often find a guitar's strumming part written out in rhythm notation. For instance, the very simple version of "Tom Dooley" from the last chapter would look like this:

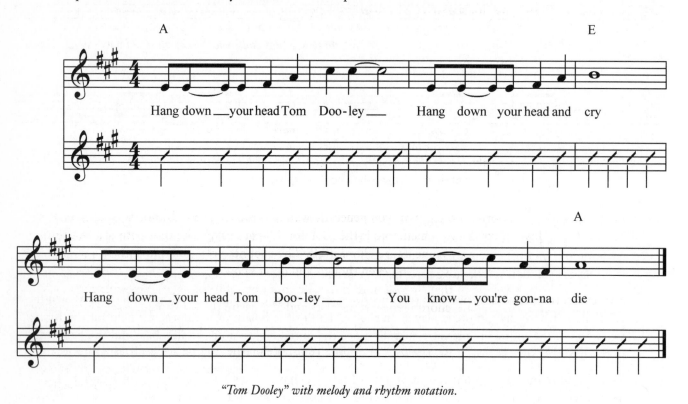

"Tom Dooley" with melody and rhythm notation.

You can see in the music that the guitar part is played with four quarter note strums of the chords (either A or E, depending on where in the song you are) in each measure, regardless of what the singer is singing.

Adding Some Pizzazz

Speaking of "Tom Dooley," you're at a point where you can get a little more adventurous with your playing, and old Tom can help. Up to now, you've been doing some very basic strumming, just playing full chords on the beats. It's time you moved beyond that.

You may not know it, but many times the only real difference between someone who has just started out on guitar and someone who is a little more advanced is that the advanced player knows a few more "tricks," or playing techniques. These techniques themselves aren't all that hard—some are actually quite easy—but they make one's playing (not to mention the guitarist) sound a lot better.

Root Notes and the "Boom-Chuck"

One of the easiest ways to spice up your strumming goes by the bizarre name of the "boom-chuck" technique. Play an A (A major) chord. Remember that you want to strum the A chord starting with the fifth string, the A string. Maybe you've been wondering why you do that instead of strumming all six strings.

Go ahead and play it again, strumming all six strings. Then try it again with just the five strings, and again with the six. Which chord sounds cleaner? Most people will agree that the five-string strum sounds better than the full six-string strum. This is because the A note, the first (and lowest) note you hit when strumming just five strings, is the *root note* of the A chord. Even though the low E is also part of an A chord, the chord sounds crisper and cleaner when the root note is also the lowest note strummed.

DEFINITION

The **root note** of any chord is the note that shares the name of the chord. For example, the root note of Em is E. The root note of E (E major, that is) is also E. The root note of A or Am is A. If you remember that sharps and flats are part of note names while "major" and "minor" are part of chord names, you'll be okay. The root note of F#m, for instance is F#, not F.

When you strum a chord on the guitar, you generally want to have that chord's root note as its bass, or lowest, note. How do you know which note is the root note? That's easy! The root note of any chord is the note with the same note name as the chord itself. The root note of A major (or just plain A) is A. The root note of A minor is also A. And even though you don't know what an Am7(♭5) chord is yet, you can say with total confidence that its root note is A. The root note of A♭ or A♭m is A♭. Just remember that "major" and "minor" are chord names, while flats and sharps are parts of note names, and you'll be okay.

To play the "boom-chuck," you play just the chord's root note on the first beat (that bass note is the "boom"), the rest of the chord (that's the "chuck" part) on the second beat, the root note again on the third beat, and the rest of the chord on the fourth beat. Playing the A chord with the "boom-chuck" should sound like this:

A

Playing the "boom-chuck."

The trick is to hit only the A string on the first and third beats and also to start your strum of the "rest of the chord" on the D (fourth) string. The bass note rings while you strike the remaining strings and gives you the feeling you're playing two instruments at once. You're on your way to being a one-man band!

Spend some time practicing the "boom-chuck" not only with the A chord, but also with Am, Em, and E. Your root note for both E and Em, as you should know, is E, the open low-E string. For both the E and the Em, you strike just the open low-E string on the first and third beats and the rest of the chord (starting on the A string) on the second and third beats.

Alternating Bass Notes

The "boom-chuck" technique is just the first of many techniques you can use to add some pizzazz to your playing. When you're confident with the "boom-chuck," you can progress to playing an alternating bass strum. It starts out like the "boom-chuck," but we change the root note in the bass on the third beat to an alternate note. Here are very basic alternating bass patterns for the four chords you know:

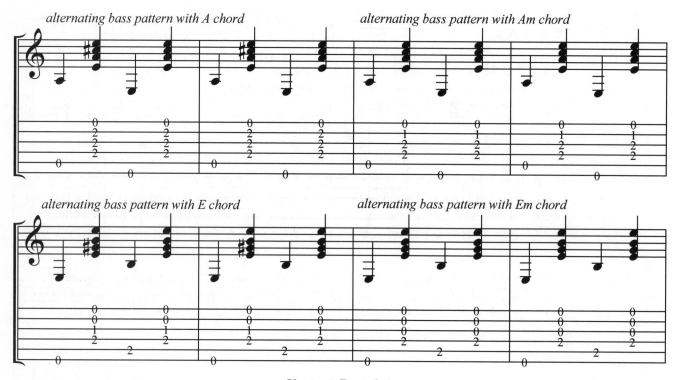

Chapter 4, Example 2.

 Track 05 (0:20)

For the A and Am chords, you hit the open low-E string (instead of the A string) on the third beat. On the fourth beat you still want to start your strum of the rest of the A or Am chords on the D string, so that means you have to skip over the A string between the third and fourth beats.

On the E and Em chords, you play the B at the second fret of the A string on the third beat, and on *both* the second and fourth beats, you want to start your strum of the rest of the chord at the D string. This is because your "alternate bass note" is on the A string, and you want it to be separate from the rest of the chord when you play the alternating bass pattern.

 LISTENING LIBRARY

Folk and country guitarists use the alternating bass strumming technique a lot. You can hear it on Johnny Cash's "Folsom Prison Blues" and Hank Williams's "Jambalaya" and "Your Cheatin' Heart."

Keeping the bass notes and the rest of the chords separate makes both bass and chord ring out cleanly. Being careful with your picking while playing these patterns requires a little practice and patience, but before you know it, you won't sound like an absolute beginner anymore.

One Last Visit with Tom

To give you a bit of practical application of the alternating bass technique, here is "Tom Dooley" one last time, arranged with a very simple alternating bass part.

Chapter 4, Example 3.

Track 06

Notice that the melody line of the song is also written out for you, but only in music notation. Usually someone is singing the melody while the guitar is playing the accompaniment. You can give yourself some extra practice by reading and playing just the melody line of this song, as well as many of the others coming up later in this book.

SOUND ADVICE

It's best to learn songs in stages, just as you've done with "Tom Dooley" in this chapter. First learn the chords and get good at making the chord changes in rhythm. When you've got it, you'll be able to play it on your own or with others. Then the fun comes in using other techniques and ideas to find ways to make the song more interesting to play and to listen to. With all the various techniques you'll learn, you'll rarely have to play a song the same way twice.

Practice, Practice

Whether you decide to read tablature, music notation, or rhythmic notation (or hopefully all three!), the best way to get good at it is to practice. That may seem obvious, but did you know that you don't even need a guitar to practice? You can do all sorts of things to become a better guitarist and musician without even touching your guitar.

If you have any music lying around the house, whether it's guitar music or piano music or flute music, you have an opportunity to recognize and memorize the notes on the treble clef. In fact, always carry some music with you, especially in music notation or rhythmic notation. When you have a spare moment, see if you can read a part of the rhythm on the page. If you can, try tapping it out on your leg or on a desk or tabletop. The more rhythms you can get into your hands, the more various strumming you'll be able to do.

You probably already tap your foot to the beat of a catchy song—you do like music, don't you? So why not take that tapping and go an extra step? Try to work out the rhythms and strumming to songs that you hear in the course of the day. Odds are, if you've taken up the guitar, you've been air-guitaring for years—and now you can actually put that "practice" to use!

There are also numerous websites, some of them free, where you can find note and rhythm recognition tests and games that can help you out. Check out Pedaplus.com, HappyNote.com, or simply type "note recognition games" or "rhythm reading games" into Google or your favorite search engine to find them. All the rhythm and reading practice you do without an instrument will pay off big time when you get your guitar back in hand.

The Least You Need to Know

- Rhythm is a very important part of music, and guitarists need to be good at playing in rhythm.
- Time signatures tell you how many beats are in a measure.
- Guitar tablature doesn't tell you anything about rhythm.
- Music notation and rhythm notation are good for reading rhythms in music.
- The "boom-chuck" and alternating bass styles of strumming can spice up your playing.

Learning to Play Rhythms

In This Chapter

- Good strumming technique
- Strumming eighth notes
- Getting beyond "down and up"
- Keeping the beat while missing strokes
- The problem with "strumming patterns"
- Playing the B7 chord

Almost everyone has some basic sense of rhythm. That's important to keep in mind, because if you really don't think you have rhythm, you might as well trade in your guitar right now! You're going to have to find and develop your sense of rhythm to become even halfway decent at playing guitar or any musical instrument.

Fortunately, it's not that hard to find and nurture your inner rhythm. If there's a "trick" to it, it's to start out very simply and to become comfortable and confident with the basics before tackling more complex rhythms—which is the same approach this book has been using for every aspect of the guitar so far.

The strumming you've done to this point has been easy and basic—simple downstrokes, playing either single notes or chords on each beat. Even the examples of the "boom-chuck" and alternating bass patterns from the last chapter were kept as simple as possible so that you could learn them easily and, hopefully, with minimal trouble on your part.

Strumming, in its simplest form, is just counting time. If you can count to four (or three, or eight) and can tap your hand on a table as you count to four, you can handle strumming. And by the end of this chapter, you should be able to perform some simple rhythms that will make you sound like you've been playing a lot longer than you have!

The Sock-Puppet Approach

Keeping time while strumming is even easier when you strum correctly. Despite what you may see during performance or on videos, strumming is subtle and doesn't require a lot of motion. In fact, the more motion you use, the more likely you are to waste energy, get tired, and have trouble keeping in time.

Smooth, even strumming comes from the wrist and forearm. Have you ever had or seen a sock puppet? Unless you happen to be a ventriloquist, a sock puppet has a limited vocabulary. It can say "yes" or "no." Hold your strumming hand in front of you, fingers together, so you can see your palm straight on. Tip your wrist so that your fingertips are the part of your hand closest to you. Now pretend that you've got a sock puppet on your hand and it's telling you "no" by shaking its head from side to side. Only your wrist and forearm should be moving—your forearm shouldn't be moving all that much. You can even hold your elbow with your other hand to confirm that it isn't really moving.

This motion of the sock puppet saying "no" is your strumming motion. Your sock puppet should be continuously saying "no" while you play. As you get better at strumming, you'll be able to stop and start at will, but for now you want to concentrate on being steady and constant with your strumming motion.

Counting by Four

Rhythm is something that you hear and feel. One of the biggest obstacles to strumming is trying to think of rhythm visually, in terms of *downstrokes* and *upstrokes*. Trying to visualize rhythm is an easy trap to fall into, particularly since one has to describe strumming in those "down" and "up" terms. If you watch someone play rhythm, trying to match them strum for strum, you're always going to be slightly behind and your rhythm will be erratic at best.

DEFINITION

Strumming the strings, from the thickest to the thinnest, in a downward motion toward the floor is a **downstroke**. An **upstroke** is a strum in the opposite direction. In both notation and tablature, downstrokes are indicated by a ⊓ symbol and upstrokes by a ∨ symbol.

This is why you need to have a good concept of rhythm in terms of counting out the beats. When you internalize this sense of rhythm, you start tapping your foot or swaying in time with the music. This means your body is counting for you and you're on your way to having a better grasp of playing in steady time.

Start with an E chord, and play it four times using only downstrokes on each beat, as in the following example:

 Track 07 (0:00)

Chapter 5, Example 1.

You're strumming in quarter notes, which you should remember from the last chapter. And whether or not you know it, you're making upstrokes while performing this last exercise. You're simply not hitting the strings when you bring the pick back up to play the next beat.

If you're tapping your foot while you're playing (and you really should get into that habit), you'll see that it's almost as if an invisible wire is connecting your toe with your strumming thumb. The toe goes down and hits the floor, and the thumb strums down on the count of the beat. The thumb rises between one beat and the next, and the toe rises from the floor. This means you're strumming steady and evenly.

Strumming by Eight

It also means that your "sock puppet" is acting as a perfect metronome, keeping the beat as it strums up and down across the strings. While you're counting out quarter notes by counting out the beat as "one, two, three, four," your hand is strumming in terms of eighth notes, going "one *and* two *and* three *and* four *and*," with each "and" being an upstroke.

Now it's time to play those upstrokes. Keep using your E chord and follow along with this next example:

 Track 07 (0:13)

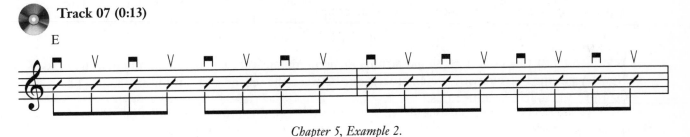

Chapter 5, Example 2.

You don't want to hit all six strings on the upstroke. Just the two or three closest to the floor are fine. Hitting all six strings on both the down- and upstrokes muddies up the sound a lot, so go easy on the upstroke. Use it primarily to get yourself in position for the next downstroke, and don't worry about how many strings you hit.

> **KEEP SHARP!**
>
> Striking the strings on the upstroke may initially throw off your timing a little. If you're strumming with your fingers, start by using your thumb for the downstroke and your index finger for the upstroke. If you're using a pick, be sure that the pick is perpendicular to the strings and that you have just a small amount of the tip of the pick exposed to the string. Otherwise, you'll find that the pick, not you, is controlling your strum.

Skipping Along

Strumming eighth notes constantly can get boring (and tiring) after a while—even if you're in a punk or metal band! Most strumming involves skipping the occasional "and" between the beat when you're counting. Here are two easy strums you can start with:

Track 08

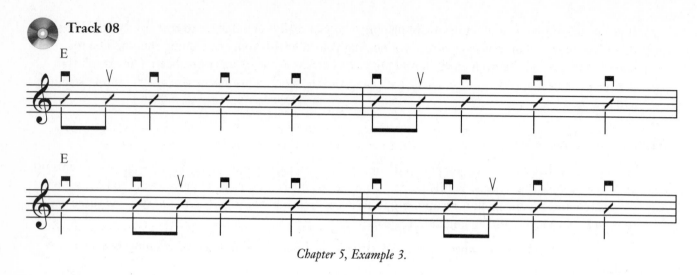

Chapter 5, Example 3.

Each of these examples involves a single upstroke at one point in the four beats of a measure. During the first strum (shown in the first line of rhythm notation), the upstroke falls between the first and second beats. It comes between the second and third beats during the rhythm of the second line.

You should hear that even these simple strums sound more musical than just strumming on the beat. Now try playing a strum with two upstrokes, one between the second and third beat, and one between the third and fourth beat, like this:

Track 09

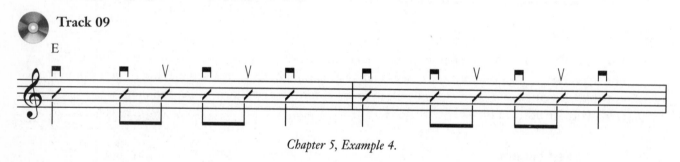

Chapter 5, Example 4.

Missing Downs

Take a little time and get this last example into your head and your strumming hand. When you're comfortable and confident that you can play it well, take a big leap and try skipping a downstroke. Here's the same pattern you just practiced, only this time you don't hit the strings on the downstroke of the third beat, as indicated by the two tied-together eighth notes (which you just read about in Chapter 4):

Track 10

Chapter 5, Example 5.

If you don't think about what you're doing and you keep the "sock puppet" motion going, you should be able to play this without too much trouble. If you watch your hands and get tense and lose your constant strumming motion, you'll have a bit of a train wreck on your hands.

> **SOUND ADVICE**
>
> Your goal with strumming is to be able to keep a good beat going, no matter what else is happening. A great way to practice this is to play a strum for a while. Don't worry if you miss a "down" or an "up"—concentrate on keeping the beat steady. Try strumming with your eyes closed, or while looking around and thinking about other things. If you can strum and hold a conversation without missing a beat, you can do just about anything!

Be loose and relaxed. The important thing to remember is that if you miss the strings on the downstroke of the third beat, you haven't lost the rhythm. It'll just sound like the strumming in Example 4, and that's okay.

Keep working at this last example until it becomes second nature. You can use this particular strum in so many songs that it's going to become one of your favorites.

Practicing Rhythms

Here are some more strums, many of them skipping downstrokes on various beats. You'll notice that these new examples involve different chords and also change chords during the strumming. The last two examples also incorporate the alternating bass technique from the last chapter.

Track 11

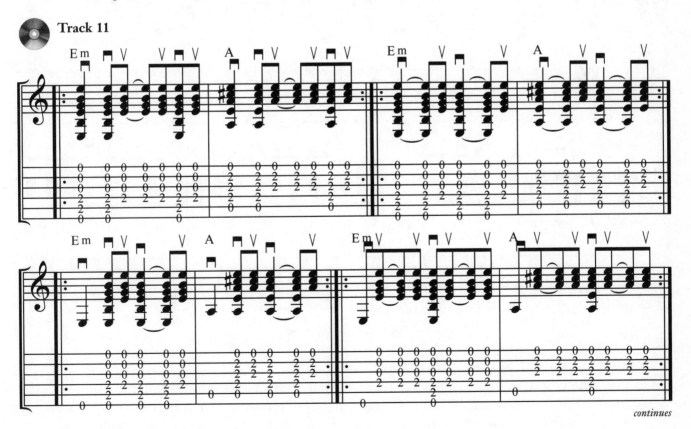

continues

continued

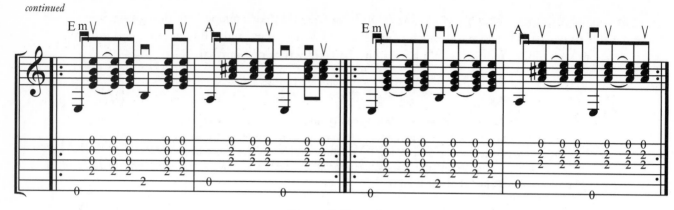

Chapter 5, Example 6.

Notice the heavy lines with accompanying dots that occur at different points in this last illustration. These are repeat signs, which direct you either back to the beginning of the piece (as shown in the second measure) or to repeat a section of a piece (as shown in the third and fourth measures).

You want to start out by practicing these rhythms and then work on mixing different rhythms together, like this:

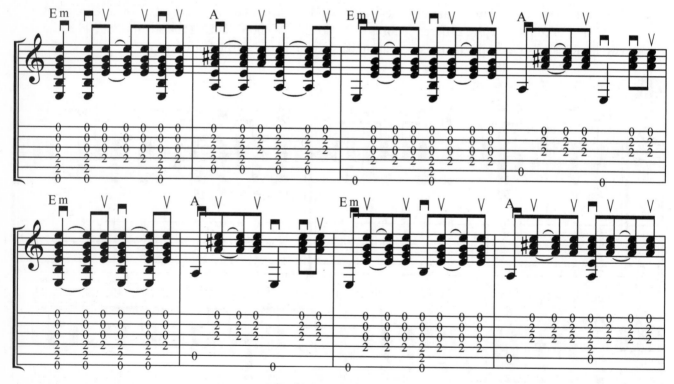

Combining various strums.

Ideally, you want to be able to call up any strum you can hear in your head whenever you want to, and to be able to do so without disrupting the beat. To do this, you'll want to have many different strums at your beck and call, and that means practicing each one to the point that you can pretty much play them all without thinking. This way, the rhythm simply flows out of you through your strumming.

The Myth of "Strumming Patterns"

Being able to switch strums in stride also makes your playing sound natural. Nobody plays robotically—at least, not for very long. Take any one of these strums and see if you can play it flawlessly for four minutes straight. Chances are, you'll occasionally slip and make some minor deviation at some point, maybe missing a bass note here or not catching a full chord there. And that's perfectly okay, as long as you don't lose the basic rhythm and tempo.

For some reason, though, people nowadays seem to obsess about what they call "strumming patterns," which they mean to be the single definitive way of strumming a song, usually by copying the strum stroke for stroke and note for note from the original recording.

But what is that original recording? It's what the guitarist played at the time that the recording took place. It's not that he meant to do exactly what was recorded, or that she played it that way the night before or at the gig last weekend. As you've just learned, it's not that easy to play the same two to four measures of a particular strum exactly the same way over and over again. The guitarist probably just strummed and didn't worry about anything other than keeping the beat steady. You don't have to make more of it than that.

Another important point to know is that strumming and rhythm in general, like most aspects of playing, tend to be stylistic to the individual guitarist. Give two guitar players the same rhythm to strum, and even though the overall rhythm may be the same, there will be little personal nuances. One may have a heavier feel on the bass notes. The other may get a distinct ring on the upstroke. Every musician's unique individual feel is part of what makes playing music so much fun.

Working the Banana Boat

You'll get plenty of practice switching between strums and chords with your song for this chapter, the traditional Jamaican folk tune called "Day-O," also known as "The Banana Boat Song."

From here on out, your song lessons in this book will mostly be written out as single guitar arrangements meant to be strummed or picked while someone sings (or plays) the melody line. The melody line will be written in notation only, which (hint, hint!) is a great way to practice reading notation. Here we go:

Track 12

continues

Chapter 5, Example 7.

New Chord—B7

This song also has a B7 chord, one you haven't played yet:

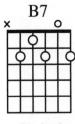

B7 chord.

Start by forming an E chord. Your index finger should be on the first fret of the G string, your ring finger on the second fret of the D string, and your middle finger on the second fret of the A string. Keep your middle finger in place and shift your ring and index fingers so that your ring finger is on the second fret of the G string and your index finger is on the first fret of the D string. Then place your pinky on the second fret of the high-E string.

> **LISTENING LIBRARY**
>
> People are probably most familiar with Harry Belafonte's version of "The Banana Boat Song" from his album *Calypso,* which spent 31 weeks at number one on the *Billboard* "Top 100 Albums" chart. Although Belafonte is often called "The King of Calypso," he was a master interpreter of many musical styles, from blues and folk to jazz standards and gospel. He found inspiration for many of his original songs in the traditional music of cultures all over the world.

This is the first chord that you've needed all four fingers to play, and you might need to make some little adjustments. Remember to keep your fingers up on their tips so they don't accidentally muffle adjoining strings.

The root note of the B7 chord is B, by the way, which is at the second fret of the A string. This is the note you'll pick for the "boom-chuck" strum in this arrangement.

Practice, Practice

Start by practicing forming the B7 chord; then practice changing between the three chords used in this song (E, A, and B7) without even thinking about tempo or timing. When you can make the changes comfortably and smoothly, try making them in rhythm, playing four beats of one chord, then changing to another for four beats, and then changing to the third chord. When you're good with this, make the chord changes every two beats.

Remember that you can use the "boom-chuck" or alternating bass strumming patterns as a way to gain a little time shifting between chords. When you change from E to B7, keep your middle finger on the second fret of the A string and shift your other fingers while you play that B note in the bass. When you move from the A chord to the B7, get the middle finger in place first so you can hit that note in the bass and move your other fingers into position as you do so.

KEEP SHARP!

As mentioned in Chapter 3, beginners tend to begin any chord change by lifting all their fingers high off the fingerboard and then repositioning them, one by one, onto the new chord. When you have to raise your finger off a string, keep it close to the fingerboard so that you can reposition your fingers quickly and easily.

Keeping the rhythm steady is the top priority in this chapter, so slow the tempo of the song, if necessary. Don't worry if you don't get the strums exactly correct. As long as you're keeping the beat, it will sound fine.

Every time you pick up a new tip or technique, you should revisit songs that you've already played and see how you can apply what you've just learned to what you already know. So take time to try out some of your new and improved strumming on "Tom Dooley."

The Least You Need to Know

- Keeping a steady, constant rhythm is important.
- You want to use your wrist and forearm to strum.
- Think of the overall rhythm in terms of beats and counts, not in terms of "downs" and "ups."
- Try to hit just two or three strings on your upstrokes.
- The more strums you know, the more easily you can shift from one to the other while playing a song.

Making Great Progress!

Now that you've learned some basic chords and rhythm, it's time to add some simple techniques to your playing that will make you sound even better. First you'll pick up the blues shuffle, and then you'll learn the C, G, and F chords—and learning these alone means you can play thousands of songs.

But you're going to go even further when you discover how easy it is to add techniques like hammer-ons and pull-offs to your strumming. You'll also learn how to play songs in different timings and to play arpeggios.

And if that's not enough, you'll find out about palm muting and percussive strokes, and you'll start adding quick little sixteenth notes to your playing. *And* you'll get an introduction to the wonderful world of finger-picking styles as a bonus. With all the new things to learn, you'll completely forget that, not long ago, you didn't even know how to play a single chord!

Swinging with the Blues

In This Chapter

- Triplets
- Swing rhythm
- Double stops
- The basic blues shuffle
- New chords—E7, A7, D, and D7
- A brief introduction to chord voicings

Being able to hear and count out rhythms is essential for a guitarist, not only because the guitar is a rhythm instrument, but also because even seemingly simple musical rhythms can sometimes be deceptive.

Listen to "Get Back" by the Beatles and compare it to "Revolution," another of their songs. You can hear that, even though both songs are played in 4/4 time, the underlying rhythmic feel of each song is different. "Get Back" has a driving beat, pushing it forward even though the overall tempo of the song isn't all that fast. The rhythm of "Revolution," on the other hand, has a loping quality. It almost seems to be limping or shuffling along.

This subtle difference occurs in almost all genres of music, so it's important to be able to identify and understand exactly what that difference is. Fortunately, it's as easy as counting to three!

Triple Time

In Chapters 4 and 5, you learned about the quarter notes (which are one beat in value) and eighth notes (which are a half beat). It is also possible to evenly divide a beat into thirds. These rhythmic notes are called *triplets*. They look exactly like eighth notes, except that they're bracketed together in sets of three and have a small "3" written above or below the connected flags, as in the following figure.

Just as an eighth note divides a beat into two equal halves, the triplet divides a beat into identical thirds. And it's the "identical" part that you have to remember when playing rhythms in triplets, even when you're playing only two of them, as you'll soon see.

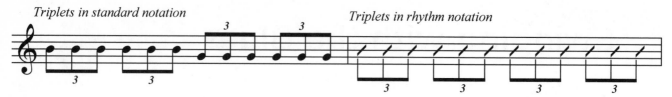

Triplets in standard notation   *Triplets in rhythm notation*

Triplets in standard notation and rhythm notation.

Playing Triplets

You count triplets this way: "one and ah, two and ah, three and ah, four and ah." Strumming triplets takes a little practice because guitarists usually approach playing them in one of two ways. Both have their merits and potential snags. The following example, which you can hear at the start of Track 13 of the CD, uses an E chord to illustrate both styles of playing triplets.

 Track 13 (0:00)

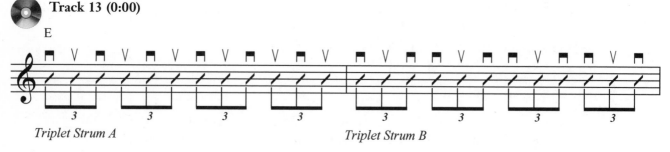

Triplet Strum A   *Triplet Strum B*

Chapter 6, Example 1.

Some guitarists play triplets with a constant "down and up" strum, shown in "Triplet Strum A" of this last example. While it does help to keep the rhythm even, one can easily get derailed playing at high speeds. This makes the triplets sound like sixteenth notes, which, as you'll read about in Chapter 9, are a quarter of a beat in duration.

> **DEFINITION**
>
> A **triplet** divides a beat, or another unit of rhythmic time, into three equal parts. Eighth-note triplets divide a single beat into three. Sixteenth-note triplets (which you'll read about in Chapter 9) divide a half a beat into three evenly spaced notes.

"Triplet Strum B" uses a "down, up, down" strum for each beat in the triplet. Playing a triplet this way gives you a strong downstroke for the beat itself, but you have to develop a slight "hiccup" in your strum because of the upstroke between the downstroke of any "ah" and the downstroke that starts the following beat.

I don't know how much scientific research has been done on this, but most of the guitarists I know or have seen play use "Strum B" more often than "Strum A." Use whichever method helps you keep the rhythm smooth and even.

Swing Eighths

Understanding triplets is vital because a lot of music is played in *swing* rhythm. That loping beat you hear in the Beatles' "Revolution" is an example of swing. Swing is mostly associated with jazz music, but you'll also find swing rhythms in country, pop, R&B, and rock music, and especially in blues.

Swing rhythm is created when you play just the first and third parts of a triplet. In other words, if you were playing while counting aloud, you would be strumming only on the beat (number) and the "ah" of any given beat, like this: "**One** and **ah two** and **ah three** and ah four and ah." Here is an example:

Track 13 (0:15)

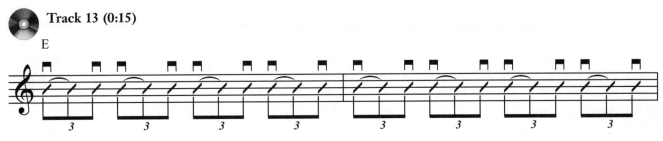

Chapter 6, Example 2.

When playing swing rhythms, guitarists usually use either two downstrokes for both parts of the triplet, as shown here, or a "down and up" strum. Often it depends on whether the guitarist is playing single notes or double stops or whole chords. Just as you did in playing triplets, find what's comfortable for you. You'll probably end up using both styles of swing strumming, as most guitarists do.

In music notation, swing rhythms are often indicated by the following equation, which is placed at the start of a piece of music.

Swing! ♫ = ♩³♪

How swing rhythm is indicated in music.

You see two eighth notes written to one side of an equals sign and a triplet on the other side. But instead of the triplet being a set of three eighth notes joined together, it has one quarter note and one eighth note. This indicates that you want to just play the first and last of the set of triplets.

In the music, any paired eighth notes you see should be played as just the first and the third part of a set of triplets. This is also called playing in swing eighths. Guitar tablature rarely, if ever, tells you a song is supposed to be played in swing eighths, so train your ear to pick out swing rhythm in a song.

Shuffling Along

Swing rhythms are also called shuffle rhythms—that loping, uneven rhythm that you hear in "Revolution" certainly sounds like someone shuffling along. When it comes to the guitar, a *shuffle* refers not only to a rhythm, but also to a specific technique. It's a special pattern of notes that are usually played in pairs on adjacent strings.

Playing these pairs of notes in swing eighths is called a *blues shuffle*.

Double Stops

Two notes on adjacent strings are called *double stops* when played at the same time. Almost all guitarists use this technique at some time. Rock and metal players pound out double stops when playing chords for rhythm, and virtually every musical genre, from classical to punk, involves double stops for playing melodies, harmonies, and lead guitar parts.

DEFINITION

Double stops are created by striking two adjacent strings at the same time, playing the notes of both stings simultaneously.

For starters, try out a simple blues shuffle using just the two lowest strings of your guitar. First, place your index finger on the second fret of the A string. Now strike both the low E and the A string at the same time for both of the swing eighth notes of the first beat. As soon as you've hit the second pair of notes, place your ring finger on the fourth fret of the A string and play the second pair of swing eighth notes. You can keep your index finger on the second fret while your ring finger is on the fourth fret. If that's too big of a stretch, then raise your index finger slightly off the frets while you put your ring finger in place, kind of like a teeter-totter. Your shuffle should sound like the one at the 29 second mark of Track 13 of the CD:

 Track 13 (0:29)

Chapter 6, Example 3.

If you're using a pick, keep the pick perpendicular to the strings and keep your picking stroke short, making certain not to touch the D string. If you're using your fingers, either you can play both the low E and A strings with a short, even stroke of the thumb or you can "pinch" the two notes, using your thumb to play the low E string in a downward motion while your index finger picks the A string with an upward sweep.

KEEP SHARP!

If you're using your whole arm or your elbow to strum, you will not be able to consistently and accurately control the strings you want to strike. Keep your strumming hand close to the strings, use your wrist, and remember to use your "sock puppet" motion, even when picking one or two strings at a time. Doing so will help you develop excellent control of your string-picking abilities.

Don't worry if something that seems like it should be easy takes a little more practice! So far, your own playing has dealt with either single notes or full chords. This is entirely new, and it will take a little time for you to get comfortable with the technique.

When you're confident that you can handle this first shuffle, try it using just the A and D strings together, and then again using just the D and G strings, like this:

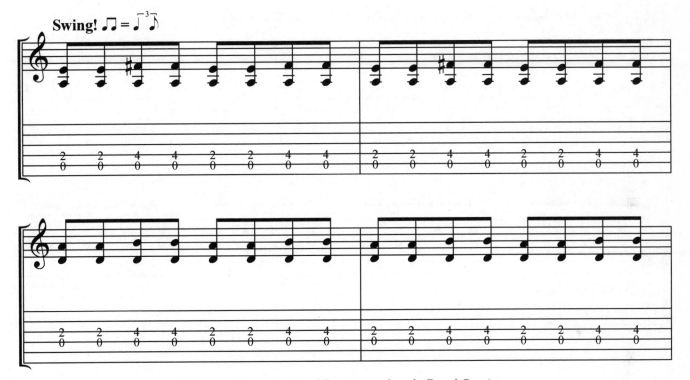

Blues shuffles on the A and D strings and on the D and G strings.

Be very careful to hit only the strings you want to when you're playing these shuffles. At first, it may seem close to impossible to not hit adjoining strings, but you'll surprise yourself by how you'll quickly get a feel for striking only the strings involved in each shuffle. A little practice is all it takes.

Blues Shuffles and Rock Shuffles

You can also play this shuffle with regular eighth notes instead of swing eighths. "Regular" eighth notes are often called "straight eighths" when someone wants to emphasize the difference between swing and regular rhythms. Also, in a few songs, like "Taylor" by Jack Johnson, the rhythm changes from swing to straight and then back again.

LISTENING LIBRARY

Listen to songs, counting the beats either aloud or in your head, to develop an ear for identifying swing rhythms. Virtually every band plays songs with both swing and straight styles. Queen's "Another One Bites the Dust" is straight; "Crazy Little Thing Called Love" is played in swing. Green Day's "Holiday" is in swing; "Good Riddance (Time of Your Life)" is in straight time.

The following example should help you clearly hear (and hopefully feel, as you practice it) the difference between swing and straight rhythms.

Track 13 (0:40)

Blues Shuffle Rhythm

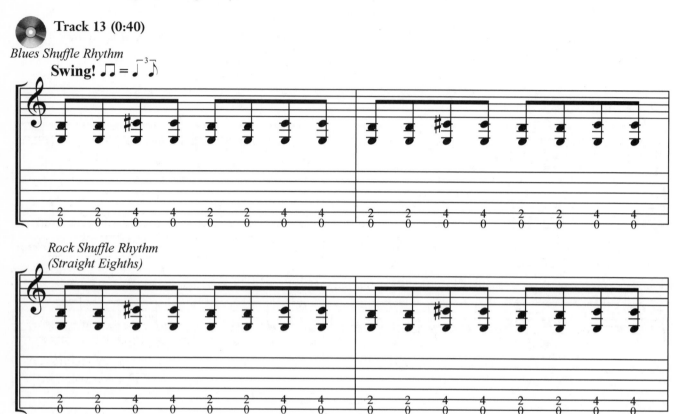

Chapter 6, Example 4.

Some More Seventh Chords

Seventh chords, which you learn more about in Chapter 13, are an important part of the blues sound. Here are the chord charts for E7 and A7:

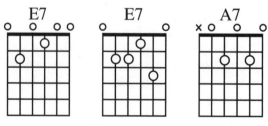

E7 and A7 chords.

Notice that you've been given two ways to play the E7 chord. The notes of E7 are E, G♯, B, and D. The easiest way to play an E7 is to start with the regular E chord and then simply remove your ring finger from the D string, which adds the D note to the E chord.

But you can also find a D note at the third fret of the B string. So another way to play E7 is to start with the regular E and then add your pinky to the third fret of the B string.

> **SOUND ADVICE**
>
> Learning new chords is a big part of the early stages of playing the guitar. You can also help yourself get even better by paying attention to which chords seem to show up in songs. As you'll learn in Chapter 15, certain chords go together well, and knowing what chords go with others will help you prepare for quick and easy chord changes.

Play both E7 chords and listen to how they're similar and different. The E7 that uses all four fingers has the D note at a higher position than the one that uses the open D string. Think of your guitar as a small choir with six people in it; each person—or each string, in this case—can sing only one note. So you have the option of telling either the "D-string person" or the "B-string person" to sing the "D" note.

The difference in sound of these chords is called a *voicing*, and you'll learn a lot more about that later. For now, it's important for you to realize that not only do you have new chords to learn, you'll also be learning different voicings for the chords you already know.

The D and D7 Chords

You need to learn two more chords at this point, D and D7. To make D, start with the A7 chord, using your middle finger at the second fret of the B string and your index finger at the second fret of the D string. Shift both fingers one string closer to the floor, so that your middle finger is on the second fret of the high-E string and your index finger sits on the second fret of the G string. Then add your ring finger to the third fret of the B string. Be sure that your ring finger stands tall on its tip and doesn't collapse and accidentally blunt out either the high-E or G strings.

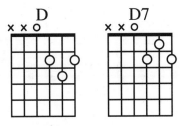

D and D7 chords.

With D7, you want your index finger on the first fret of the B string. Then place your middle finger on the second fret of the G string and your ring finger on the second fret of the high-E string.

As you have in the earlier chapters, play these chords over and over again, and work on changing from one chord to another in every possible combination. I can't stress enough how important it is for you to know your chords and to be able to change smoothly between them. The fastest way to get better at this is simply to use the steps outlined at the end of Chapter 3 over and over again. It may seem like a lot of work now, but you'll be glad you stuck with it. It will make most of the techniques coming up later in the book a lot easier for you to grasp quickly.

The Complete Idiot's Blues (Take 1)

And to give you a break from practicing your chord changes, here's your first blues song! Actually, it's more of a "rhythm template" for a blues song, one of two that you'll see throughout this book:

 Track 14

Chapter 6, Example 5.

When you can play a basic blues shuffle such as this one, you can play literally hundreds of songs. And not just blues songs—many rock, folk, country, and pop songs use very similar chord progressions or simple variations on this one.

LISTENING LIBRARY

Many songs in just about every musical genre use similar, if not identical, chord changes as blues songs. Early rockers like "Blue Suede Shoes," country songs like "Folsom Prison Blues," and even swinging jazz numbers like "Jump, Jive and Wail" are based on blues chord changes, as are hard-rocking numbers like Led Zeppelin's "Rock and Roll" and Jim Carroll's "People Who Died."

We'll be revisiting this "template" in Chapters 18 and 24, when you learn about fills, soloing, and blues music, so don't just learn it and set it aside.

Stretching Out the Shuffle

In fact, you can begin to embellish this basic shuffle almost immediately by expanding the number of notes you play on the string you're fretting. The following examples start out the same as your previous shuffles, but after you play the note on the fourth fret of any given string with your ring finger, you use your pinky to get the note at the fifth fret; then you let it up, keeping your ring finger at the fourth fret and starting the shuffle cycle all over again:

Expanding the blues shuffle.

Do try to use your pinky for the notes at the fifth fret. This is a good exercise to get the pinky involved with your playing. Aside from the B7 and E7 chords you've just learned, you probably haven't used it since the "one finger, one fret" exercises in Chapter 2. You definitely should keep your pinky ready and in shape because it has a lot of important things to do as you move forward with your guitar playing.

The Complete Idiot's Blues (Take 2)

Let's take this expanded shuffle and work up a different arrangement of "The Complete Idiot's Blues" to play. This one also involves changing between playing the shuffle and playing chords and has a cool surprise ending.

Track 15

Chapter 6, Example 6.

Some Quick Changes and a New Voicing

If you've listened to this last song and taken a look at the music and tablature, you've undoubtedly found some spots that require your attention. The shuffle changes strings during each of the first three measures, then does something totally different in the fourth measure. There the B note (second fret of the A string) remains constant while you create a moving bassline on the low-E string. Keep your index finger on that B note and use your middle finger for the F♯ (second fret of the low-E string), your ring finger for the G (third fret), and your pinky for the G♯ (fourth fret).

SOUND ADVICE

More often than not, short runs of single notes (which are called *fills*) are based around the fingering of basic chords. Before you go lifting all your fingers off the strings to play a few single notes, see what chord you're fretting (as well as which chord you might be changing to) to see if the fingering of the chord lends itself to easily reaching the necessary single notes.

You start measure 11 with one beat of the low E/B on the A string double stop. After hitting that, you want to form a D7 chord, but instead of playing it on the first and second frets, you play it on the third and fourth frets. Doing so changes the D7 to an E7, giving you a totally new voicing of the E7 chord.

The strumming, beginning with the second beat of measure 11, changes to triplet strumming. First, you strum a triplet of this new voicing of E7 and then shift the entire chord down one fret so that you're playing it on the second and third frets. This is D♯7, but don't worry about that too much for the moment. After a triplet of D♯7, shift your fingers down another fret, and you'll find yourself playing a regular old D7, just like you learned a few pages ago.

The last measure starts with a full E chord, played as a half note, so it gets two beats. Finally, you play an E7 chord—the four-finger version this time—to end the piece.

Practice, Practice

Not all of the songs you'll be learning later in this book will be as jam-packed with new material as this last one. Still, you want to be careful and smart about how you practice. Some parts of this song will be easy, and others will require work.

KEEP SHARP!

If you're practicing a song and make a mistake, resist the temptation to go back to the beginning and start again. Instead, focus on the trouble spots, just as you've read in this chapter, and try to play just that one section six times or so without a mistake before moving on.

If you continually go back to the beginning and start again, you're very likely to make the same mistake at the same trouble spot—and then you're just practicing mistakes!

As you practice, make note of where the trouble spots are for you. Let's say, for example, that you're doing great up to measure 4 and then things kind of go wonky on you. That's okay! You just started learning this song moments ago, so what did you expect? But what you do next is very important. First, work only on measure 4, and do it just as you would when learning a new chord. Don't worry about the timing; concentrate instead on getting the fingering smooth so that you are confident you know exactly what you want your fingers to do. Then start keeping time at a very slow tempo and work your way up to an acceptable speed.

That's just the first step, though. Next you want to work on connecting this trouble spot to the rest of the song. Begin with measure 3 and see if you can play that measure seamlessly into measure 4 and then go without a hitch into measure 5. Again, start at a very slow tempo until you are confident you can put it all together.

Practicing a piece "in pieces" like this can be very helpful, especially when you are faced with a tricky passage of music. But you want to also practice connecting all the pieces; otherwise, your song is going to sound as if the tempo changes from section to section, according to how well you know the section. You want the entire song to be smooth and even, so take the time to both work out the trouble spots and also make them fit seamlessly into the whole of the song. It should sound like one piece, not several pieces.

The Least You Need to Know

- Triplets are one third of a beat.
- Swing rhythm is based on playing the first and third of the set of triplets.
- Double stops involve playing two adjacent strings at once.
- Any chord can have a different voicing, another fingering of the guitar strings.
- It's helpful to practice the trouble spots of any song by themselves, and then to work them into the rest of the song.

Stretching Out with Three New Chords

In This Chapter

- Playing the C chord
- Distinguishing the many fingerings of the G chord
- Using simple walking basslines
- Tackling the F chord
- Playing the Dm chord

For the beginning guitarist, chords can seem a bit like playing pieces in a strange game. The more chords you "collect"—the more chords you know and the more easily you can change from one to another—the more songs you can play. Songs, after all, are *chord progressions*, combinations of chords that change over a specific rhythm pattern.

So are you ready to be able to play *thousands* of songs? Adding just three more chords—C, G, and F—to your chord catalog will exponentially increase your potential song repertoire. Each of these chords poses a bit of a challenge, not only in fingering, but in the logistics involved in making chord changes. But you're ready, so let's get to it and make some more music!

Stretching Out

These three new chords are also important because they involve some of the biggest stretches you've made on the fingerboard, in terms of both length and width. If you've been keeping up with your "one finger, one fret" warm-up exercise and keeping your fingers up on their tips when forming chords, you should get used to these new chords fairly quickly.

Up to this point, all the chords you've learned have been within a span of two frets. And except for the B7, which uses four fingers across five strings, you haven't had to worry about covering the first and sixth strings at the same time.

Both C and F require you to cover three frets along the fingerboard. And playing G involves fingering notes on both the first and sixth strings. Taking on each of your three new chords one at a time, looking at the nuances of each chord, and practicing forming them (as well as making changes between the new chords and the old chords) as diligently as you've done in your earlier lessons will take you quite a ways down the road in your guitar journey.

SOUND ADVICE

You've probably noticed by this point that your fingers (on your fretting hand) are hurting a little—maybe even a lot. Don't worry, this is normal! You're building up calluses on your fingertips, and it will take a while to develop them.

When your fingers start to hurt, take a short break. For a while, possibly even a month or so, you'll practice in 10- to 15-minute chunks. And that's a lot better than not playing at all.

Remember that the more you play, the sooner you'll get through this stage. But do yourself a favor and take breaks whenever you have to. Playing in pain is not fun, and you've got a long life of playing ahead of you. You'll get through this phase of learning fairly quickly.

The C Chord

Start by fingering an Am chord. Your index finger is on the first fret of the B string, your ring finger should be on the second fret of the G string, and your middle finger sits on the second fret of the D string. Keeping your index and middle fingers in place, pick up your ring finger and reposition it at the third fret of the A string, like this:

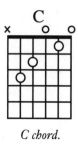

C chord.

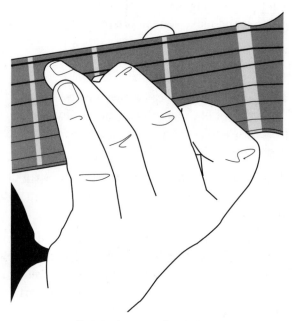

Finger placement for C chord.

C is another chord that you want to strum from the A string downward. First of all, make sure you're getting a good C note (the third fret of the A string) in the bass. Shift all your fretting fingers a little toward the body of the guitar, if necessary. You've got more room on the fingerboard to play with than you might think.

KEEP SHARP!

If you're not getting a clean chord when playing the C chord, make sure you have good position with your ring finger on the C note at the third fret of the A string. You can adjust your other fingers, especially the index finger, once you have the ring finger in place.

You also want to be careful to keep your fingers up on their tips. Collapsing the middle or ring fingers will result in "tunks" or muted (or, worse, semimuted) notes. And if you're grabbing the neck too much (remember, you can tell that you are if you can feel the bottom edge of the neck along the palm of your fretting hand), you won't get a clean note from your open high-E (thinnest) string.

C Chord Alternating Strums and the C7 Chord

You can also play a four-finger version of C by using your pinky in place of the ring finger at the third fret of the A string and then placing your ring finger on the third fret of the low-E (thickest) string, as shown in the following chart.

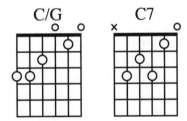

Variation of the C chord and the C7 chord.

Many guitarists refer to this fingering as "C/G," which is musical shorthand for playing a C chord with a G note in the bass (instead of the usual root note of C). This sort of chord is called a *slash chord*, and you'll be reading about these in Chapter 13.

The previous illustration also contains a chart for C7. Playing C7, as with fretting B7, involves all your fingers. Start with the basic C chord and then add your pinky to the third fret of the G string.

If you want to play an alternating bass strum for C or C7, you have many options:

C

continues

continued

C 7

Various alternating bass strums for C and C7.

Usually one uses a G note, either the open G string or the one at the third fret of the low-E string. When using the low G, you can use the four-finger version of C, which puts your fingers in place for both notes. Many people, though, simply move their ring finger from the A string to the low-E string as they change the bass note. It's not hard to get used to, with a little practice.

You can also use E as an alternating note, but use the E note at the second fret of the D string. The open low-E string muddies up the sound when used for an alternating bass.

The G Chord

Once you know the C chord, learning how to shape the G chord is easy—but figuring out which fingers to use may take a little extra work. Starting with the basic three-finger C chord, you pick your index finger totally off the fingerboard. Then shift both your ring and middle fingers to the next-thicker string. Your middle finger will be on the second fret of the A string, and your ring finger on the third fret of the low-E string. Finally, add your pinky to the third fret of the high-E string. Your fingers should be positioned as shown in the following chord chart.

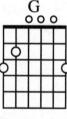

G major chord.

Many guitarists do *not* play the G chord with this fingering; they find it uncomfortable. Instead, they use the index finger on the second fret of the A string, the middle finger on the third fret of the low-E string, and the ring finger on the third fret of the high-E string. Try out both fingerings and see which you feel more comfortable with. Use that as your "default" position, but do try to become somewhat adept at both fingerings, because each one has its uses.

More G Options

You want to be aware of two other voicings of the G chord, each used for a different reason.

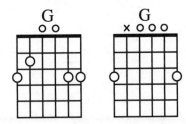

Other options for playing the G major chord.

The notes of a G chord are G, B, and D. In this first voicing, the B note of the open B string is replaced with the D note at the third fret. Use your ring finger to play this added note, and place your pinky on the third fret of the high-E string.

KEEP SHARP!

When playing the G chord, be very careful to apply even pressure to all the fretted notes. Beginners tend to push the G note on the low-E string too hard, either pulling the string in toward the middle of the fingerboard or pushing it off the edge of the neck. Without meaning to do so, they bend the note and make it sharp, which makes the whole chord sound out of tune, even though the fingers are on the correct frets.

The second voicing shown here makes use of string muting, which you'll learn more about in Chapter 10. You'll notice an "X" above the A string in the chord chart, which you know means that you don't want to play that string. But when you strum across all six strings, it's impossible to not hit the A string!

What you do here is use either your middle finger (and that should be your first preference) or your index finger to play the third fret of the low-E string. But instead of keeping your finger up on its tip, flatten it slightly so that it lightly touches the A string. This mutes the string. When you play just the A string with your fingers in this position, you'll hear a dull, muted "tunk" instead of a clean note. That's exactly what you want. Now, when you strum across all six strings, the ringing notes will drown out that weak, muted string and you'll have your G chord.

G and the Alternating Bass

As with the C chord, you have a couple options for playing alternating bass strums with G:

G

continues

continued

Possible alternating bass for the G chord.

Most people prefer to alternate the low G (third fret of the low-E string) with the D note of the open D string, but you can also use the B note (second fret of the A string) as an alternate bass note. You can also mix the two alternating strums, as shown in the second line of this example.

Changing G to C

More songs use the C and G chords than you can possibly imagine, so you have to be able to change between these two chords smoothly and efficiently. That's not easy for a beginner, especially if you use the "typical" fingering of G, with the middle finger on the third fret of the low-E string, index finger on the second fret of the A string, and ring finger on the third fret of the high E.

If you opt for this fingering, take this trial test: get your fingers in place, and then play the G chord four times and switch to the C. Watch your fingers as you do so. More likely than not, you try to place your index finger down first (at the first fret of the B string) when making the C chord. This means you're waiting until you have the entire chord in place before making your strum.

SOUND ADVICE

Guitar music uses G, C, and D chords all the time. Spend as much time as you can practicing the change between these three chords. Remember to use all the steps outlined at the end of Chapter 3.

More times than not, you'll make chord changes on a downstroke, so get in the habit of placing your fingers from the low strings up whenever possible. This means getting the ring finger down first when making a C chord—which can be tricky.

Let Your Fingers Do the Walking

Fortunately, there are ways to train yourself to get the fingers you want where you want them to be. One cool-sounding way to help you develop this habit with the switch from the G chord to the C chord is to use a *walking bassline*, as shown here:

Track 16 (0:00)

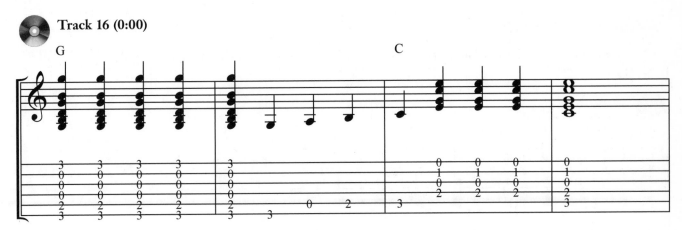

Chapter 7, Example 1.

Play the G chord five times very slowly. After the fifth time, pick just the G note (third fret of the low-E string) by itself. Then lift all your fingers off the strings (not very far off!) and pick the open A string. Then place your middle finger on the B note at the second fret of the A string and play that. Finally, place your ring finger on the C note at the third fret of the A string. As you do so, get the rest of the C chord into place by moving your middle finger to the second fret of the D string and your index finger to the first fret of the B string.

 DEFINITION

A **walking bassline** is a short series of low (bass) notes used as a fill to connect chords.

If you practice this example diligently, working slowly through the changes to make certain that you're getting the right fingers on the right frets, you'll soon be automatically making the C chord by leading with your ring finger.

LISTENING LIBRARY

You can hear guitarists using walking basslines all the time. Johnny Cash's "I Walk the Line" is an excellent example. The walking bassline descends during the first line of the chorus ("… because you're mine …") and ascends during the "I walk the line" part.

The second half of this example reverses the process, moving from C to G. Be sure to practice this as well. Start with the C chord, then play just the C note and use your middle finger (shifted from the D string) to get the B note (the second fret of the A string). Pick up all your fingers (lifting them just enough to clear the strings) to play the open A string and use that moment when all your fingers are off the strings to reposition them for playing the G chord. Be sure to first set the finger on the third fret of the low-E string, since you'll be playing that first.

Adding the D or D7

You can use a slight variation of this walking bassline to move from the G chord to either D or D7, like this:

Track 16 (0:18)

Chapter 7, Example 2.

Handsome Molly

Even though you're using these walking basslines as a method to smooth out chord changes, they are wonderful musical phrases in and of themselves. Your first song for this chapter uses them to help you practice both the walking basslines and the chord changes from G to D and from C to G:

Track 17

Well I wish I____ was in Lon-don____ or some oth-er sea-port town   I'd

Chapter 7, Example 3.

This song also makes use of the both the B and D notes when alternating the bass on the G chord.

One Tough Chord

You've done a lot of great work so far in this chapter, so give yourself a well-deserved pat on the back! You've tackled both the C chord, getting yourself to stretch your fingers across three frets to make the chord, and the G, which involved fretting both the low- and high-E strings. So relax, shake out your wrists, and unwind before moving on.

F, the last of the three new chords, is like C, in that you'll be stretching across three frets. But it also introduces you to the concept of barring the strings, which is laying one finger out flat to cover two or more strings. Placing a finger, usually the index finger, across all six strings is called a *full barre*. Covering any other number of strings, from two to five, is called a *half barre*. Any chord that you create with a barre, whether a full barre or a half barre, is usually referred to as a *barre chord*, and you'll learn all about those in Chapter 14.

Working the Half Barre

Start by fingering a three-finger C chord. Keep your index finger in place at the first fret of the B string and shift your middle and ring fingers up one string. Your ring finger will now be on the third fret of the D string, and your middle finger will be on the second fret of the A string. Finally, slightly adjust the position of your index finger so that you can flatten it out to cover the first fret of *both* the high-E and B strings, like this:

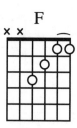

The F chord.

If you're having trouble with the fingering, don't panic! The F chord gives everyone fits the first time—sometimes the first hundred times! Try working the fingering backward so you can get your fingers in place. Put your index finger on the first fret of the high-E string and place it flat instead of having it on its tip. Pick the high-E string with your finger in place to make certain you've got a good, clean note. Then shift your index finger to cover both the high-E and B strings at the first fret. Again, play both strings to be sure you've still got good notes sounding when you pick the strings. Your index finger should be parallel to the fret; feel the edge of the fret along the side of your finger closest to the body of the guitar.

When you're good with the first two strings, add your middle finger to the second fret of the G string and again test all three strings for clean-sounding notes. Your middle finger, unlike the index finger, should be up on its tip so that it doesn't accidentally brush up against the adjacent strings.

Finally, add the ring finger to the third fret of the D string. Your ring finger should be up on its tips as well. Strum the complete F chord from the D string down.

Viable Options

Because you've been working on your other basic chords first, and because you've gotten used to stretching across three frets with the C chord, you should have a much easier time with the F chord than you would if you'd had to learn it first! But this is the most difficult chord you've attempted. Be patient if it doesn't come immediately.

The F chord consists of the notes F, A, and C, so there are other ways to play it if it's giving you fits. The easiest way is to use an F major seventh chord (Fmaj7, for short), as shown in either of these two chord charts:

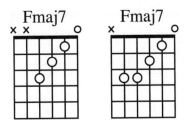

The F major seventh (Fmaj7) chord.

The first version uses the index finger on the first fret of the B string, the middle finger on the second fret of the G string, and the ring finger on the third fret of the D string. In the second, you place your pinky on the D string and then add your ring finger to the third fret of the A string.

The Fmaj7 chord, as you'll learn in Chapter 13, adds the E note to the rest of the F chord, and it often can serve as a substitute for F. To just play the notes of the F chord, simply avoid both the high and low E strings when strumming. That, too, takes a bit of practice, but it's a good technique for you to work on.

Alternating bass notes with F is also much like the C chord:

Alternating bass for the F.

It's very rare to use the open A string for your alternating bass note. You certainly can, but most people find that the C note at the third fret of the A string works best.

Walking C to F and Back

You can also use a walking bassline to practice getting your ring finger down on the fingerboard first when playing an F chord. Changing from C to F (and back) works like this:

C to F walking bassline.

Rowing the Boat Ashore

Now it's time to take on a song that uses all three of your new chords, plus your old friend Em and one more new chord, D minor (Dm, for short), which also covers the span of three frets.

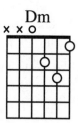

The Dm chord.

Most people finger the Dm with the index finger on the first fret of the high-E string, the middle finger on the second fret of the G string, and either the ring finger or the pinky covering the third fret of the B string. Both fingerings have advantages, so (as always) try them both and see which you like.

Notice, at the end of the fourth measure, that you can use most of the walking bassline from C to F to make the change from C to Em.

You're also introduced to first and second endings (in this case, first, second, and third endings, since there are three verses!). In the last line, you find a repeat sign at the end of a measure that is underneath a bracket labeled "1, 2." When you reach this repeat sign, go back to the repeat sign at the start of the first full measure and proceed through the verse of the song again, including playing the measure under the "1, 2" bracket.

After playing the song twice, you play it a third time. This time you don't play the measure under the bracket labeled "1, 2." Instead, you skip over it entirely and play the measure under the bracket labeled "3," which is the end of the song.

Track 18

Chapter 7, Example 4.

Practice, Practice

The point of all the songs in *The Complete Idiot's Guide to Guitar* is to help reinforce the ideas and techniques that you're picking up as you learn your instrument. But that doesn't mean you have to play them as they're written out.

LISTENING LIBRARY

Both songs in this chapter are traditional tunes with impressive and surprising histories. You can hear "Handsome Molly" on Mick Jagger's solo album *Wandering Spirit,* and Bobby Darin has a very cool jazzy version of "Michael Row Your Boat Ashore" that you can find on YouTube.

For example, both songs in this chapter involve your new chords, plus the new idea of walking basslines. They also both use the alternate bass strumming that you learned in Chapter 4. For some, that's a lot to take on at once. A good idea is to start by just seeing if you can make the chord changes using simple strums. Then see how you do by adding the alternating bass. Get comfortable and confident playing the song in this simpler version before adding on the walking basslines.

Conversely, each time you learn something new, it's an excellent idea to go back over old songs, especially ones you really like, and see if you can apply these new ideas to them. Some ideas, like the walking bassline, may need a bit more explaining (which you'll get in Chapter 12) before you can get them to the point that they work in the old songs, but just hearing how they might work in your mind can be a big start.

The Least You Need to Know

- The C, G, and F chords are used in thousands of songs.
- You can play the G chord in many different ways.
- You usually want to form chords by getting your fingers on the lower strings (low E and A) first.
- Walking basslines can help you get better with your chord changes *and* they make changing from chord to chord sound cool!
- Fmaj7 can substitute for F, but it's still good to work on playing the F chord. Hang in there!

Making Your Guitar Sing with Slurs

In This Chapter

- Hammer-ons
- Discovering grace notes
- Proper pull-offs
- Sliding from note to note
- String bends
- Combining slurs with strumming

Learning chords—how to play them and how to change smoothly from one to another—and learning how to strum with a steady beat are the first major goals for the beginning guitarist. Whether you want to sing songs with your family and friends; play intricate, multivoiced classical or jazz pieces; or even shred a lightning-fast flamenco or rock solo, it all begins with chords and rhythm.

Adding these three newest chords—C, G, and F—to the chords you learned in the earlier chapters means that you can now strum along with thousands of songs, as long as you know which chords to use and are able to keep a steady beat.

You've come quite a long way in such a relatively short time, but the fun is only beginning. You're now ready to make your strumming and chord playing a lot more musical. Working through the "one finger, one fret" exercises of Chapter 2 helped your fingers learn how to create clean, clear-sounding notes and got them limber for fretting chords and smoothly (and cleanly) changing your chords—all in rhythm.

Now you're going to see how knowing your chords, combined with the finger dexterity you've developed to this point, can make you sound like more than a beginning guitarist. Quite often, the only difference between an absolute beginning guitarist and an "intermediate beginner," if you will, is simply that the intermediate beginner knows a few tricks.

Introducing Slurs

Up to this point, your left hand and right hand have been working as a team to produce a note. Your left hand frets the note on the fingerboard and your right hand picks the string. It's all nice and uncomplicated, and both hands know their respective tasks.

When you play a note in this fashion, it's called an *articulated note*. A *slur*, or a slurred note, is created using one of four special techniques—hammer-ons, pull-offs, slides, and bends—that are usually done by the left hand on the fingerboard without picking by the right hand.

DEFINITION

Slurs, in guitar music, are notes that are produced by a means other than picking the string, usually by using the fretting hand to create the note on the neck. The four basic types of slurs are hammer-ons, pull-offs, slides, and bends.

In music notation or guitar tablature, slurs are indicated by the same arc that is used to tie notes together (from Chapter 4). You can tell the difference between a tie and a slur because the notes tied together in a tie are the same note (in terms of note name) and those linked together in a slur are different notes.

Tied notes

Slurs

The difference between ties and slurs.

Because slurs involve individual notes rather than chords, you won't usually find slurs in rhythm notation.

The Mighty Hammer-On

Playing any of the four different guitar slurs is fairly simple—you just do what the name says! To play a hammer-on, you hammer a finger of your left hand onto a specific fret of a specific string *after* you have already picked, plucked, or strummed that string. A hammer-on is usually indicated by a small "H" placed above the arc of the slur.

In the following example, you first pick the open A string and then hammer a finger (use your index finger to start with) onto the second fret of the A string. Bring it down onto the string hard and fast!

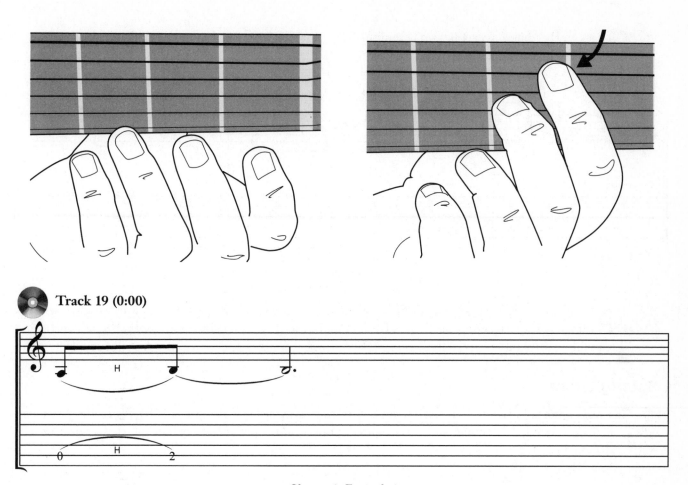

 Track 19 (0:00)

Chapter 8, Example 1.

Pick the A string only once! Your index finger hammering the string creates the second note (B at the second fret of the A string) in this example.

 SOUND ADVICE

When learning hammer-ons, it helps at first to exaggerate the motion of the technique. Really whack the finger onto the string, putting some speed and strength into it. And make certain to use the tip of the finger, as you do when regularly fretting a note. As you get more accustomed to playing hammer-ons, you'll find you don't have to exaggerate so much to get the speed and strength you need.

As with all slurs, this is simpler to explain than to execute. You're not used to performing this technique and haven't yet built up the finger strength needed to be consistent and accurate in making hammer-ons. But you will.

KEEP SHARP!

Make it a point to work *all* your fingers in the slur examples in this chapter. You need all your fingers, especially the ring finger and pinky, to be able to perform slurs well.

Go back to the "one finger, one fret" exercises from Chapter 2, but adapt them specifically for developing your skills at hammer-ons.

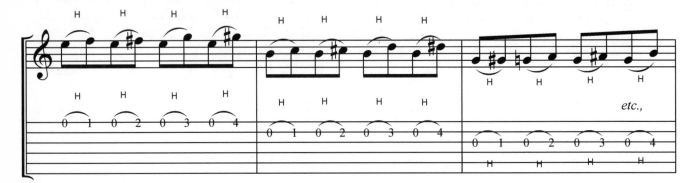

One finger, one fret exercises for hammer-ons.

Even though you want to use enough finger strength to sound the hammered note cleanly and clearly, you ultimately want to keep your fingers fairly close to the strings, ideally not more than a half-inch. That will be difficult at first, but as you gain both finger strength and confidence, it will get easier.

Saving Grace

It's very important to note that slurred notes have timing values just as regular notes do. In the previous "one finger, one fret" hammer-on exercises, each note, whether articulated or slurred, is an eighth note and should receive half a beat.

 KEEP SHARP!

While slurs like hammer-ons and pull-offs can almost immediately make you a speedier guitarist, you have to remember to watch your timing! Just because you can use a hammer-on to move quickly from one note to the next doesn't mean you should. Be sure to read the rhythm values of slurs and play them with the appropriate timing.

Sometimes, though, slurs are played very quickly, almost as if the guitarist played the first note, the articulated one, by accident and thought "oops" and used the slur to cover his mistake. These "oops" notes, played as fast as one can change them, are called *grace notes*. They're indicated in both music notation and tablature as tiny notes right before the slurred note.

Track 19 (0:06)

Chapter 8, Example 2.

It's incredibly important to take notice of the timing between the articulated note and the slurred note. You can inadvertently fly through a series of slurs when you're meant to string them along to a specific rhythm. A good method of keeping your mind on the task is to change the timing around using the "one finger, one fret," like this:

Track 19 (0:13)

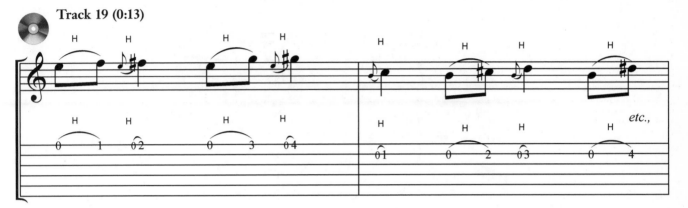

Chapter 8, Example 3.

Fret-to-Fret and Multiple Hammers

Paying attention to timing, as well as developing strength in all your fingers, becomes more important when you start working on hammer-ons from one fretted note to another and multiple hammer-ons, such as in the following example:

Track 19 (0:29)

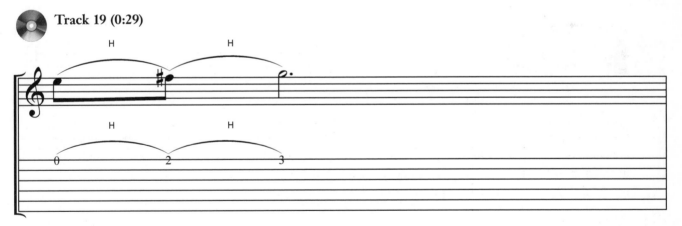

Chapter 8, Example 4.

The trick to these is to keep the finger fretting the first note on the string when hammering with the next finger. This is where all your practice in keeping your fingers on their tips when playing chords comes into play. You may want to go back to some of your earlier songs and exercises, and try playing the ascending walking basslines as hammer-ons.

Pull-Offs

The pull-off is almost like an "anti-hammer-on." You start with a finger fretting a note and then, after picking the string, you pull your finger off the string and it sounds the note of the open string. A small "P" placed above the arc of a slur shows you when to play a pull-off.

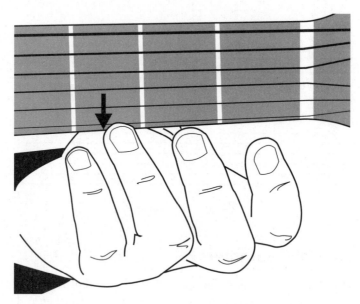

Track 20 (0:00)

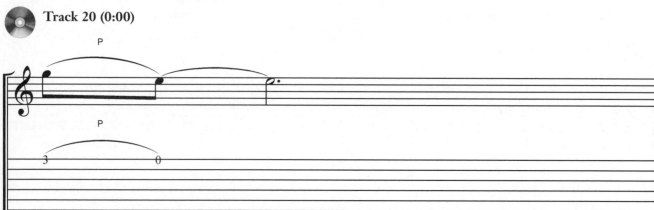

Chapter 8, Example 5.

How you take your finger off the string is the key to playing a successful pull-off. Merely lifting the finger from the string won't result in much sound; you want to *pull* your finger off the string, using a slight downward (toward the floor) motion. Your fingertip pulls the string and then releases it, essentially picking the string again without your right hand doing the picking. This "pick from the pull" makes the second note sound.

Multiple Pull-Offs

Pull-offs quite often occur between one fretted note and another, as in the following examples:

 Track 20 (0:06)

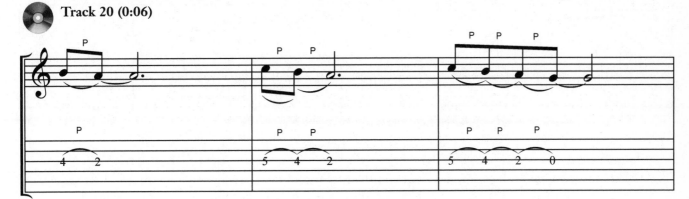

Chapter 8, Example 6.

To play the example in the first measure, put your index finger on the second fret of the G string and keep it in place as you add your ring finger to the fourth fret of the same string. Pick the G string with your right hand and then perform a pull-off with your ring finger, still keeping the index finger in place.

> **SOUND ADVICE**
>
> Pull-offs become even easier to play as you start developing calluses on your fingertips. The rough edges of the calluses will catch and pull the string for you!

The second measure adds another note to the mix. You place both your index and ring fingers on the second and fourth fret, respectively, of the G string and add your pinky to the fifth fret. After picking the G string with your right hand, you perform a pull-off with your pinky, which sounds the B note that is still held by the ring finger at the fourth fret. The ring finger then performs a pull-off that sounds the A note still being held by the index finger at the second fret.

The final example, shown in the third measure, is a repeat of the second example, except that you finish with the index finger performing a pull-off to sound the note of the open G string.

Combining Hammer-Ons and Pull-Offs

As you improve your skills with hammer-ons and pull-offs, it will become second nature to you to mix them together, as in the following example:

Track 20 (0:19)

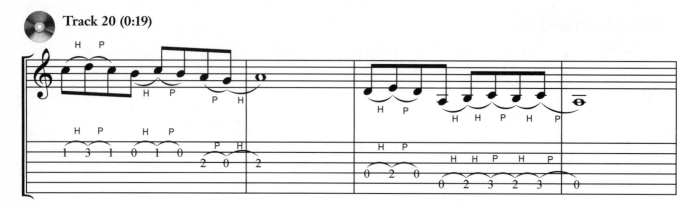

Chapter 8, Example 7.

Start this example with your index finger on the first fret of the B string and use either your ring finger or your pinky for the D note at the third fret of that string. Use your middle finger for notes at the second fret of any of the other three strings and your ring finger for the C note (third fret of the A string) in the next-to-last measure.

A quick, repeated combination of hammer-ons and pull-offs between two notes is called a *trill*. In notation, it is indicated with a thick, wavy line accompanied by the letters "tr."

Track 20 (0:30)

Chapter 8, Example 8.

In guitar music, a trill often starts as a grace note to indicate which two notes are involved in the trill. In the previous example, you are trilling between the D note of the open D string and the E note at the second fret of the D string.

Slides

Slides are probably the most deceptive of slurs. They sound impressive and look easy enough to do, but they can initially drive you to distraction. Like hammer-ons and pull-offs, you're going from one note to another, but instead of slamming a finger onto a fret or pulling it away, you're keeping contact with the string the whole time. After picking the string to sound the initial note, you then let your finger glide over the frets to a second, targeted note somewhere along the same string.

Successful slides are a matter of touch. When you first pick the string, fret the note as you normally do. As soon as you start your slide, ease up slightly on your fretting finger so it will glide smoothly over the frets to the next note. Too much pressure, and your finger won't slide; too little, and you won't create the sound of the slide.

The note you're sliding to is actually more important than the note you started on! Think of it as trying to land your finger directly on a target. Once you reach your desired note, reapply pressure with your fingertip; otherwise, that note won't sound.

Slides require some practice and finesse. Beginners often find themselves picking the string before making the slide and again after reaching the target note. But with repetition and confidence, you'll soon find that your fingers will develop the strength and coordination to make the target note ring out after you've slid up (or down) to it.

Slides are indicated by diagonal lines connecting notes in notation (or numbers in tablature), like this:

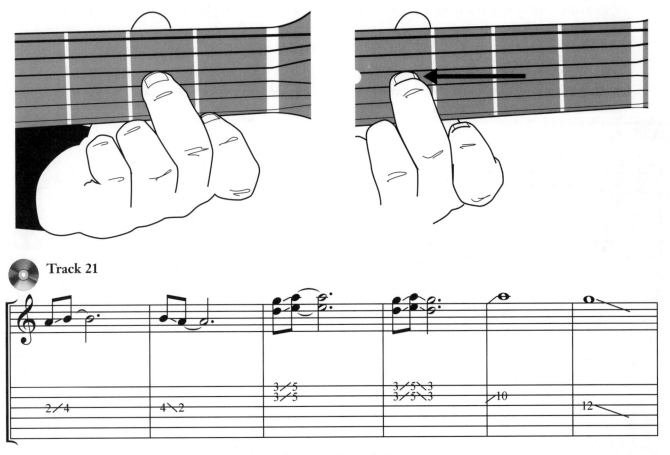

Track 21

Chapter 8, Example 9.

In the first measure of this example, you have a finger (try the ring finger) on the A note located at the second fret of the G string. After you pick that note, slide the ring finger up two frets so that it sits at the fourth fret of the G string.

Slides can go either up or down the neck. The second measure of the previous example has a downward slide, moving from the body of the guitar toward the headstock. Slides can also be done on more than one string at a time, as shown in the third measure.

There are also "undefined" slides, meaning that the starting or ending point isn't given in the music or tablature. In the fifth measure, you'll see first an upward slide, starting from an unspecified note moving up to the tenth fret of the B string. Most guitarists tend to start an undefined slide from either two or three frets away from the target note, but usually where one starts the slide depends on what happened immediately before it, musically.

To play slides starting on specific notes and ending on an undefined one, as shown in the sixth measure, simply ease off on the pressure of the fretting finger as you slide and let the sound trail away.

Bends

Normally when you fret a note, you push it straight down on the fingerboard. When you push or pull a string up or down, you are *bending* the string. This causes the fretted note to go sharp. Depending on how much you bend the string, you can change the note up to a step and a half higher than the original.

Bending strings doesn't require strong fingers as much as it does good ears. You need to be able to hear the note you want to achieve on the bend in order to successfully perform this slur. And when first learning how to bend, it's best to have all your fingers involved.

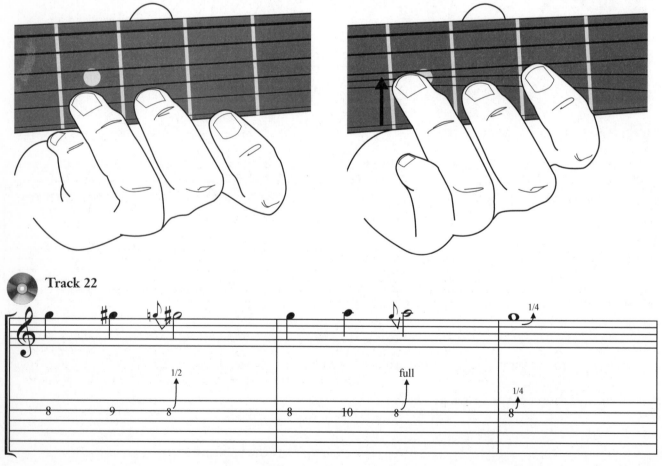

Track 22

Chapter 8, Example 10.

Start with the "half-bend" or "half-step bend" in the first measure. Before you even attempt it, play the G note at the eighth fret of the B string. Then play G♯ at the ninth fret. Try to set both notes (especially the G♯) front and center in your brain. The G♯ is your target, the note you want to achieve on the bend.

Now place your ring finger on the eighth fret of the B string, just as you would to play the note normally. Then place your middle and index fingers on the seventh and sixth frets, respectively, of the same string. Your ring finger is going to bend the note, and the other fingers are helping provide support.

Your wrist actually provides the "muscle" when it comes to bending. You want to use a motion like turning the key in the ignition of a car. As you make that motion, your fingers will push the B string along the fingerboard toward the center of the neck, raising the pitch of the note from G upward. When you hear yourself hit the G♯ note, you've achieved your target and can stay put for the rhythmic duration of the target note.

SOUND ADVICE

You can bend strings in either direction. Most guitarists tend to bend toward the center of the finger-board, pushing the three high strings (the high E, B, and G) and pulling the low ones. It's much easier to bend the thinner strings, and it's also easier to perform bends higher up on the neck, as you're doing in the examples in this section. As you become more confident in your abilities, try working your way down the neck to the lower frets.

In the second measure of the previous example, you perform a "full bend," meaning that the note achieved by the bend will be one full step higher than the starting note. Do yourself a favor and play the A note at the tenth fret of the B string, and fix your ears on your new target. Then repeat the steps you just took to get that note.

In some styles of music, especially in blues, Celtic, and rock, you will run into "quarter bends," shown in the third measure of the previous example. Here your target note technically doesn't have a name. It's kind of halfway between G and G♯. All you need to do is give the string a little nudge to knock the note slightly sharp.

Quarter bends are used to give the guitar a bit of a personal quality, allowing it to be slightly out of tune for a brief moment before righting itself, much like a singer or an unfretted instrument such as a violin. The effect is both haunting and arresting when done well.

Putting It All Together

As you might imagine, slurs are used extensively in guitar solos. Anyone playing speedy lead lines is probably well versed in executing hammer-ons, pull-offs, slides, and bends.

But inserting even a single slur into your strumming expands your rhythmic vocabulary almost as much as adding the C, G, and F chords expands your potential song repertoire. Just to get you started, here are examples of a very basic strum of the E minor chord, each augmented with one or more of the four slurs you've learned.

Track 23

Chapter 8, Example 11.

The first two measures, labeled "Section A," give you a basic alternating bass strum for the Em chord. In "Section B" (the third and fourth measures), you add hammer-ons to this basic strum. Instead of hitting just the B note (second fret of the A string) on the third beat, you hit the open A string and then hammer onto the B note. Be sure that both notes are an eighth note in duration. The fourth beat repeats this process, except that the hammer-on occurs on the D string.

Keep your fingers in place with this Em chord until you are at the proper beat to perform the hammer-ons. The more you get used to being able to play hammer-ons and pull-offs while maintaining the chord you're playing, the smoother your rhythm will be. You probably can already hear how much more musical the hammer-ons make even this simple strum sound.

"Section C" uses pull-offs instead of hammer-ons for the third and fourth beats. When you make the pull-off, remember to keep your fingers very close to the strings so you can reform the Em chord again on the first beat of the following measure.

You get almost the whole kitchen sink thrown at you in "Section D." On the third beat of the first measure, you pick the E at the second fret of the D string and then slide it up to the F♯ at the fourth fret at the second half of the third beat. Follow that with a downstroke and upstroke of the three high strings on your guitar, then hit the F♯ again on the first beat of the next measure, and then slide it back to E on the second half of the first beat. A pull-off from B (second fret of the A string) to the open A comes on the third beat, and on the fourth beat you play the G note at the third fret of the low-E string and give it a slight tug, bending it a quarter-tone.

Wayfaring Stranger

After you've taken some time using this last example to add slurs to your strum, you can tackle the following song, "Wayfaring Stranger," which combines some of the measures of the last example with some new material.

 Track 24

continues

Chapter 8, Example 12.

The introduction of the song is a composite of "Section B" and "Section D" of the last example, and is used in many places throughout the song. You will also run into some walking basslines (measures 8, 16, 22, 24, and 26).

LISTENING LIBRARY

Like "Michael Row Your Boat Ashore" from Chapter 7, "Wayfaring Stranger" is an old spiritual whose appeal spans almost all musical genres. It's been covered by folk artists (Pete Seeger and Peter, Paul and Mary), bluegrass players (Alison Krauss, Tony Rice, and Bill Monroe), country legends (Dolly Parton, Johnny Cash, and Emmylou Harris), pop and rock performers (Neko Case, Jerry Garcia, Eva Cassidy, Roger McGuinn, Natalie Merchant, Duane Eddy, and Jack White), and even jazz musicians (Charlie Haden Quartet).

Practice, Practice

Even though they may seem easy, you want to put in a lot of time practicing slurs, paying particular attention to adding them to your strums. As mentioned, the "one finger, one fret" exercises are great for building finger strength and coordination for hammer-ons and pull-offs.

You can practice slides almost anywhere and anytime, but you have to do three things:

1. Work on the mechanics of the slide, making sure you're sliding smoothly and evenly over the string and not getting snagged in the frets because of too much pressure by the finger.

2. Work on the accuracy of your slide to ensure that you land on the right note.

3. Work on getting the notes on either end of the slide to sound clean and true.

Bending involves developing both your ear, to hear that you've achieved the correct note in your bend, and your mechanical technique, to perfect hitting the note on time. When you pick the note you're going to bend, see if you can sing the target note if it's a half-step or whole step higher. Try matching the note you're singing to the note at the next fret (if you're targeting a half-step bend) or two frets away (for a whole-step bend) and see how on or off you are. Try to start hearing the note you want in your head before you even make the bend.

The Least You Need to Know

- There are four main types of slurs: hammer-ons, pull-offs, slides, and bends.
- Hammer-ons and pull-offs can add speed when playing individual notes.
- Good sliding technique relies on having a light touch.
- Bending a string causes it to go sharp. By controlling the amount of bend, you can raise your initial note a whole step (and higher).
- Combining slurs with strumming really spices up your playing!

Strumming by the Measure or by the Note

In This Chapter

- Recognizing dotted notes
- Playing in 3/4 time
- Playing in 6/8 time
- Perfecting your accents
- Adding arpeggios to your playing
- Mixing arpeggios and strumming

Slurs offer you a first look at a very important concept in playing guitar, namely that the little touches can add an incredible amount of variety and interest to your playing. You were hopefully both amazed and pleased with how mixing in a hammer-on here or a pull-off there to your strumming makes you sound more like what you think a guitar player should sound like.

Three's a Crowd

All the songs you've learned so far are in 4/4 time. Most songs are, for that matter. But there are millions of songs, and you're bound to run across songs that aren't in 4/4 time, that have a different rhythmic pulse. You have to be ready to play music with a different feel than the music you already play.

After 4/4 time, you're most likely to run into songs in 3/4 time. Obviously, the first thing you want to do when playing a waltz is to change your rhythm when counting out the beats. Instead of counting "one, two, three, four, one, two, three, four," count "one, two, three, one, two, three, one, two, three" and so on. As with counting to four, you want to keep steady and even. Don't count "one, two, three" and then pause slightly before returning to one. Think in triplets!

Dots

You also need a way to notate notes of three beats. Fortunately, music notation already has this figured out for you. A half note that has a dot placed after it is held for three beats:

Dotted half note and dotted quarter note (standard notation)

Dotted half note and dotted quarter note (rhythm notation)

Use of dots in music and rhythm notation.

Dots are shorthand for "add one half the value of the previous note to that note." That sounds more complicated than it is. Simply put, a dotted half note is three beats:

> Half note (2 beats) + Quarter note (1 beat) = 3 beats

The half note is, as you know, two beats. The dot means you add half the value of the half note (one beat) to it. That gives you three beats. Using this system, a dotted quarter note is a beat and a half in length:

> Quarter note (1 beat) + Eighth note (half a beat) = 1½ beats

Because you usually run into only two types of dotted notes in almost all music, it makes more sense to just memorize their values instead of worrying about all the calculating. You probably can memorize them before you finish reading this page!

Basic 3/4 Strumming

Waltzes are very easy to arrange for guitar. You can simply strum a chord for three beats, as shown in the first line of the following illustration:

Track 25 (0:00)

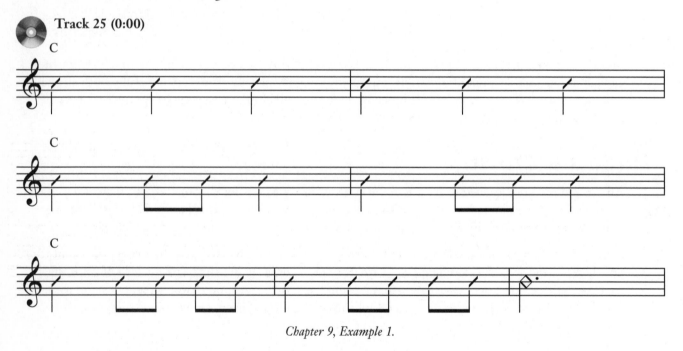

Chapter 9, Example 1.

Lines 2 and 3 demonstrate other strums using a combination of quarter notes and eighth notes.

Typically, though, waltzes are played with the "bass/strum" method. You strike the root note of the chord on the first beat and play the rest of the chord on beats two and three, as shown here:

Track 25 (0:24)

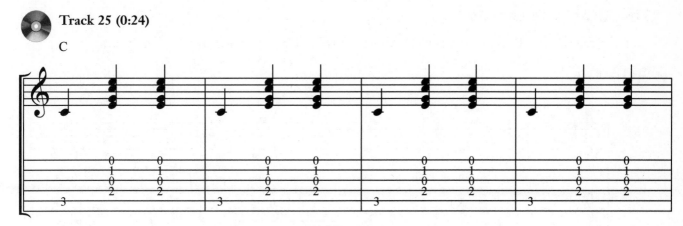

Chapter 9, Example 2.

Think "oom-pah-pah" and you'll soon be playing this strum in your sleep!

Adding an Alternate

One common variation of this strum is to substitute the first quarter note (the root note of the chord) with two eighth notes, the first being the root note of the chord and the second being an alternate bass note, usually on the next-higher string, like this:

Track 25 (0:36)

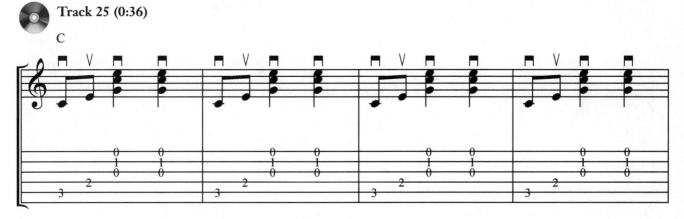

Chapter 9, Example 3.

If you're using a pick, pick down on the first eighth note of the first beat and up on the second eighth note. The following quarter notes (the chords) are downstrokes. You can use your thumb, with a downward stroke, on all the notes and chords if you're playing with your fingers.

Another technique is to use your thumb (picking down) on the first eighth note, pick upward with your index finger on the second eighth note, and then flick your index finger down across the string for the second and third beats. This gives you a different kind of sound because it's the nail of the finger making the downstroke as opposed to the flesh.

It can be a little weird getting used to having your nails hit the strings, so take some time to practice this technique. You also can try out using your middle and ring fingers instead of or in combination with your index finger when making the downstroke. Listen to the different sounds you can get as you play and experiment with them.

"The Streets of Laredo"

Here's a traditional cowboy song to help you practice both 3/4 time and this new strumming style.

 Track 26

Chapter 9, Example 4.

Measure 7 has a new kind of hammer-on that combines the slur with the use of double stops. On the first beat of that measure, you strike just the G and B strings (your index finger should already be on the first fret of the B string), then hammer your middle finger onto the second fret of the G string. On the second beat, you remove your middle finger and play just the G and B strings again; then on the third beat, you strike just the open D and G strings and hammer your middle finger onto the second fret of the D string.

The next-to-last measure combines a walking bassline (using the notes G, A, and B in the bass) with the open strings of the G chord. Play the bass notes with a downstroke and catch the open B, G, and D strings on the upstroke.

Charting the Pulse

Pulses of three are fairly common in music. You know this already from your brief introduction to blues and swing rhythms back in Chapter 6. Music that has a "triplet feel" to it, though, tends to have a different overall vibe than a waltz has.

This is because there are all sorts of ways to subdivide a rhythm—and, just as important, there are different ways of stressing certain beats. In music, particularly in rhythm notation, *accents* are symbols used to show when to stress a beat. They look like "greater than" symbols (>) placed over a note or chord.

DEFINITION

Stressing a particular beat by strumming it harder or louder is called an **accent.** Accents are used to create dynamics and variety in strumming as well as in single note playing.

Suppose you played a few measures of 3/4 time all in eighth-note strums. You usually accent it in either of these ways:

Track 27 (0:00)

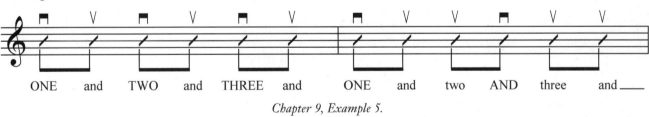

Chapter 9, Example 5.

The first measure accents each beat, and you can hear how it stresses the "three" of 3/4 time. In the second measure, though, the stress is on the first and fourth eighth notes, which gives the measure more of a triplet feel.

Six Eight

Songs that have this "two divided by three" pulse are usually written in 6/8 time. The top number of the time signature indicates that there are six beats in each measure. The bottom number indicates that each eighth note receives one beat, as opposed to the quarter note getting one beat in 4/4 or 3/4 time.

LISTENING LIBRARY

Some songs in 6/8 time that you may know:

- "Nothing Man," by Pearl Jam
- "Norwegian Wood," by the Beatles
- "Breaking the Girl," by the Red Hot Chili Peppers
- "Nothing Else Matters," by Metallica
- "We Are the Champions," by Queen

Here is a basic strum for 6/8 time that uses an alternating bass pattern. You play a bass note (an eighth note in duration) to start with and follow that up with four sixteenth notes of chord strumming. (You'll be learning all about sixteenth notes in the next chapter.)

 Track 27 (0:12)

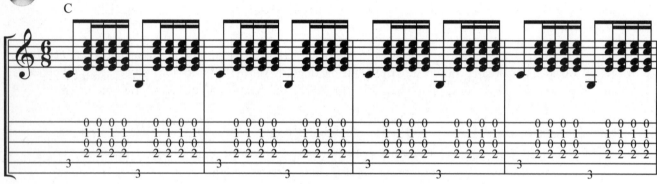

Chapter 9, Example 6.

Because the emphasis in 6/8 time is on the first and fourth beats, you often see dotted quarter notes (which you just recently learned are a beat and a half in length) used as part of the rhythm notation.

Changing on the Fly

You can have songs in all sorts of rhythms and time signatures besides 4/4, 3/4, and 6/8, but these three time signatures account for probably 99 percent of the songs you'll run into. But you do have to be on the lookout for songs that change their time signatures within the song themselves.

In the middle section of the Beatles' "Here Comes the Sun," for instance, the 4/4 time signature switches to one measure of 7/8, then a measure of 6/8, and then a measure of 5/8 before returning to 4/4, but only for a single measure—and then the whole process repeats itself several times. This is certainly on the extreme side, but keep in mind that time signatures can suddenly change on you.

Arpeggios

One easy way to change your strumming style is to use arpeggios instead of full chord strums or alternate bass strums. To play an arpeggio, you hold a chord but hit each string individually in a rhythmic pattern, letting each note ring out on its own. Instead of getting a rush of notes blending together into a chord when you strum all the strings at the same time, you hear each note individually, and the ringing of the individual notes creates the chord.

To understand the difference, try the following:

Track 28

E m

Chapter 9, Example 7.

First, play an Em chord. Next, play an Em chord, but this time hit all the strings as eighth notes and let them continue to ring out as you move from one string to the next.

You can play arpeggios with either upstrokes or downstrokes, or you can change from one direction to another, as shown in the third, fourth, and fifth measures in the previous example.

"The House of the Rising Sun"

To help you work on your arpeggios, and to help you get a little more comfortable in 6/8 time, here's a song I'm sure you've heard before. This is a slightly different, simpler arrangement than you're probably used to.

Track 29

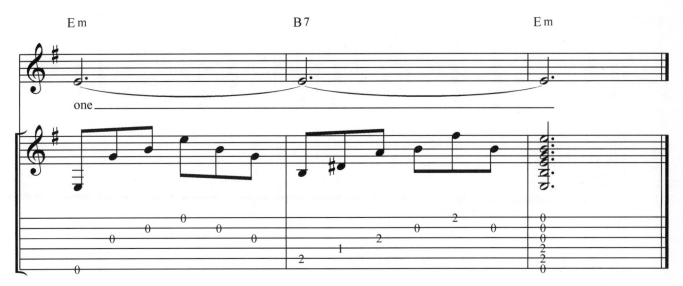

Chapter 9, Example 8.

The arpeggios in this version of "The House of the Rising Sun" are very simple. For all the chords except the B7, you first hit the root note of the chord in the bass; then you skip to the G string and pick the G, B, and high-E strings, and then the B and G strings again, as an arpeggio. On the B7 chord, depending on where you are in the song, you will run into different variations, so listen and read carefully!

If you're using a pick, use downstrokes on the first three notes of the arpeggio and use upstrokes (starting with the first stroke on the high-E string) on the last three. If you're using your fingers, you have many options. I recommend that you try using your thumb for the bass note, whether that note falls on the low-E or A string, and then use your index finger to play any note on the G string, your middle finger for the notes on the B string, and your ring finger for the notes on the high-E string. Your thumb also handles the D string on the B7 chord.

Mixing Things Together

Just as you've combined slurs with strumming, you want to play around with mixing arpeggios into your rhythm. And you can certainly have a lot of fun stringing together arpeggios, strums, and slurs in your rhythm playing! Here are some possibilities, just a few of the many you can come up with:

Track 30

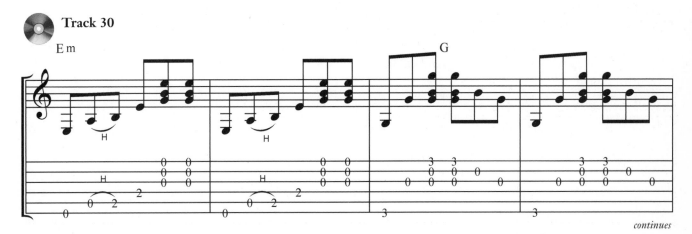

continues

continued

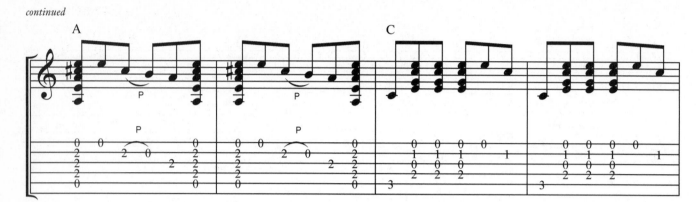

Chapter 9, Example 9.

All of these examples are in 6/8 time, and all involve chords from this chapter's arrangement of "The House of the Rising Sun" for a reason! Try using any of them as substitutes for the appropriate measure in the first version.

And don't be afraid to come up with some of your own as well. When you understand that there's more than one way to play any given measure of music, you'll play with more confidence. As long as you have your chord in place and are keeping proper time, you'll sound like you know what you're doing, even if you don't—and you'll be making the music your own!

Practice, Practice

When practicing arpeggios that run both down and up, it's a good idea to get used to using the highest string you play as a "turnaround point" for your strumming. For example, if you're playing all six strings of the Em chord, use downstrokes for the first five strings you strike (low E, A, D, G, and B), but then use an upstroke on the high-E string to start your change of direction.

The Least You Need to Know

- A dotted half note has a rhythmic value of three beats. Dotted quarter notes are a beat and a half in length.
- Songs can come in many time signatures, but 4/4 time and 3/4 time are the most common.
- In 6/8 time, the pulse is usually on the first and fourth beats of the measure.
- Arpeggios are chords that you strum one string at a time instead of all at once.
- You can mix slurs, arpeggios, and strums.

Stop and Go

In This Chapter

- Strumming sixteenth notes
- Musical rests
- Left-hand string muting
- Palm muting
- Percussive strumming

As you read in earlier chapters, a big part of learning to play music is learning to listen. And strange as it may seem, another big part of learning to play music is learning how to occasionally *stop* playing— that is, to stop playing notes and to use your guitar strictly as a rhythm instrument.

Just as there are many ways to play, there are numerous ways to *not* play, from total silence, to soft string muting, to percussive hits on the guitar that can seem as ferocious as an electric guitar through an amplifier turned up to 11.

Further Subdivision

First, though, you need to learn one more rhythmic value of notes—the sixteenth note. Sixteenth notes are half the value of eighth notes, meaning that they are a quarter of a beat. In music notation or rhythm notation, they look just like eighth notes, except that they have two flags on their stems instead of one. When joined, they are linked by a double beam:

Sixteenth notes in music notation and rhythm notation.

Strumming sixteenth notes involves the same process of strumming that you've been using up to this point. You're simply playing downstrokes on each half beat (eighth note) instead of just on the beat (quarter note).

Track 31 (0:00)

Chapter 10, Example 1.

In the previous example, you can hear that the rhythm is kept steady throughout. As long as you can keep the count and keep your sock puppet motion going, you won't have problems with sixteenth notes.

SOUND ADVICE

A great practice exercise to help you both hear and play the rhythmic differences between notes is to first play a single measure (four beats) of a single chord strummed as quarter notes. Follow that with a measure of eighth notes, a measure of triplets, and then a measure of sixteenth notes. Make sure there's a distinct difference between the triplets and sixteenth notes. Then try using two beats each for each rhythmic value, and then switch from quarter notes, to eighth notes, to triplets, to sixteenth notes on each beat.

As far as strumming goes, you'll most often encounter strums used as accents in songs of slower tempos, as in these samples:

 Track 31 (0:11)

Chapter 10, Example 2.

You can play these with all downstrokes on the eighth notes, using upstrokes only on the sixteenth notes; or you can play as you normally would (down on quarter notes and up on eighth notes) and "double up" when you come to a set of sixteenth notes.

KEEP SHARP!

Don't fall into the trap of thinking that more notes equals faster tempos! The overall beat of a song, the "one, two, three, four," is supposed to remain steady and constant, whether you're playing quarter notes, eighth notes, sixteenth notes, or triplets. You can find yourself speeding up in spite of yourself, so keep your foot at a steady "four on the floor."

For instance, in the first measure of the previous example, play down on the quarter note of the first beat, down and up for the eighth notes of the second beat, down again on the quarter note of the third beat, down on the first half of the fourth beat (the eighth note), and down and up on the two sixteenth notes making up the second half of the fourth beat.

Also notice the sneakily placed dotted eighth note used in the last line of the previous rhythm samples. That will receive three quarters of a beat.

Making a Rest

Rests in music, like notes, are identified by their individual symbols, which are the same in both music notation and rhythm notation:

Rests in music notation.

The tricky ones here are the whole rest (four beats) and the half rest (two beats). An easy way to tell them apart is to think "hole = whole," because the rest sitting below the line looks like a hole, and "hat = half," because the rest looks like a hat when it sits atop the line.

To play a rest, you want to deaden all your strings. The easiest way to do that is just to lay your fretting hand lightly across all six strings, touching them lightly enough to stop any vibrations. You can do this subtly or quite dramatically, as you'll soon see.

SOUND ADVICE

You can come up with all sorts of ways to practice adding rests to your strumming and rhythm playing. Go back to any of the strumming examples in previous chapters and add a quarter note rest at one point in any given measure. Be sure to change it around a bit, putting the rest on the first beat in one measure, on the third in another, and so on.

You can also create a rest with your fretting hand by lifting the fingers slightly off the strings while still keeping enough contact to stop the notes from sounding.

Rests as Rhythm

Many guitarists use rests and various muting techniques as part of rhythm. Cutting a chord short with a quick percussive hit, or strumming while muting the strings with the left hand, allows the guitar to be a pure rhythm instrument, like a drum or any other member of the percussion family. You can play any guitar this way, whether it's acoustic, classical, or electric. In some genres of music, the percussion quality of a guitar is as important as the notes it can play.

Strictly speaking, there's a definite distinction between a true rest (a total absence of sound) and a mute, which is usually used to produce a percussive sound out of the guitar. Mutes are usually denoted in all forms of notation (music, tablature, and rhythm) as "X" symbols, usually attached to an appropriate rhythmic note stem in music and rhythm notation, like this:

muting in music notation and rhythm notation

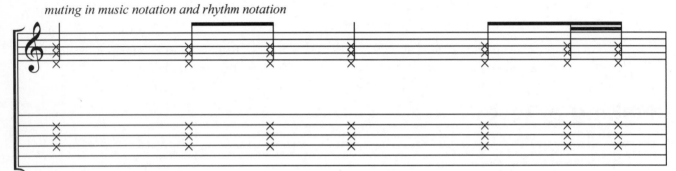

muting in guitar tablature

Muting in music notation, tablature, and rhythm notation.

Left-Hand Muting

The easiest way to perform left-hand muting is to simply lay all the fingers of your fretting hand lightly across the strings, dampening them just enough to keep them from ringing when you strike the strings with your right hand. Here are a few measures of left-hand muting to practice:

Track 32

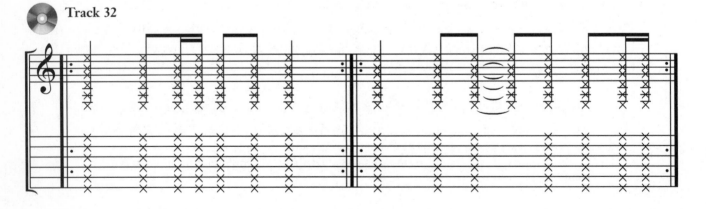

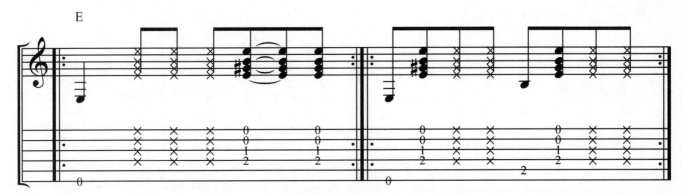

Chapter 10, Example 3.

The first two measures are all muted, while the second two combine the strumming of chords (and bass notes) with muting. When switching from a full chord to a left-hand mute, let your fingers go slack enough to cover as many strings as you can. As you get more comfortable with this technique, you'll start to think of muting as just another chord shape to change to from other chords.

Palm Muting

Palm muting is actually done with the heel of your hand, the edge along the far side of your pinky. It's the part of your hand that would strike the table first if you gave it a karate chop.

When you strum, keep this edge in contact with the strings, applying just enough pressure to slightly dampen the sound instead of totally muting the notes. You can vary the tone of the palm-muted notes by the amount of pressure you apply with the heel of your hand:

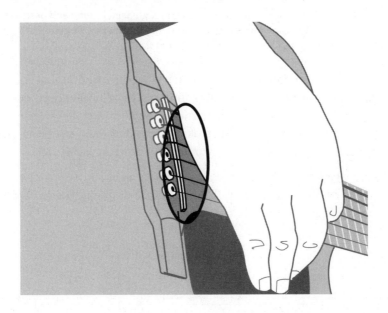

Track 33

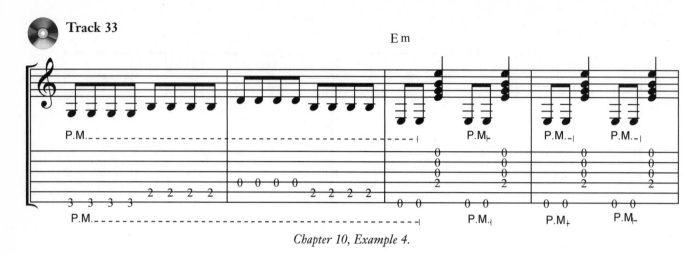

Chapter 10, Example 4.

Palm muting requires a bit of patience and persistence. Listen to the tone you're getting and work at achieving a particular amount of palm muting at will. As with many other guitar techniques you've attempted up to this point, it will come along the more you work at it. One day you'll be able to do it without even thinking about it.

Percussive Stroke

A percussive stroke differs from palm muting, in that it is a sharp, biting, and potentially explosive sound. The simplest way to achieve it is to simply slap the palm of your strumming hand across the strings, making contact with the body of the guitar. Please be gentle when first trying to do this!

KEEP SHARP!

Go easy and be patient when you first start working on both palm muting and percussive strumming. As with slides, both techniques are a matter of developing a proper sense of touch. Someone can show you how he or she does it, but you still have to get the feel for it yourself.

This "slap" technique can add quite a punctuation mark to your rhythm, but it can be disruptive when trying to incorporate it into more of a steady strumming style. Another method is to perform a typical strum with your right hand while making contact with the heel of your hand across the strings at the same instant your pick (or fingers) makes the stroke. It's kind of like giving the guitar an oblique karate chop at a slant to the strings at the same time you make a downstroke strum.

Percussive strokes are written out the same way as string muting, unless you have notation that is especially written out for flamenco music. Often the choice of mute, whether left hand on the strings or right-hand percussive, is up to the guitarist:

Track 34

Chapter 10, Example 5.

As with palm muting, playing percussive strokes effectively will probably require patience on your part. They add a lot to your playing, so don't be discouraged if it takes a while to get good at them.

"The Gallows Pole"

Your song for this chapter is "The Gallows Pole," a folk song that's been around for centuries. It is in 2/4 time. Here is a basic strum, incorporating chords and slurs:

Track 35 (0:00)

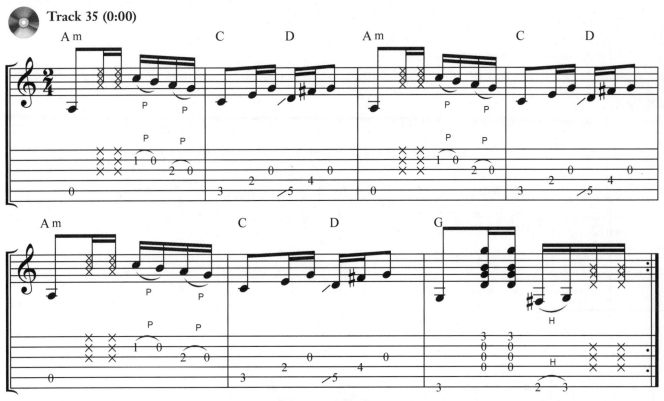

Chapter 10, Example 6.

The easiest way to play the second measure is to start with a C chord and then slide the entire chord two frets up the neck. This gives you a variation of the D chord (labeled in the music as "D" for convenience) that sounds a little dissonant and ominous.

Since the song basically repeats this progression over and over, don't worry about nailing this basic strum perfectly each time. Instead, mix in some of the rests and muting techniques you've learned in this chapter. Here are some possible variations to try:

Track 35 (0:21)

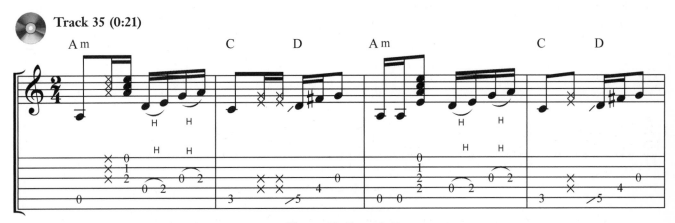

Chapter 10, Example 7.

As with your songs from earlier chapters, feel free to experiment and try out all sorts of combinations. There's no right or wrong way, as long as you make the chord changes at the appropriate time and keep the rhythm steady and even.

To encourage you to play as many different variations as possible, the final transcription of this arrangement is written in rhythmic notation. On Track 36 of the CD, you'll notice that I use quite a few variations of the basic strum when backing up the singer. There's also a neat little series of arpeggios that serve as an ending to the song.

Track 36

continues

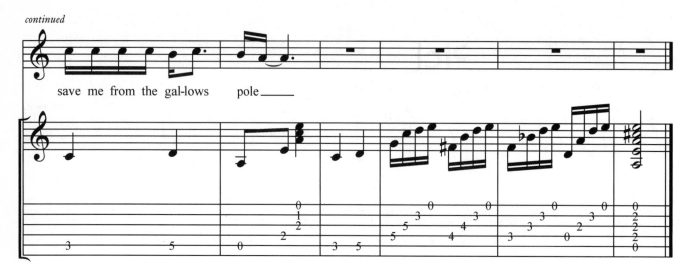

Chapter 10, Example 8.

Practice, Practice

One good way to practice percussive strokes and muting is to take any strum that you know and like and substitute a percussive stroke for any single quarter-note downstroke. Start out with just one in each measure. Then try adding left-hand string mutes for any downstroke/upstroke combination of eighth notes—again, no more than one per measure to start.

Working percussive strokes and muting into your basic strumming helps you get these techniques quickly into your hands and head. You'll soon find yourself using left-hand muting to help you make quicker chord changes. You use the mute while you're changing a chord on the beat before the chord change. It's easier than you think and helps you get your hand in place for the next chord.

What's more, both of these techniques give you more choices when it comes to strumming in general. You've probably already forgotten that you were once happy to simply strum four quarter notes, all downstrokes, in a row!

The Least You Need to Know

- Strumming sixteenth notes requires the same care and attention to timing, if not more, as strumming eighth notes.
- Rests and muting are important parts of playing.
- Different muting techniques have different sounds and tonal qualities. It's important to experiment with all of them.
- Effective palm muting and percussive strumming require practice.
- Combining muting and percussive playing with the techniques you already know gives you more stylistic choice when strumming.

Finger Picking in Style

In This Chapter

- Playing arpeggios with your fingers
- Using the "pinch" technique
- Pedal points
- Introduction to Travis-style picking
- Two very basic Travis patterns
- Adding pinches to Travis picking

Music is a means of expression, and, regardless of which instrument you play, each musician's expression is somewhat unique. Give five guitarists the chord sheet of any song, and you will get five different versions of that song. Some differences may be quite small—a chord may not be strummed confidently or fully, a root note may get more stress from the guitarist who has a heavier stroke—but some differences can be quite marked. One guitarist might strum with a pick, while another might play in various finger-picked patterns, letting each note ring out and overlap the next in a waterfall-like cascade.

Many beginning guitarists initially shy away from finger picking because it seems complicated. Nothing could be further from the truth! It's easy to pick up a few easy picking patterns, but the real challenge is not to keep using the same one over and over. Lots of easy songs sound absolutely breathtaking when played with even the simplest finger-picking styles.

Fortunately, too, there's a wealth of material to draw on for anyone interested in coaxing beautiful music out of his or her fingers. Some of it has been played for 200 years. Some of the earliest guitar masters left behind a wealth of music, from concert pieces to study exercises for their students. There's no reason to pass up that much help when it comes to your own playing.

Pick a Finger

The first question everyone has when finger picking is which finger, or fingers, to use. Starting out, I recommend trying the typical classical approach—using your thumb to pick the three lowest strings (the low-E, A, and D strings) and assigning a finger for each of the three high ones. Your ring finger picks the high-E string, the middle finger plays the B string, and the index finger picks the G string.

Most guitarists hold their right hand at a slight angle to the strings. If you think of the strings running along the neck to the headstock as being "9 o'clock" on a watch, your right wrist should be approaching the strings from between "4 o'clock" and "5 o'clock." Your fingers should be slightly curled and poised over their assigned strings while your thumb hangs close by the low strings.

SOUND ADVICE

Most classical guitarists, and many acoustic guitarists as well, will tell you that picking the strings with your nails gives you the best sound. Others prefer using the pads of the fingers to convey more expression. Both choices have their points.

If you use your nails, you need to have them just long enough to catch and pick the string. If your nails are too long, they'll likely get snagged on the string and eventually break. Be prepared to spend time caring for your nails by trimming, filing, and shaping them for play.

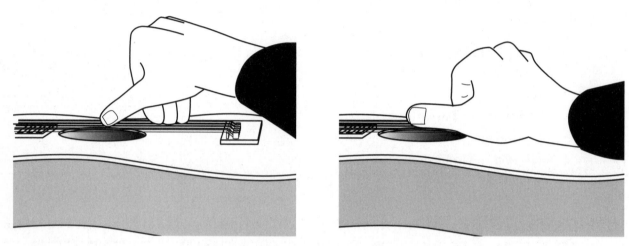

Two positions of the right hand for finger picking.

Some people find it more comfortable to keep the thumb both parallel and in contact with the bass strings, as shown in the second illustration. This position is especially useful if you want to apply a bit of muting to the bass strings (as you learned about in Chapter 10) because it keeps the heel of your hand close enough to the strings for contact.

Whichever thumb position you use (even if you use both!), you want to make certain that the thumb is extended and that the fingers pick inward toward the palm. This way, you won't have your thumb and fingers colliding when picking.

KEEP SHARP!

You might notice that some guitarists place the pinky (and sometimes the ring finger as well) of the right hand just below the sound hole to serve as an anchor while they pick. For some players, having an anchor gives them a sense of security when doing detailed picking work. It's a completely personal choice. When starting out, most teachers recommend not using an anchor, simply to keep all your fingers involved in picking the strings.

Also, keeping all finger movement to a minimum is essential to good finger picking. Try to keep the fingers you're not using close to their strings.

Revisiting Arpeggios

Here's an arpeggio example to get you going:

Track 37

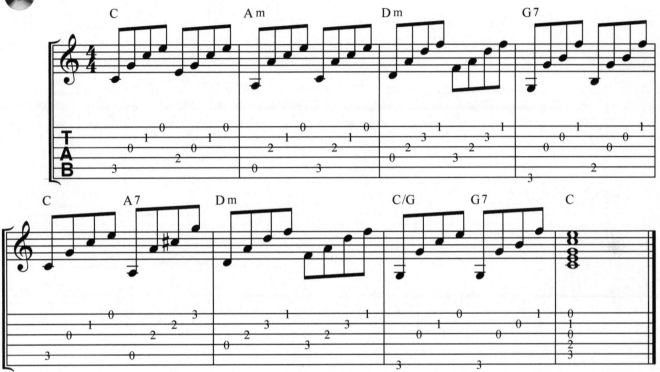

Chapter 11, Example 1.

Use the chords as guides to tell you where to position your left hand on the neck. The first measure, for instance, is a C chord, so if you have your left hand fretting a C chord, you don't have to move those fingers at all; you can focus on your picking hand. Be sure to let the bass notes ring out

The second measure uses two notes of the Am chord, so place your index finger on the first fret of the B string and your middle finger on the second fret of the G string. This allows either your ring finger or your pinky to play the C note at the third fret of the A string at the start of the third beat in this measure.

LISTENING LIBRARY

The first two examples in this chapter were written by Matteo Carcassi (1792–1853), a great guitarist, composer, and teacher. His method book is still used today by guitar students and teachers around the world, and you can easily find recordings and video performances of much of his music, some by the greatest classical guitarists of our time, in stores and libraries, as well as on the Internet.

The chord of the third measure is Dm, and you might find the measure easier to play if you use your pinky on the D note (third fret of the B string) when forming the chord. Doing so frees up your ring finger for the F note (third fret of the D string) that appears halfway through this measure.

Take your time and get comfortable with the idea of using all your fingers in this manner. With a little practice, you'll probably find your fingers taking to it quite readily.

Pinches and Pedals

Now that your fingers are getting warmed up, it's time to give them something even more coordinated to do. This next finger-picking technique is called a *pinch*, and, like many guitar techniques you've learned, the name tells you just what to do.

Take a look at the first pair of notes in this example:

 Track 38

Chapter 11, Example 2.

Here you have a C note (first fret of the B string) and an E note (second fret of the D string). You want to play both notes simultaneously, so the pinch allows you to do just that. Pick the E note with your thumb using a downward motion and, at the same time, pick the C note with your middle finger using an upward motion.

Be careful not to hit the G string with either your thumb or your middle finger; you want to hit the G note separately with your index finger next. Try to let all the notes, the pinched pairs and the single G string, ring out until you either pick them again or move your fingers off the strings to play different notes.

SOUND ADVICE

When changing chords, particularly when finger picking, it's good to keep the idea of "constant contact" in mind. Don't move a finger from the note it's on until you have to. This cuts down on unwanted string noise and unintentionally picked strings.

In addition to the pinch, this example introduces you to the concept of a *pedal point*, which is also called a pedal note or a pedal tone. A pedal tone is a repeated note that stays constant while other single notes, pairs of notes, or even chords are changing around it. It's usually played every other note when it occurs, such as the G note that appears every other note in this last example, until the middle of the seventh measure, when it changes to D and remains as a D pedal for the next measure and a half.

DEFINITION

A **pedal point,** or pedal tone, is a note that is played steadily over a period of time (usually a measure or more), alternating with other single notes and chords. It serves as a focal point for the other notes and chords, often creating interesting harmonies.

For an excellent example of the use of a pedal point, listen to "Blackbird" by the Beatles.

The picking pattern changes in the second set of four measures. Here you want to use your ring and middle fingers to pick the notes on the two high strings (the high E and B), and you can use either your index finger or your thumb to pick the G string. When you get to the D note in the bass at Measure 7, definitely go with the thumb.

Basic Travis Picking

When you are fairly comfortable playing these two basic finger-picking styles, you can move on to Travis-style picking. You may not be familiar with the name, but Merle Travis was a legendary guitar player throughout the 1940s and 1950s. He could play many styles, from ragtime to country, to gospel, to folk, but he is primarily associated with a finger-picking style that relies on a steady use of the thumb to play the bass notes while the fingers dance on the high strings.

Since the thumb is the "steady" part of the rhythm, it's smart to work with it first. Form an Am chord and use your thumb to play an alternating bassline as follows.

Think of your thumb as the metronome, counting off the beats for you, hitting the root note of A (the open A string) on the first and third beats of the measure and the E note (second fret of the D string) on the second and fourth beats.

Typical bass movement in Travis picking.

Being Contrary and Picking Parallel

When you can keep your thumb steady and even on the bass notes, add your fingers to the mix. First try this "contrary motion" pattern, using your middle finger to play the C note (first fret of the B string) between the first and second beats and again between the third and fourth beats. Your index finger plays the A note (second fret of the G string) between the second and third beats and on the last half of the fourth beat.

Track 39 (0:00)

Chapter 11, Example 3.

This may initially be difficult, but you'll be amazed how quickly your fingers will take to this style. To help your progress, try not to look at your fingers picking the strings. That may seem strange, but it really does help. Yes, you will make mistakes and hit the wrong string occasionally, but you will develop a better feel for where your fingers want to go.

After practicing with the Am chord for a while, try picking A or C, using the same fingers and strings as part of your pattern:

A

Travis picking on the A and C chords.

Then try all three chords again, but use your ring finger and middle finger to play the notes on the high-E and B strings instead of the B and G as you had been doing.

Variation on contrary motion.

Finally, go through the E, Em, G, D, and Dm chords. Remember that the root notes of E, Em, and G are on the low-E string, and the root notes of D and Dm are the open D string, so you probably want to just try out the thumb part first, as shown:

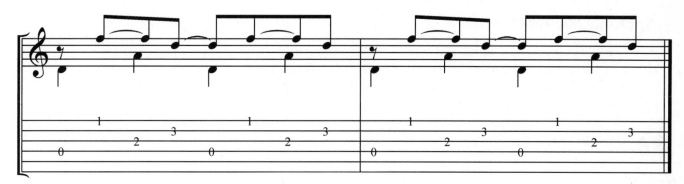

Contrary motion with E, Em, G, D, and Dm.

You can experiment with different string combinations, too, just as you did earlier with the Am, A, and C chords.

 KEEP SHARP!

When your right hand can play a given pattern well enough that you can let your attention wander a bit, or even hold a conversation while playing, try making chord changes while keeping the picking pattern going steady and strong. Don't stop your pattern if your left hand is slow with changing chords. Instead, slow down the tempo of the picking so that you can work on making the chord changes on the fly.

Hopefully you can hear that, even when you make a mistake by hitting the wrong string, the picking doesn't sound wrong in the least. This is because every note you're playing is part of the chord. And, truth be told, no one besides you even knows that you've made a mistake. So don't tell!

Picking in contrary motion is just one of many possibilities. You can also play Travis style in parallel motion, as shown with these chords:

 Track 39 (0:17)

A m

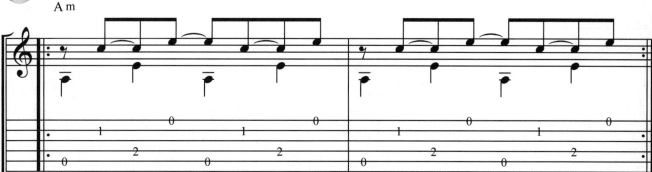

Chapter 11, Example 4.

As you get used to this new motion of picking, play around with the various possible string combinations, as you did with the contrary motion picking. Also choose a single chord and try switching smoothly from parallel to contrary, or vice versa.

Pinching Mr. Travis

As cool as all your newfound Travis-style finger picking may sound, it'll get a huge boost when you start adding pinches to the mix. Start out with Am again and, instead of hitting just the root note on the first beat, pinch both the open A string (with the thumb) and the C note at the first fret of the B string (with the middle finger).

  Track 39 (0:32)

Chapter 11, Example 5.

Because you play the pinch on the first half of the first beat, using both thumb and middle finger, there's no note to play between the first and second beat as there is in both the contrary and parallel motion patterns. This means that you really have to keep your thumb steady on the beat, or you'll skip a half beat when playing. If you're having problems, first do just the bass notes with the thumb and count the timing aloud, then continue counting as you add your fingers to the picking.

Adding pinches to the two basic Travis patterns you've learned will help you develop melody and harmony lines as you pick out chords. And as you get more confident with your picking, you'll be able to add moving basslines and then even harmonize the two. Here are some simple examples to get you started:

Track 40

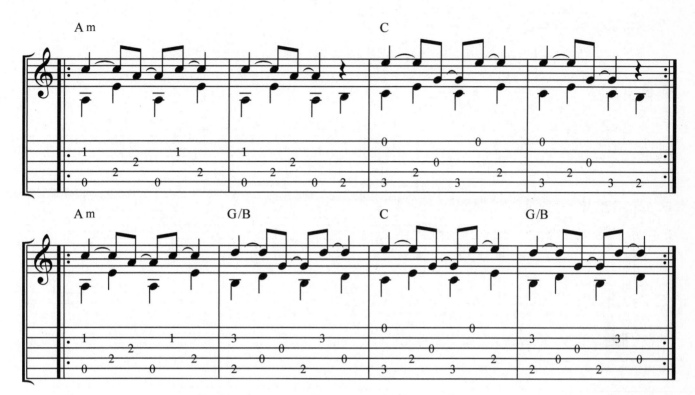

Chapter 11, Example 6.

The first line demonstrates a simple moving melody line played over a single chord. Try to keep the Am chord shape in place as much as you can. Use your pinky to play the D note at the third fret of the B string, and keep your index finger in place at the first fret while you do so. Remove it only when you need to play the open B string.

Also notice in this example that the note on the second half of the fourth beat in the second measure has been taken out to keep the picking pattern from sounding too busy. That's just one of many options you have when playing.

A walking bassline, both ascending and descending, is added to the picking of the second line. Pay close attention to the timing as the picking changes in the third and fourth measures. The finger notes drop out on the third and fourth beats, leaving just the thumb to play the basslines.

The last line combines both the pinch notes in the melody and the thumb notes on the bass strings. Take this example very slowly when you first try it out. This C-to-Am change happens quite a bit in music, and you'll find that this little bit of picking can make a typical chord change sound a lot more interesting.

"The Cruel War"

Now it's time to try combining the many ideas from this chapter into a single song.

Track 41

Chapter 11, Example 7.

In measures 7 and 8 (and measures 15 and 16 as well), you'll find an interesting G to C to G change. Form the initial G chord in measure 7 as you usually do, but when you switch to C, keep whatever finger you have on the G note at the third fret of the high string in place. Shift only your two fingers on the low-E and A strings up to the A and D strings. This isn't a full C chord, but if you're careful and don't pick the B string during this change, no one will know. That's another fun thing about getting good at picking—quite often you can get away with fingering only parts of chords.

Practice, Practice

Practicing finger picking is, in many ways, a lot like practicing chord changes. First focus on the pattern that your right hand plays, and try to get the picking on autopilot. Start with a single chord and pick and pick until your fingers are doing exactly what you want.

Early guitar masters such as Matteo Carcassi, Mauro Giuliani, and Fernando Sor left a treasure trove of guitar music to the world. Because they effortlessly combined excellent technique, strong melodies, and interesting harmonies, even the easiest pieces they wrote for their students are worth seeking out to play.

Be sure to work at varying your picking patterns. It's too easy to get hooked on one and never change, so make a point of keeping your fingers on their toes, so to speak! Play two measures of a contrary motion pattern, then add a pinch or two, then start picking in parallel motion. There's no end to the mixing and matching you can do, and you want to be able to change patterns as you see fit while playing.

Above all, try to not make a habit of watching your fingers pick the strings. Yes, at first you want to make certain you're playing the ones you want, but as soon as you can (sooner, really!), try playing by ear without looking. You'll definitely make mistakes, but as long as you keep the chord with your fretting hand, it will be nearly impossible for anyone to know you made a mistake—unless, of course, you make a big deal about it!

The Least You Need to Know

- Finger picking is a very expressive way to play guitar.
- Pinching involves playing two notes at once, one picked with the thumb and the other with a finger.
- Travis-style finger picking has a steady bass picked on the beat by the thumb while the fingers play notes between the beats.
- Combining pinching and Travis picking produces very cool-sounding music.
- Classical guitar exercises can help you quickly develop your finger picking.

Learning a Little Local Lore

If all you want to do with the guitar is strum a few chords, you're already good to go! But if you want to get even better, it's time to get your brain as involved in your playing as your fingers are.

The good news is that almost everything you need to know about music theory is as easy as counting to 13. If you can do that, you will have no trouble learning how scales are made and how to figure out the notes used in any chord you can think of (and some that you might not know exist).

The better news is that you can use this knowledge to learn how to play barre chords, opening up the entire fingerboard to your creativity. You can also create more interesting chord voicings that will enhance your guitar playing with complex and intricate sounds.

A guitarist who can think as well as play will always be discovering new adventures, so take a few moments now and be rewarded with more musical roads to travel.

A Major Step Forward

In This Chapter

- The steps and half-steps between notes
- The pattern of the major scale
- Learning scales in closed position
- Working scales together with chord strumming
- Getting your brain involved with your learning

You've read about how a guitarist needs to use his or her fingers and how important a guitarist's ears are when it comes to playing. You've been working on your posture and your sense of rhythm and timing, and you've been developing muscle memory so that you can smoothly and effortlessly change from one chord to the next.

Now it's time to start working on your brain. In case you haven't caught on by now, your creative brain plays a very important part in learning to play guitar. It tells you, "You know, maybe that hammer-on you played on the Em chord in 'Wayfaring Stranger' could also work on 'House of the Rising Sun,' even though you're playing an arpeggio instead of a full chord."

The biggest challenge for any guitarist, aside from the many things to explore and discover about both music and the guitar, is getting the brain, ears, and fingers functioning at the same level at the same time. And just as the ears and fingers get better with practice, your brain needs practice, too.

Fortunately, the best way to train your brain is to have it learn the very basics of music theory, which will also translate immediately into improved performances from both your fingers and your ears. Also fortunately, these basics are as easy to learn as "do, re, mi."

The Steps (and Half-Steps) to Building Scales

That last bit about "do, re, mi" wasn't a joke. Nearly everything concerning music theory revolves around the major scale, the "do, re, mi, fa, sol, la, ti, do" from the song you might remember from *The Sound of Music*. If you want to know how to create any chord, figure out what chords are likely to be in a song (even a song you've never played), come up with a cool-sounding riff or fill to spice up your strumming, or play a rocking guitar solo, the major scale is the place to start.

Before looking at the major scale, though, you might want to know exactly what a scale is. Simply put, a scale is a specific combination of musical steps and half-steps that starts with any given note and ends when you reach that starting note again.

SOUND ADVICE

Scales are usually called by two names, such as the "C major" scale or the "G minor pentatonic" scale or the "B♭ blues" scale, just to give you a few examples. The first part of the name is always a note. This gives you the tonal center, or root note (starting point), of the scale. The second name, "major," "minor pentatonic," "blues," and so on, is a descriptive name. As you'll learn, each descriptive name has its own pattern of whole-step and half-step combinations.

Hopefully you remember learning about notes in the first chapter in this book. Notes are named by the first seven letters of the alphabet, going from A to G as you go higher in tone. When you reach G, the note names cycle around again, so A is the note after G, but at a higher pitch (vibration frequency) than the A that started the sequence.

A   B   C   D   E   F   G   A   B   C   …

You also learned about accidentals, notes that are either sharp or flat. When you raise a note, such as G, a half-step in tone, it becomes G♯. Lowering the G a half-step in tone turns it into G♭.

Arranging all the notes, A through G, in order in terms of half-steps looks like this:

A   A♯/   B   C   C♯/   D   D♯/   E   F   F♯/   G   G♯/
     B♭   D♭   E♭   G♭   A♭

Knowing the notes in terms of half-steps is important to the guitarist because the note of each fret along the fingerboard is one half-step away from its neighbor. Whole steps are two frets apart. When you put your finger on the first fret of the A string, you raise the A note of the open string one half-step higher, turning it into A♯ (which you can also call B♭). Placing your finger on the second fret of the A string raises the note an additional half-step, making it B, which is one whole step higher than A.

KEEP SHARP!

There's a B♯ note, as well as E♯, C♭, and F♭, but they appear very rarely in music. It's certainly easier to think of B♯ as C, since C is a half-step higher than B. But it's good to know that sometimes you'll see that note written as B♯.

A scale called the *chromatic scale* starts on a given note and proceeds in half-steps until you reach your starting note again. For example, you play the A chromatic scale by starting with the note of the A string, which is the *root note*, or first note, of the scale and playing each fret up to and including the twelfth fret of the A string, like this:

Playing the A chromatic scale.

The Major Scale

To make any scale, then, you must know two things: the specified root note and the pattern of whole steps ("W") and half-steps ("H") that define the desired scale. The pattern of the major scale is as follows:

Root   W   W   H   W   W   W   H (Root again)

Let's put it to the test. Here's the A major scale:

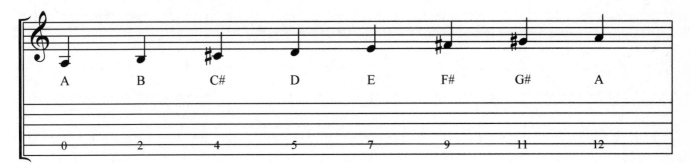

Playing the A major scale.

Starting with the A of the open A string, you then play B, which is a whole step higher than A. C♯ comes next because it is a whole step higher than B. D, one half-step up from C♯, is the fourth note of the scale. Then comes E, F♯ (a whole step up from E), and then G♯ (a whole step up from F♯). Going one half-step higher than G♯ brings you back to A and completes the A major scale.

Scales by the Dozen

Since you can start on 12 different notes, there are 12 different major scales. Here's the C major scale:

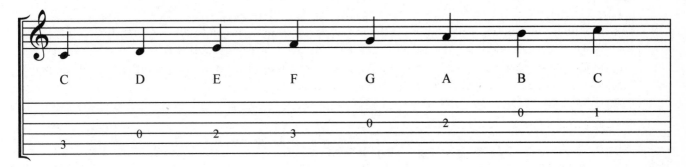

Playing the C major scale.

The C major scale is important, in that none of its notes are accidentals—it has no flats or sharps. As you'll learn in Chapter 15, each major scale has a unique number of either flat notes or sharp notes. This knowledge can help you recognize what key a song is in, as well as which chords you're most likely to come across in that particular song.

Open and Closed Scales

Playing 12 different major scales may seem a bit daunting, but it's actually easier than you think. Because your guitar is tuned to specific notes, you can learn one major scale, tweak it a bit, and then automatically know how to play all 12, as long as you know where your root note is on the low-E string.

Start with the G major scale. This is a good one because you can run through it twice using the notes across all six strings.

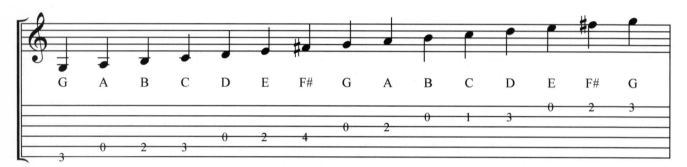

Playing the G major scale across all six strings.

Closing Positions

When you play a scale using open strings for some of its notes, as you have with all three scales so far in this chapter (the A, C, and G major scales), you are playing open-position scales.

SOUND ADVICE

Saying the name of a note aloud as you play it is an excellent way to remember where notes are on the fingerboard. It's also an excellent way to memorize which notes are used in any particular scale.

As you know, you can play most notes on the guitar at more than one place on the fingerboard. You could play A, the second note in this last scale, with the open A string, as shown, or also at the fifth fret of the low-E string. Here's the same G major scale as before, but this time all the notes of the open strings have been replaced with notes at fretted positions:

Playing the G major scale in closed position.

Playing this scale, or any riff, fill, or chord, with no open strings is called playing in *closed position*. The best way to play this scale is to use your middle finger to start on the G (third fret of the low-E string) and think in terms of your "one finger, one fret" exercises. That means your index finger plays any notes on the second fret, your middle finger handles any notes at the third fret, your ring finger plays any notes on the fourth fret, and your pinky plays all the notes at the fifth fret.

Moving Around the Fingerboard

The real advantage of closed positions is that you can play them anyplace on the fingerboard, provided you have a reference note. For instance, you know that the fifth fret of the low-E string is A, so if you shift your finger position, placing your middle finger on that A note, you can play the A major scale in closed position without even thinking about it:

A Major Scale - Root 6 Closed Position

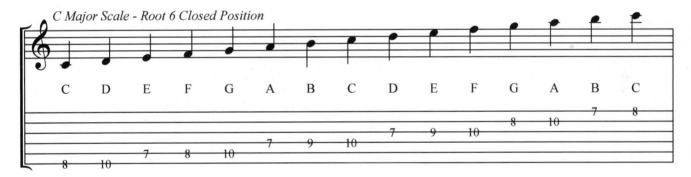

C Major Scale - Root 6 Closed Position

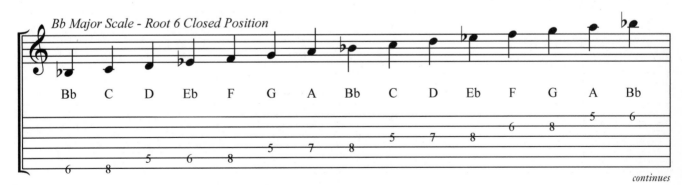

Bb Major Scale - Root 6 Closed Position

continues

continued

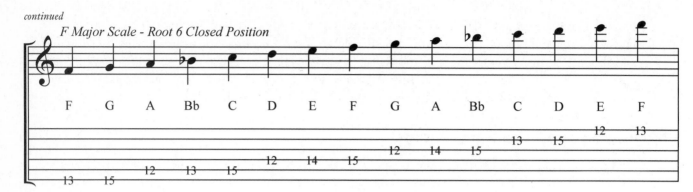

The A, C, B♭, and F major scales in closed position.

As long as you know where your root note is on the low-E string, you can play any of the 12 major scales in this manner. This pattern is often called the *Root 6 major scale* because the root note is on the low-E, or sixth, string.

Root 5 Major Scales

You can use the same logic to come up with a pattern for any major scale when you want to use the root note on the A, or fifth, string. Here's the C major scale you played earlier, first in open position and then closed:

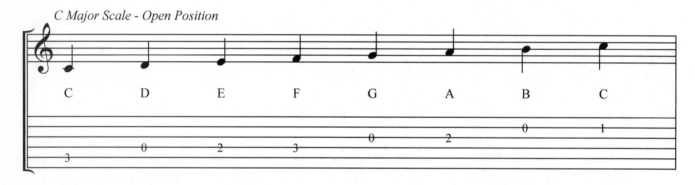

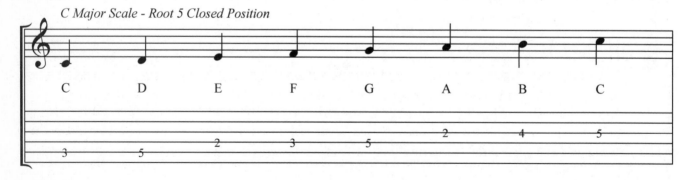

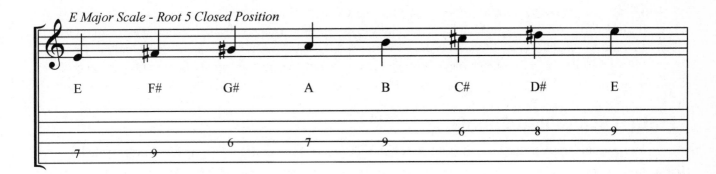

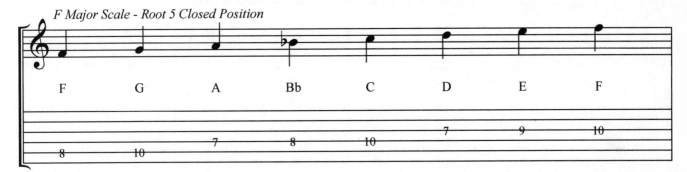

Major scales in Root 5 (closed position).

Following this closed-position C major scale, this last example also lays out the E and F major scales for you in Root 5 closed position.

SOUND ADVICE

Playing scales in closed position, as with your "one finger, one fret" exercises, is an excellent way to warm up your fingers at the start of a practice.

Between both the Root 6 and Root 5 closed positions, you should be able to comfortably play any of the 12 major scales anywhere on the neck. That will come in handy when you start playing riffs and solos later in Chapters 18 and 20.

Walking in Steps

You still want to know many of your scales in open position, though, because they can help you when it comes to adding basslines or simple little fills or even melody lines. You've played some walking basslines in earlier songs, like "Streets of Laredo" and "Handsome Molly." You may have noticed that the individual notes of these simple basslines were, for the most part, very easy to reach from either the chord you started on or the one you finished with. It didn't require a lot of effort to add them to your playing, and once you practiced them a bit, they might even have become second nature to you.

KEEP SHARP!

Whether practicing scales as part of strumming or just practicing them by themselves, always try to keep your fingers close to the strings and in a position where they can readily return to fretting a chord instead of playing single notes. Being able to shift from single notes to chords and back will be useful no matter what style of music you play.

When you're playing a song, you don't want to worry about where your fingers are going to end up. This is why most of the walking basslines and the little guitar fills you hear in songs usually aren't that hard to play. The person who came up with the fill doesn't want to think that hard, either! These bits of musical magic are often played someplace on the fingerboard around either a chord shape or a scale—usually both.

Putting Scales into Chords

You can understand this idea a little better through practice. Here are two simple examples to help:

Track 42

Walking Bass / Chord Exercise with C Major Scale

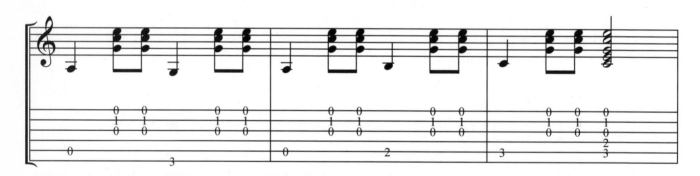

Walking Bass / Chord Exercise with G Major Scale

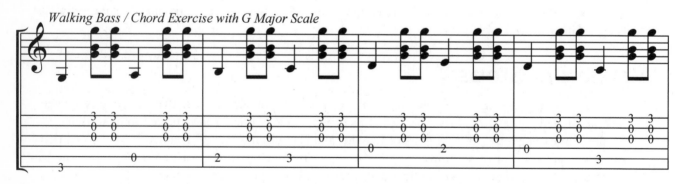

Chapter 12, Example 1.

The first two lines are essentially a C chord using various notes of the C major scale (in open position) for its bassline. When you practice this, keep your index finger on the C note at the first fret of the B string the entire time, and try to keep *all* the notes of the C chord in place. Use your pinky, for example, to finger the F note (third fret of the D string) while keeping your ring finger on the C at the third fret of the A string.

Obviously, you need to move fingers around, but the closer you can keep your fingers to the strings, the faster you can get back to the full C chord when you want to play it.

The third and fourth lines of the last example employ the same idea, but this time you're using a G chord and notes from the G major scale in open position. You'll be moving your fingers around a lot more, but do your best to keep the G at the third fret of the high-E string in place for the entire example.

"Oh! Susanna"

Your song for this chapter incorporates basslines with chord arpeggios and even throws in the occasional slur.

A lot of different musical techniques and ideas are at work in this relatively easy song! Obviously, you want to start slowly, and breaking down the song into sections of four measures each will probably help you learn it quickly. Remember that you've already done the little bits that make up this song—you just haven't done them all in this order!

If you prefer to play this song with a pick instead of using your fingers, you certainly can. Be sure to simply strum a G chord with your ring finger at the D note (third fret of the B string) instead of the G note on the high-E string at the start of the second measure of the second line on the second page (the "don't" of "don't you cry for me"). And when you strum that G chord, strum down only to the B string, to emphasize that D note before making the pull-off.

Track 43

Chapter 12, Example 2.

LISTENING LIBRARY

This arrangement of "Oh! Susanna" is inspired by the descending walking basslines of songs like "Friend of the Devil," by the Grateful Dead, and Green Day's "Wake Me Up When September Ends," but you can also find whole major scales popping up throughout music. There's a descending C major scale played by the piano in the chorus of Cat Stevens'"Wild World." And each verse of Desmond Dekker's classic reggae song "The Israelites" (one of the first Jamaican songs to be a major hit worldwide) ends with an ascending C major scale even though the song is in A major.

Practice, Practice

As mentioned at the start of this chapter, you're at the point where you need to get your brain actively involved if you want to continue to develop and grow as both a guitarist and a musician. In addition to practicing with your fingers and hands—making notes and chords and working on rhythm—you need to add in some work for your brain.

This can be tricky because you really don't have anyone besides yourself to report to. You won't be taking any tests on scales in the foreseeable future. And the construction of the major scale isn't going to come up at any family meals.

The best thing you can do to immerse yourself in music theory is read, write, discuss, and listen. You can find a wealth of material to read, either in books or online, including some great resources listed for you in Appendix C. In addition to reading, testing your knowledge on the materials studied—actually writing things down—will help imprint music theory on your brain. You can start writing out the notes of some major scales. Start with C, G, D, A, and E, since guitarists often play those particular chords.

When you've written out the scales, map out where the notes are on the fingerboard. You can download blank guitar fingerboard charts, not to mention chord charts, blank tablature pages, blank notation sheets, and more for free on the Internet. Use your maps to learn where various notes are located on your instrument.

If you run into questions, discuss them with teachers or other musicians. There are also many guitar forums on the Internet where you can pose questions—and you can also feel free to e-mail me any questions you might have! My address is at the end of the Introduction of this book.

Above all, listen. Right now you probably feel like you're doing more listening than playing, but it will all be worth it when you can identify different aspects of music and guitar techniques in the music you hear. You can probably already pick out various slurs and maybe even tell the difference between major and minor chords. It's only going to get better from here!

The Least You Need to Know

- Scales are specific patterns of steps and half-steps.
- The major scale is probably the most important scale to know.
- You can play any chord or scale in either open or closed position.
- Knowing the pattern of the major scale in closed position allows you to play all 12 major scales.
- You can use open-position scales to play walking basslines with strumming.

Building Chords from Scratch

In This Chapter

- Intervals of the major scale
- Creating chords
- The four basic chords
- The many types of sevenths
- Extended chords
- Slash chords

The beginning guitarist's life can almost be broken down into three stages. First, he learns some basic chords. Then he discovers that there are even more chords to learn than he thought possible. And then he finds out that there are dozens of ways to play all those chords he's learned, seemingly anywhere on the fingerboard. It can be a little overwhelming, to say the least!

The good news is that chords are easy to understand, and understanding means that you can often come up with creative ways to voice chords on your guitar. Knowing the makeup of chords also allows you to make chord substitutions from time to time, to give a song a different feel or flavor. Instead of being overwhelmed by chords, you'll soon be making them without even using charts.

An Interval on Degrees

To understand how chords are constructed, go back to the major scale. Each note of the scale is given a degree, a number that corresponds to its ordered place in the scale. This is the C major scale, with the notes and degrees charted out for you:

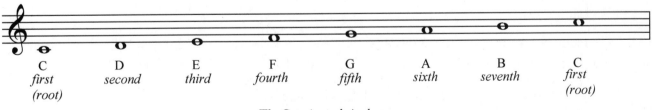

The C major scale in degrees.

These degrees are also used to describe the *intervals* between two notes in relation to the major scale. An interval is the space from one note to the next. The interval between C and D is a whole step, so it is called a *major second*. The interval between C and E (two whole steps) is called a *major third*.

Fourths (two and a half steps, remember) and fifths (three and a half steps) are called *perfect*, and sixths (four and a half steps) and sevenths (four and a half steps) are also major sixths and sevenths.

The tricky part of this is that intervals are all in relation to the major scale of the starting note. For instance, C to E is a major third. F to A, which is also two whole steps, is also a major third. But D to F or E to G is a step and a half, called a *minor third*. Here's a chart to show you all the possible intervals:

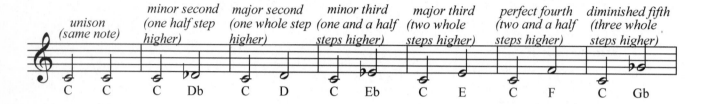

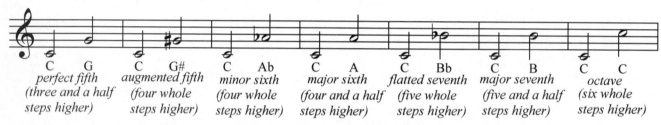

How intervals are measured and named.

Notice how some intervals are named. Some musicians use *minor* and *flatted* interchangeably. But as you will soon read, doing so can lead to problems, especially when the seventh is involved. Likewise, the terms *augmented* and *diminished*, used with the fifth, are important to help you remember your basic chords.

SOUND ADVICE

Listening to intervals is one of the best ways to develop your ear. Start by playing the major scale—any one will do—and sing or hum the notes as you do so. Then hit the root note and see if you can sing the octave. Then try hitting the major third or fifth.

Many Internet sites have free ear-training "games" to help you practice your interval recognition. Just enter "ear training" or "ear-training intervals" into your favorite search engine to find them.

Triads

Harmony, at least in the music of the Western Hemisphere, is based on the interval of the third, and on having at least three notes to work with. For instance, if I gave you two notes—say, the G and B of the open G and B strings—and asked what chord it is, you might say G. You could also say Em. If you knew them, you could also say Cmaj7 or A9 or even Em9, as shown here:

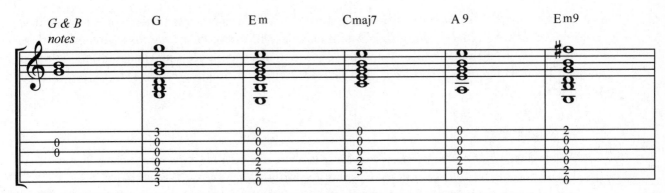

Some of the possible chords using the same two notes.

And these are just *some* of the possibilities. So the convention in music theory is to have at least three notes: the root note, the third, and the fifth. This may seem a little arbitrary, but think of it this way: You take the first note of the major scale and then add the third. Then you take the third of that note (which is the fifth of the original note), and there's your chord.

Building Four Basic Chords with Thirds

Thinking of building chords in thirds also helps you discover (and remember!) the four basic kinds of chords used in music. Since there are major and minor thirds, you have four possible ways to combine three notes:

>   Root + Major third + Minor third = Major chord
>
>   Root + Minor third + Major third = Minor chord
>
>   Root + Major third + Major third = Augmented chord
>
>   Root + Minor third + Minor third = Diminished chord

To demonstrate how these different chords sound, play the D major chord. The root note of D major is D, found at both the open D string and the third fret of the B string. The major third is F♯ (second fret of the high E), and the perfect fifth is A (second fret of the G string). Here are some charts to help:

 Track 44 (0:00)

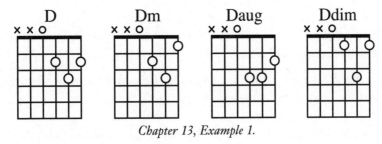

Chapter 13, Example 1.

You're already familiar with both the major and minor chords. The augmented chord sounds transitory. It certainly isn't going to linger for any length of time. The diminished chord sounds even more restless. Usually both augmented and diminished chords are used to make an interesting change from one chord to another. Instead of going straight from D to G, for instance, one might go from D to D augmented and then to G.

SOUND ADVICE

Augmented is usually listed in chord charts as "aug" for short, although you'll also see it as a plus sign (+) and occasionally as ♯5. "Caug" or "C+," for instance, would be C augmented. C7♯5 would be a C7 chord with the augmented fifth (G♯ instead of G).

These four basic chords also demonstrate the importance of language. On chord charts, you'll never see the word *minor* (or the corresponding "m," as in Em) unless it's referring to the third of a chord. *Augmented* always lets you know that the fifth has been raised, and *diminished* means that both the third and the fifth have been lowered a half-step.

Chords Without Thirds

Like almost everything in music, there are exceptions to convention. Having just learned that chords are made up of the root, third, and fifth, you also need to know the two types of exceptions.

The first is actually not a chord to anyone but guitar players, and that is the 5 chord. In a 5 chord (which guitarists often refer to as a "power chord"), the only notes used are the root and the perfect fifth. You can play just the two notes using two strings, or use all six of the guitar's strings if you know where to find the notes! Here are the different ways of playing E5, which are just the notes E and B:

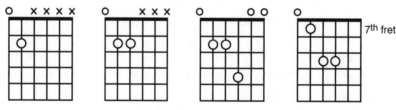

Various voicings for E5.

First play an E chord and then an Em. Then play these various voicings of E5 and listen to the differences. Some people think E5 sounds major and some think it sounds minor, but it's actually neither. Think of it as a "tonally ambiguous" chord.

Another chord that doesn't use the third is the *suspended* chord. In a suspended chord, labeled "sus" for short, the interval of the third (whether major or minor) is replaced with a different note, usually the perfect fourth. These are usually labeled "sus4." Sometimes you run into chords that replace the third with the major second and are labeled "sus2." If you see a chord simply labeled "sus," the safe bet is to use the fourth. Here are some common suspended chords:

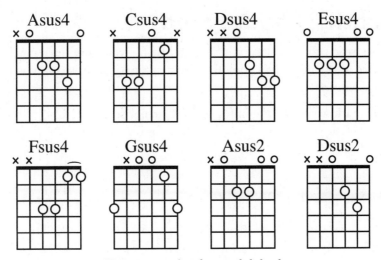

Various examples of suspended chords.

Suspended chords are usually used as a way to play around with a chord that you're strumming for some time. Instead of playing eight beats of A, for example, you might try something like this:

Track 44 (0:18)

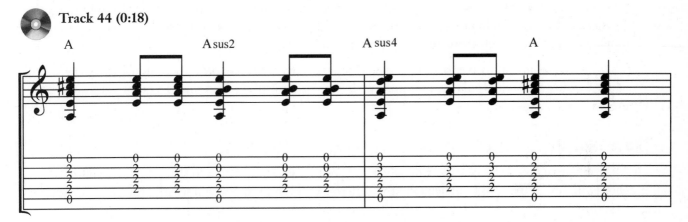

Chapter 13, Example 2.

It's also good to note here that *you should take the time to play around with chords!* Many guitarists, despite their "music theory means no creativity" stances, are slaves to chord and tablature sheets. Unless a piece of music clearly spells out a D to Dsus4 to D to Dsus2 chord change, it might never occur to some guitarists to try it out and make their playing more interesting.

The whole reason for learning different chords is to add spice and creativity to your playing, so knowing how chords are put together and then experimenting with them on songs you already know can lead to some wonderful musical moments.

Sixths, Sevenths, and Beyond

When you have the basic chord—the root, third, and fifth—you can pretty much add to it as you see fit. Usually the name of the note gives you all the instruction you need, but you do have to make an adjustment in your counting.

Take a piece of paper and write out the notes of the C major scale on two different lines, like this:

C   D   E   F   G   A   B

C   D   E   F   G   A   B

Now add the degree numbers over the top of the first line, and on the second line continue numbering the notes from 8 to 14:

1   2   3   4   5   6   7
C   D   E   F   G   A   B

8   9   10   11   12   13   14
C   D   E   F   G   A   B

The root, third, and fifth are already spoken for in the basic chord, so you don't need the numbers 8, 10, and 12. The second and fourth are used for the suspended chords, so you usually won't see those numbers, either (although there are exceptions, as you'll see!).

The convention in chord construction is to add the sixth and seventh notes when indicated by the chord name. For instance, C6 would be a C chord with the sixth note (A) added to it. In other words, C6 is made up of C, E, G, and A.

Five Sevenths

All that clarity takes a bit of a vacation when you get to sevenths. There are five types of seventh chords, and it's important to understand the differences, even though you'll usually run into only the first three types in most music:

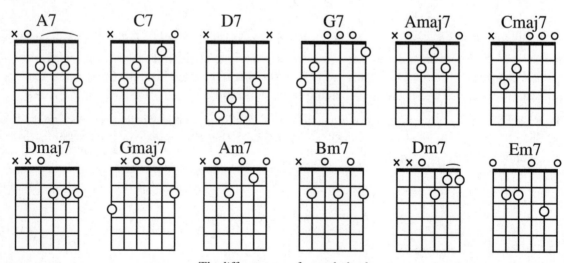

The different types of seventh chords.

When you see the number "7" tacked onto a chord, it means to use the interval of the *flatted* seventh. That's the note one full step below the *octave* of the root note. So when you read C7, you add B♭, not B, to the C chord, meaning that this chord is made up of the notes C, E, G, and B♭.

DEFINITION

An **octave** is the interval from a single note to the next note that shares the same name—from A to A, C to C, or F♯ to F♯, for example. The term is slightly confusing because the octave is always 6 full steps (12 half-steps) away from the root note, but in the major scale, counting the root note as "one," you reach the root note again at "eight." This is where the "oct" of *octave* comes from.

"Maj7" indicates that you add the interval of the *major seventh*, the seventh note of the major scale, to the chord. Cmaj7 is made up of C, E, G, and B. Note that this is the only time you see the word *major* used in a chord. Usually you default to a major chord unless the chord name indicates otherwise, with the word *minor* ("m"), *augmented* ("aug" or a "+" sign), or *diminished* ("dim" or a ° symbol). Seeing "maj" always tells you that you're dealing with the major seventh.

In minor sevenths ("m7"), the *minor* refers to the interval of the third. So this means to play a minor chord ("m") and add the *flatted* seventh ("7") to it. Cm7, then, is C, E♭, G, and B♭.

This is important because there are also "minor major seventh" chords that add the interval of the major seventh to the minor chord. Cm(maj7) is C, E♭, G, and B.

Finally, there are two types of diminished seventh chords. First, there's the "half-diminished seventh," which is the basic diminished chord (with flat third and flat fifth) that has the flatted seventh added to it. These are usually labeled as minor seventh chords with "♭5" added. Cm7♭5, for instance, is C, E♭, G♭, and B♭. A "full" or "regular" diminished seventh means flatting the seventh twice (making it the same note as the sixth) and then adding that to the basic diminished chord. Cdim7, for example, is C, E♭, G♭, and A ((technically B♭♭).

Beyond the Octave

After sixths and sevenths come ninth, eleventh, and thirteenth chords, which are called *extended chords*, since notes are being added from beyond the octave. When it comes to the various extended chords, it's assumed that you're keeping the seventh note as part of the chord. C9, for instance, is C, E, G, B♭, and D. Cmaj9 means that the B (the interval of the major 7) is used instead of B♭, so it is made up of C, E, G, B, and D. C11 is C, E, G, B♭, D, and F. Cmaj13 is C, E, G, B, D, F, and A. That's every note of the C major scale!

And you might be wondering how on Earth you can play a chord with seven notes on a six-string guitar. The answer is, you can't. Guitarists will usually drop notes from extended chords not only because there are so many of them but also for voicing purposes, as you'll read about in Chapter 28, which gives you a brief introduction to jazz. If only one note is meant to be added to the basic chord, you'll usually see this indicated as "add," such as Cadd9, which is C, E, G, and D. Depending on who wrote the music, you can sometimes find chords like "C2" or "C4," but you should think of those as "Cadd9" or "Cadd11," respectively.

Finally, you can also have accidentals added to the mix. For instance, C7(♯9) is C, E, G, B♭, and D♯; and C7(♭13) is C, E, G, B♭, and A♭.

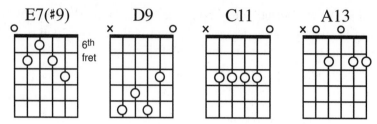

Various extended chords.

I can't stress enough that most beginning guitarists won't run into these sorts of chords unless they have a strong interest in jazz or pop music from the middle of the last century. But it's important to have an understanding of how they're created so that if you do run into one, you'll know what to play. When all else fails, default to one of the four basic chords. For instance, if you're playing a song and you see "A11" pop up, you can play A and be totally fine. If you don't know "Em9," you can get away with Em until you learn it. Any chords that include accidentals on the fifth (♯5 or ♭5 chords such as Dm7♭5, for example) indicate that either an augmented or diminished chord is the basic chord being used.

Slash Chords

Sometimes a songwriter decides that a chord should be played with a specific note in the bass that is *not* the root note of that chord. To indicate this specific new bass note, slash chords, such as C/B, Am/G, or D7/F♯, are used.

LISTENING LIBRARY

If you hear a song with a prominent descending walking bassline, chances are likely it will have some slash chords in it. For example, "Bell Bottom Blues," by Eric Clapton back in his Derek and the Dominoes days, starts with a C chord followed by E/B and then Am. The Kinks' "Sunny Afternoon" is another great example of the use of slash chords.

Reading a slash chord is simple. The chord name is to the left of the slash. The new bass note is to the right. Here are some common slash chords you'll find used by guitarists:

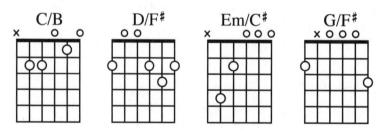

Chapter 13, Example 10.

The important point to remember when playing slash chords is to keep as much of the chord intact while still fingering the new bass note. Using a "bass/strum" or "boom-chuck" approach can help. For example, playing C/B in the previous example, you first hit the new bass note (B at the second fret of the A string) and then skip over the D string and strike the rest of the C chord on the three high strings.

Remember, too, that if you're playing with a bass player, she can handle the bass side of the slash chord and you can just play the chord side!

Practice, Practice

Knowing how chords are made, you can easily figure out the notes to any chord and then find those notes on the fingerboard of the guitar to create new and interesting chord voicings to enhance your playing.

And even though it may seem a bit daunting at first, it's not a big step to start memorizing the notes that make up chords, especially chords you play all the time. Pick one chord—G, for instance—to start with. You now know that the notes of G are G, B, and D. Take a day (or two or three) to memorize that. When you have that information hardwired, it's a snap to figure out Gm (G, B♭, D), Gaug (G, B, D♯), and Gdim (G, B♭, D♭). Then when you're ready add G7, Gmaj7, and Gm7 to your list. You'll surprise yourself at how easy it is to know the notes of chords.

Learning how different chords sound is just as important as learning the chords themselves. Take the time to listen to the differences between the four basic chords—major, minor, augmented, and diminished—and see whether you can identify each type by its sound.

When practicing hearing the differences between chords, it's not important to *exactly* identify a chord, like E minor or D major. All you really want to focus on is the difference in the *type* of chord, such as how the major sounds different from the augmented. Start with just the four basic ones, or even with just the major and minor chords, since they're the ones you'll hear most often.

When you're good at identifying both major and minor chords, test your ears with sevenths, primarily the dominant seventh, major seventh, and minor seventh. These differences will be more subtle. You may first identify the chord only as major or minor. But keep at it and practice listening. When you can pick out these three seventh chords, you'll be able to identify most of the chords you hear in recordings.

You also want to be able to identify chords visually, whether you read notation or tablature (or both). This may seem a little strange, but it can be very helpful. Here are six of the most common open-position guitar chords:

Common guitar chords in notation and tablature.

Now here are the last few measures of "Caprice in G," written by Ferdinando Carulli about 200 years ago:

The ending of "Caprice in G," by Carulli.

The first measure is the G major scale (played from B to B instead of G to G), and the second measure uses the open G string as a pedal point. Now take a look at the notes of the third measure and compare them to the C chord in the previous example. Whether you read either the tablature or the notation, you should be able to see this measure of notes and think "C chord" to yourself.

Most beginning guitarists read from note to note or number to number instead of taking the notes in a measure at a time. If you think about it, this makes sense because it's also how you learned to read ages ago. First you learned the individual letters, and then you grouped them into small words; with practice, you got to the point that you could take in whole lines of words at once.

It's the same with reading music or tablature. If you can make the connection between the individual notes and chords, you'll automatically know where to put your fingers to best play a measure or small musical passage. In this last line of the example, the first measure is an arpeggio of a G chord followed by a D7 arpeggio. And if you finger a G chord after that, you'll be able to play the notes of the last two measures without moving a muscle in your fretting hand.

The Least You Need to Know

- Basic chords are built with the root, third, and fifth notes from their major scales.
- The four basic kinds of chords are major, minor, augmented, and diminished.
- Seventh chords come in many varieties.
- Slash chords indicate that a note other than the chord's root note will be played in the bass.
- Reading chords, in both notation and tablature, can help you develop a better understanding of where to position your hands along the fingerboard when playing.

Barre Tending

In This Chapter

- Some easy half-barre chords
- Root 6 (E-shaped) full-barre chords
- Turning any barre chord into a dozen barre chords
- Switching between Root 6 and Root 5 barres
- Barre chords as slash chords and "5" chords
- Root 4 barre chords

Every undertaking has its set of trouble spots, and sometimes these little bumps are more worrisome because of what we've heard from others. For the beginning guitarist, playing *barre chords*, which require you to fret all six strings with one finger, has that sort of "just wait till you try it!" reputation.

Getting Ready to Barre

Take a look at the palm side of your index finger. You're going to want that to lay flat across six strings so that it can fret each note and make it sound. And that's the first obstacle you must overcome because, unless you were in a bizarre dry-cleaning accident, chances are, your finger isn't flat. It's got creases and joint lines that are very convenient for a string to hide in.

DEFINITION

A **barre chord** is formed, in part, by laying the index finger across a number of strings on the same fret. When you use the index finger across all six strings, it is called a *full barre*. Laying the finger across two, three, four, or five strings is called a *half barre*.

Also take a look at your posture, whether you're sitting or standing when playing. Your fretting hand should be about chest level so that your index finger can easily reach across all six strings.

Half a Barre

Instead of starting right out with a full barre, work your way into it by practicing some half barres. First play the F major chord that you learned back in Chapter 7, just to get yourself warmed up. When you're comfortable, give this Gm chord (technically "Gm/D," as you learned just last chapter) a try:

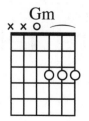

Gm as a half-barre chord.

For the Gm chord, lay your index finger across the first three strings (the high E, B, and G) at the third fret. Try to keep your finger parallel to the frets. Some guitarists like to feel the edge of the fret along the guitar body side of the finger. Get just enough of the finger to fret the G string. Don't jam your hand into the side of the neck closest to the floor.

Strum each of the three strings to make sure you're getting good, clean notes. Then strum across four strings, starting with the open D string. If you're getting dead notes, adjust your index finger so that you aren't catching one of the three strings in the joint.

Four, Five and Six Strings

Now move your index finger up to the fifth fret and barre across the four highest strings (high E, B, G, and D):

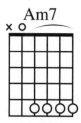

Am7 as a half-barre chord.

Again, strum each string individually as an arpeggio to hear whether each string is giving you a clean, clear note. Adjust your index finger accordingly if you find any clunkers.

Sticking at the fifth fret, adjust your index finger so that it covers all the strings except for the low E and see how well you're doing. Make adjustments if you have to (and don't be afraid of starting over again, barring just two or three strings).

Full Barre

Rest for a moment and shake out your left hand before attempting your first full-barre chord. When you're ready, make a regular open-position E chord. Reposition your fingers on the chord so that your index finger is free. This means using your middle finger to play the first fret of the G string, your pinky to play the second fret of the D, and your ring finger to play the second fret of the A string. Strum the chord a few times to get your fingers used to the new position and to ensure that you're playing all the notes cleanly.

Now shift your entire hand five frets up the neck. Your middle finger should now be at the sixth fret of the G string while your pinky and ring fingers are on the seventh fret of the D and A strings, respectively. Strum all six strings again to make sure your fingers are in good position.

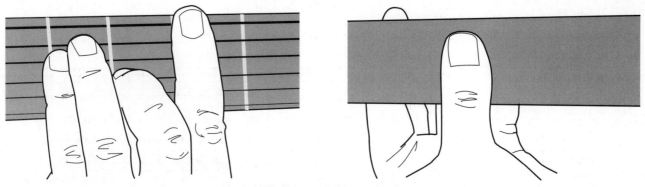

Position for a full-barre chord.

Finally, drop your index finger to form a barre across all six strings at the fifth fret. Remember to not squeeze too tightly; use just enough pressure to sound the notes on the low- and high-E strings and the B string.

Name That Chord!

Now it's time to put your brain to work. You started with an E major chord. Laying your index finger across all six strings closed the position of the chord, and you then shifted the whole thing up five frets. The note at the fifth fret of the low-E string is A, so you might logically conclude that this barre chord is an A major chord. And you'd be right!

Moving the whole barre chord up two more frets gives you a B major:

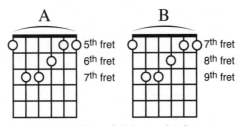

A and B as full-barre chords.

Once you lay your index finger across all the strings to form a barre chord, you create a closed, moveable shape. If you play this barre chord shape at the first fret, it is an F chord. Many guitarists come to find the barre shape easier to play than the half barre you already know.

This E-shaped (or F-shaped, if you prefer) barre chord is also called a *Root 6 barre chord* because the root note of the chord is on the sixth (low-E) string. The note your index finger is covering when barring this note is the root of the chord.

"Down by the Riverside"

Here's a song using the regular E, plus your new A and B barre chords. It's written out in rhythm notation, so you don't have to worry about reading the tablature. Just use the E shape and move to the B and A positions when needed.

Track 45

Chapter 14, Example 1.

If you find it too difficult to manage all the barre chords, try using open-position A in the chorus and substitute the open-position B7 for B in the chorus as well, but still try to make the B barre chord in the verse.

Cheaper by the Dozen

Because barre chords are based on open-position chords you know, you can easily translate "families" of open-position chords to barre chords. For instance, since you know E, Em, E7, and Em7 in open position, converting them to barre chords is a snap:

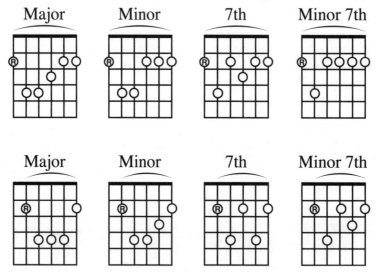

Major, minor, seventh, and minor seventh barre chords.

The family of open-position A chords you've learned so far (A, Am, A7, and Am7) can also be played as barre chords, as you see in this last illustration. Because the root note of these A chords is the open A (fifth) string, these barre chords are called "A-shaped" or "Root 5" barre chords. As with open-position A chords, you usually want to strum these Root 5 barre chords from the A string down, striking just the five high strings.

The A major position is the hardest of the four because most guitar players can't get three fingers cleanly on the D, G, and B strings in the same fret while barring with the index finger. Some guitarists use only two fingers to fret the nonbarred notes, having the ring finger get the notes on both the D and G strings while the pinky plays the note on the B.

Some guitarists are able to get their ring finger to buckle slightly backward, allowing it to fret all three strings and still clear the high-E string. Most, though, use their ring finger to barre across the four high strings and avoid hitting the high-E string when strumming. Others let the same ring finger mute the high-E string totally. Either technique will serve you well, but either (and it goes without saying that ideally you want to learn both) will require a bit of practice.

"Motherless Children"

Your second song for this lesson ups the ante and uses only barre chords.

Prepare for playing this song by first practicing switching between the Am and Dm7 barre chords without even thinking about rhythm or strumming. Then get the rhythm and strumming down (you can use any chord you want for this) so that you can play it without thinking. Only then try to play it while changing from the Am barre chord to the Dm7 barre chord. Stick to a very moderate to slow tempo!

Track 46

continues

Chapter 14, Example 2.

Turning Barres into Slashes and 5s

Barre chords, especially Root 5 barre chords, are sometimes used as slash chords. For example, if you play all six strings of the Dm Root 5 barre chord, it would be Dm/A.

And if you're careful with your strumming, any barre chord can easily become a "5" chord—or power chord, if you prefer. Hitting just the low-E and A strings, or even the low-E, A, and D strings of the first A barre chord you played, means that you're playing only the notes A (fifth fret of the low-E string and seventh fret of the D) and A (seventh fret of the D string), so there's no third in the chord. Therefore, you've played A5.

"Jesse James"

Because barre chords take practice and repetition, not to mention patience and perseverance, you get three songs to learn in this lesson! This last one uses quite a few barre chords, as well as some open position chords (noted as "open" in the music):

Track 47

steal ___ from the rich he would give to the poor he had a___

hand and a ___ heart and a brain _____ Now Jes-se ___ had a

wife to mourn for his ___ life three child - ren they were

brave _____ But that dirt - y lit-tle ___ coward who shot Jim - my

continues

continued

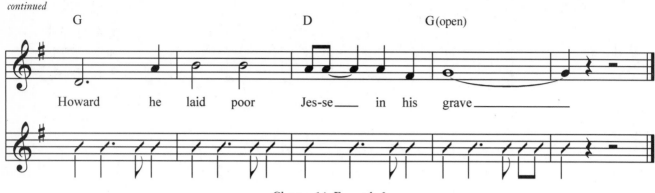

Chapter 14, Example 3.

This song requires a number of quick changes. Work through them first without thinking about tempo. Changing from the first G barre chord to Bm/F♯ looks harder than it actually is. You want to slide the index finger making the barre from the fifth fret to the fourth. Your other three fingers maintain their shape but shift one string higher, just as you first learned to change from E to Am.

SOUND ADVICE

Sometimes the difficulty in changing between barre chords isn't making the barre, but using your other fingers to form the chord! Practice changing your open-position E and A chords (including the minors and sevenths) using only your middle, ring, and pinky fingers, keeping your index finger out of the mix. Working on getting the ring finger and pinky good at making chord changes also helps them develop the strength and coordination needed for techniques like hammer-ons and pull-offs.

Practice, Practice

In case you didn't let it sink in, playing barre chords smoothly and cleanly takes time and practice. The more you can work barre chords into your playing, the sooner you'll get better at them. Take a simple song you can already play well, like "Tom Dooley," and change one of the open-position chords to a barre chord, to get more practice.

The Least You Need to Know

- There are full-barre and half-barre chords.
- When playing barre chords, the position of the index finger is more important than the amount of pressure you use.
- Learning any one barre chord translates into knowing 12 different chords.
- Most barre chords are either Root 6 (E-shaped) or Root 5 (A-shaped).
- The action of your guitar can affect how easily you can make barre chords.

Using Your Intelligence

In This Chapter

- Keys and key signatures
- Assembling diatonic triads
- Discovering the relative minor
- Three minor scales
- Tweaking a chord progression
- Using partial barres

With your knowledge of the major scale, combined with your knowledge of how chords are formed, you can now figure out quite a lot of music theory on your own. Using that same knowledge of the major scale in tandem with your newfound knowledge of barre chords will help you apply music theory directly to your guitar.

You also need to understand a lot more about what, exactly, the knowledge you have means. Yes, you know some things about music and how it's made and what chords are, but have you thought about what, if anything, this music theory can do to help you as a guitarist? Many guitarists know the same basic theory that you do at this point. But most of them haven't taken the extra step to discover that the knowledge they have can do a lot to make them better musicians and guitar players.

The Key to Keys

The *key* of a song is its tonal center. It's usually major or minor and centers on a specific note or chord. Often, it's the first chord played in a song. More often, though, it's the last chord played, the one that makes you feel like the song has ended in the best possible spot. Try playing through "Jesse James" or any of your earlier songs and see if you like ending on any chord other than the final one. You probably won't. The song won't have a sense of closure, of a satisfying conclusion.

Twelve Major Keys

Keys are based upon scales. If you did your practice assignment back in Chapter 12 and wrote out each of the 12 major scales, you may have wondered whether to use flats or sharps to mark the accidentals of each scale. The G major scale, for instance, is G, A, B, C, D, E, F♯, and G. Why F♯ and not G♭? Using F♯ instead of G♭ allows you to use each letter of the musical alphabet one time. That certainly makes things easier when writing out notation! Likewise, the fourth note of the F major scale is B♭, not A♯, because you already have A as the third note of the scale.

DEFINITION

Keys and **key signatures** are *not* the same thing! A song's key is its tonal center, its sense of "home," if you will. A key signature merely tells you the number of flats or sharps in the major scale used for that particular song. As an example, it's possible for a song with a tonal center of E minor to have a key signature of D major.

The number of flats or sharps in any major scale is called the *key signature*, and this can be found on any line of the music notation of any song. Each of the 12 possible keys has a unique key signature, so you can look at any piece of music and have a good idea of the key you're in.

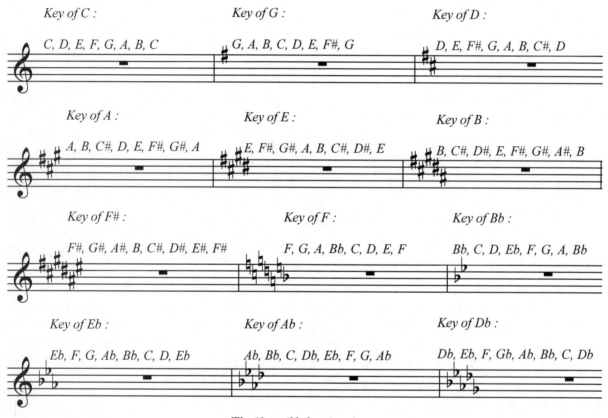

The 12 possible key signatures.

Pallet of Chords

Knowing the key of a song means that you also can know what chords you're mostly likely to encounter when playing that song. To figure this out, you start with the major scale of the key in question and then build diatonic triads on each note of the major scale. *Diatonic* means using only notes from that key.

As an example, start with the key of C major. The diatonic triads can include only notes from the C major scale, so there are no flats or sharps in any of the chords created. The first triad starts on the first degree of the scale (C), and then, using C as our root, we add E (the third) and G (the fifth). This makes a C major chord.

SOUND ADVICE

Roman numerals are usually used to generically denote diatonic triads of a key. Often the major chords (I, IV, and V) are capitalized, while the minor chords (ii, iii, and vi) are lowercase.

The second degree of the C major scale is D. Using D as the root of the second triad, you add F (the third of D) and A (the fifth of D). These notes, D, F, and A, are the D minor chord.

Continuing with this process, the entire set of diatonic triads in the key of C major looks like this:

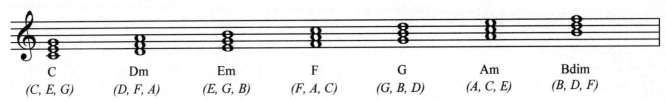

Creating the diatonic triads for the C major scale.

This pattern of diatonic triads holds true for *every* major key. The triads at the first, fourth, and fifth degrees are major; the triads at the second, third, and sixth degrees are minor; and the triad at the seventh degree is diminished. For most music, you can pretty much discard the seventh triad.

This means that if someone tells you a song is in the key of C, the chords you're most likely to find in the song are C, F, and G (the I, IV, and V chords), as well as Dm, Em, and Am (the ii, iii, and vi chords). Charting out all 12 keys by their first 6 diatonic triads (remember that the I position is the key in question) looks like this:

I	ii	III	IV	V	vi
C	Dm	Em	F	G	Am
D♭	E♭m	Fm	G♭	A♭	B♭m
D	Em	F♯m	G	A	Bm
E♭	Fm	Gm	A♭	B♭	Cm
E	F♯m	G♯m	A	B	C♯m
F	Gm	Am	B♭	C	Dm
F♯	G♯m	A♯m	B	C♯	D♯m
G	Am	Bm	C	D	Em
A♭	B♭m	Cm	D♭	E♭	Fm
A	Bm	C♯m	D	E	F♯m
B♭	Cm	Dm	E♭	F	Gm
B	C♯m	D♯m	E	F♯	G♯m

This chart will be incredibly handy for you. Almost all blues songs use only the I, IV, and V chords of any given key. So if someone told you they wanted to play a blues song in the key of D, you'd know that the song would probably just have D, G, and A chords in it. So make your own copy and keep it close!

KEEP SHARP!

In any song, any chord can occur! The diatonic triads give you a very good *educated guess* on the probable chords in any song in any key, but you have to remember that just about anything can happen.

Minor

There are minor keys as well as major keys, as you probably guessed from going back through some of the songs you've learned. Every major scale has a *relative minor* scale (also called the *natural minor* scale) that uses the same notes but starts on the sixth degree. In the key of C, the sixth note is A, and the A natural minor scale is A, B, C, D, E, F, G, and then back to A again.

The chords created by the diatonic triads of the A natural minor scale are the same as those in C major, just in a different order:

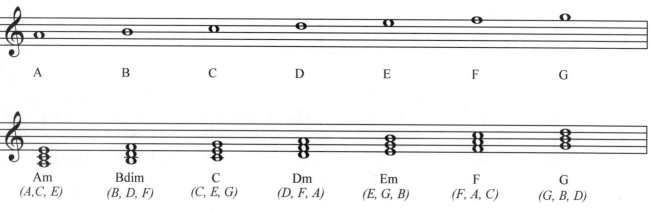

The diatonic triads for the A natural minor scale.

As you see, the i, iv, and v are minor chords, while the III, VI, and VII are major chords. The diminished chord has shifted from the vii position in the major scale to the ii position here in the natural minor.

Harmonic Minors

The trouble is, though, there are *three* different minor scales. In addition to the natural minor scale, there's also the *harmonic minor* scale and the *melodic minor* scale.

The harmonic minor is the same as the natural minor, except that the seventh note of the scale is just a half-step lower than the octave. Here's the A harmonic minor scale and its diatonic triads:

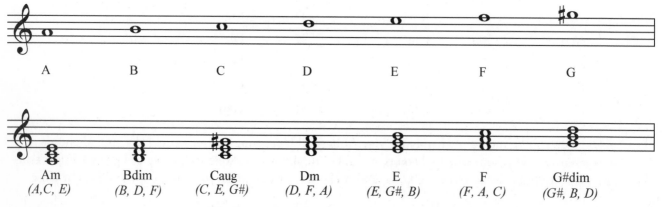

The diatonic triads for the A harmonic minor scale.

Changing the seventh note of the harmonic minor scale results in two very interesting things. First, you've got an interval of a step and a half between the sixth and seventh notes of the scale. This gives the harmonic minor a very exotic sound that most people associate with Asian and Arabian music.

Just as important, the change of the seventh note makes the chord at the fifth degree a major chord instead of a minor one, creating a stronger sense of key for the root chord when played one after another.

Melodic Minors

Just to add to the confusion, the melodic minor scale is different depending on which direction you go in. Ascending the scale, it's just like the regular major scale, only the third is a minor third instead of a major third. The descending melodic minor scale is exactly the same as the descending natural minor scale.

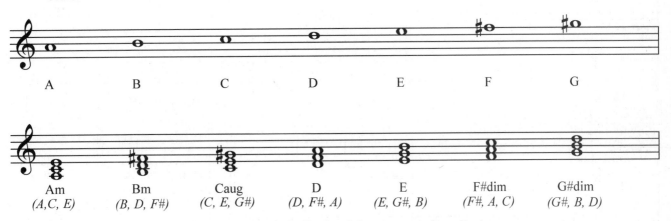

The diatonic triads for the A melodic minor scale (ascending).

This set of diatonic triads makes things even more interesting. The root chord is minor, while the IV and V chords are major.

Starting to Put Pieces Together

There's a lot to digest here, so don't let it overwhelm you. All this information will eventually find a place in your brain where you can access it. And, truth be told, you won't need it all at once, nor will you need much of it in the immediate future.

But you do want to start to apply little touches here and there, using ideas that you've gathered from both your reading and that you've picked up from the songs themselves. Don't fall into the trap of thinking that a particular musical phrase or a technique is the property of one specific song or style of music. Experiment with what you've learned and see (and hear) what you come up with.

Connecting the Dots

Take the idea of walking basslines, for example. Up to this point, you've probably used them only when they've been written out in the notation or tablature of a song, but there's no reason you can't come up with your own whenever you feel like it. The main thing to remember is to get to your "arrival" chord's root note on time.

SOUND ADVICE

Always look at the chords of any song to see where you might be able to toss in a bassline or two. Any chords whose roots are the interval of a third apart (G to Em or Am to C, for example), or fourths or fifths have the potential for walking basslines, provided there's enough time between the chords.

Suppose you have two measures of G right before a measure of C. Here are just a few possibilities of the walking basslines you could play:

Three different G to C basslines.

Remember that music is about rhythm as well as notes. You can take the same notes of any bassline and dramatically alter its feel simply by giving the notes different timing. Likewise, adding rests or hammer-ons or pull-offs will give you different ways to play any given line.

Chord Embellishment and Substitution

You should always look at a chord sheet as a guideline, not as some arcane ritual to be performed precisely as written. For example, suppose the chords for a certain song are G, Em, C, and D. You can create some interesting music by tweaking the chords a bit:

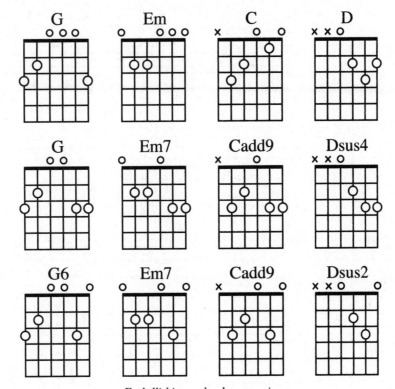

Embellishing a chord progression.

This is an example of how just a little bit of music theory can give you a lot of ideas. The G chord is made up of the notes G, B, and D. G and B are also part of Em (and D is part of Em7) and Cmaj7 (adding the D makes it Cmaj9). Adding an E to the G chord gives you G6. Replacing the F♯ of the D chord with either G or E gives you a D-suspended chord. And all of these choices give the progression a much different sound than it does playing just the regular chords.

Using similar logic, the only difference between the chords C and Am7 is the A note, so using Am7 in place of C can be a viable and interesting chord substitution.

But you won't know this unless you try it yourself and see what you like and what you don't like. Sometimes tweaking the chords sounds good in one song but not another. It really depends on the kind of mood you want to set. Having a bit of music theory under your belt allows you to be creative without falling on your face as often as you might using just trial and error.

"John Barleycorn"

To demonstrate some of these ideas, have a go at "John Barleycorn."

Before diving in too deeply, listen carefully to the rhythm of the picking in the introduction. This rhythmic pattern recurs throughout the song, so get it fixed in your head from the start.

Track 48

Chapter 15, Example 1.

Partial Barres

This arrangement of "John Barleycorn" incorporates the technique of partial barre chords. Using just the three high strings of an E-shaped barre chord played at the fifth fret for the A chord, and then at the third fret for the Em7, gives the opening two measures the same musical feel as the opening of James Taylor's "Fire and Rain."

This works for many reasons. The partial barre is an A chord; you're just using the open A string as your bass note instead of barring across all six strings for the A note at the fifth fret of the low E. When you slide the partial barre down the neck two frets, you're playing G, D, and B (the notes of the G chord) with your fingers, and, as you just learned with a different voicing of this in Example 6, adding the note of the open low-E string in the bass gives you Em7. Not a bad trick!

Thumb Wrap

You can also find a few D/F♯ slash chords. Many guitarists find that the easiest way to play this particular slash chord is to do something you've been told not to do: wrap your thumb around the neck of the guitar. (Remember, you were also warned that there are exceptions to almost everything!)

When attempting this maneuver for the first time, start by having your D chord in place and keeping your thumb centered in the middle of the back of the neck. Gradually slide your thumb up to the edge until you can just get a bit of the low E string. You should be making contact with it just between the first joint and the bottom of the thumbprint area. This definitely takes a little getting used to.

If you're using a classical guitar or an acoustic with a wide neck, you might want to try a different fingering. Place your index finger on the F♯ at the second fret of the low E, and put your middle finger on the A at the second fret of the G string. Keep your ring finger at the D (third fret of the B string), and leave the high-E string open.

Practice, Practice

Experimentation is an important part of practice, not only for your fingers, but for your ears and brain as well. Make notes of the different chords you try as embellishments or substitutes.

When you find something you like, try to determine whether the chord progression or just the overall tone of the song makes it work.

Also make notes, at least mental ones, of the ideas that don't work. Your ears and brain will eventually start working together. You'll be able to try out more ideas on the fly when you have a good preconception of what it's going to sound like.

The Least You Need to Know

- The tonal center of a song is known as its key.
- There are 12 different major keys, each with its own key signature.
- Within any song in any given key, you can have a good idea of which chords will be used.
- There are three different minor scales—the natural minor, harmonic minor, and melodic minor.
- Experiment with tweaking chords and adding little touches like basslines when you can.

Exploring Even Further

With the musical knowledge and techniques you've already learned, it's a small step to explore the rich worlds of song arrangements, transposing, alternate tunings, and more.

You'll learn how to create fills and spice up your guitar playing with short, tasteful (and tasty!) musical phrases that make your music sound even better.

You'll also give your guitar a chance to do some singing all its own by playing single-guitar chord-melody arrangements, where your one guitar serves as a three-piece band—lead, rhythm, and bass all in one! And speaking of lead guitar, how about spending some time discovering how to create your own solos?

Add some alternate picking and crosspicking techniques to all of this, and you'll find that you've made your biggest strides since taking up the guitar!

Clipping on a Capo

In This Chapter

- The process of transposing
- Making a song more "guitar-friendly"
- Getting help from the capo
- Using a capo to create two-guitar arrangements

You may have noticed—between the songs you've learned and your chapters on the 12 major scales and the 12 different major and minor keys that songs may be played in—that certain chords (C, G, Am, Em, and so on) seem to come up a lot in guitar music, whereas others, like A♭, just to pick an example, don't. But with your knowledge of barre chords, it's easy to play these rarely used chords when needed.

However, part of the guitar's sound comes from the ringing of the open strings, particularly when you play with finger picking or add some bass notes while strumming chords.

Some chords, though, like the A♭ mentioned earlier, can be played only as barre chords. Songs played entirely with barre chords have no ringing strings and have a decidedly different tonal texture than those that use only open chords or even a combination of both open and barre chords.

So what do you do if you've got a song in the key of A♭ and you want to give it the ringing sound of open strings? First, you let something else barre the frets for you, leaving all your fingers free to play. That something is called a *capo*. Second, you use the knowledge you gained in Part 3 of this book to *transpose* the chords from one key to another. You won't believe how easy this is to do!

Transposing

The tuning of a guitar has come about so that you can play a wide number of chords in open position. These open position chords—C, G, D, A, and E—are also the root chords of the keys that guitarists usually find themselves playing in. It's no coincidence that most songs guitarists play are in the keys of C, D, G, A, and E (and their relative minors—more on that in Chapter 18).

But there are many keys—12 major and 12 minor. Some keys, particularly those with flats in the key signatures, have diatonic chords that can be played only as barre chords. And the diatonic chords in some "guitar friendly" keys, such as C♯m, which is found in the keys of E and A, aren't always chords that a beginning guitarist (or even an experienced guitarist) might like to play.

> **DEFINITION**
>
> A **capo** is a clamp that uniformly raises the pitch of the guitar's six strings. Placing a capo on the first fret of the neck raises each string a half-step in pitch. When placed on the second fret, each string is now a whole step higher. A capo attached at the third fret raises each string a step and a half higher, and so on.
>
> **Transposing** is changing the key of a song. There are all sorts of reasons for doing so, from finding a key that better suits someone's vocal range to making it easier to play on a particular instrument.

You know how chords are made in any given key, and you know how to read the generic Roman numeral notation given to the diatonic triads based on their degrees of the major scale, so you can do a little transposing to make your life easier. To transpose, musically speaking, means to reproduce in a different key. For example, suppose that a song is in the key of A♭, where the diatonic chords are:

I	ii	III	IV	V	vi
A♭	B♭m	Cm	D♭	E♭	Fm

Wouldn't you rather play it in the key of G, where the diatonic chords are:

I	ii	III	IV	V	vi
G	Am	Bm	C	D	Em

Given the choice between these chords, most people definitely prefer playing in G.

Secret Decoder Ring

Transposing is like making one of those "secret codes" you might have done as a child, where one letter substitutes for another. For example, say the chords of a song in A♭ are as follows:

A♭	Fm	B♭m	D♭	E♭7	A♭maj7

You want to start by thinking "generically." A♭ is the I chord in the key of A♭. Fm is vi, B♭ is vi, and so on. Labeling the chord progression generically looks like this:

I	vi	ii7	IV	V7	Imaj7
A♭	Fm	B♭m7	D♭	E♭7	A♭maj7

Notice that some of these chords are sevenths and major seventh chords. You want to carry any "baggage" the chord might have with it. The Roman numerals indicate whether the chord is major (uppercase, like I, IV, and V) or minor (lowercase, like ii, iii, and vi), so you need to add the extra chord names like 7, maj7, and so on. You also carry along labels like augmented and diminished if they're part of the original chords.

> **SOUND ADVICE**
>
> If you're transposing to have easier (or more guitar-friendly) chords to play, you usually want to transpose *downward* to a lower key. This allows you to use a capo to raise the transposed chords back to the original key.

Now take a look at the generic equivalents in the key of G:

I		ii	III	IV	V	vi
G		Am	Bm	C	D	Em

Substitute the appropriate corresponding generic chord from G into the A♭ chord progression. G is the I chord, so it takes the place of A♭. Em, being the vi chord, fills in for Fm, and so on:

I		vi	ii7	IV	V7	Imaj7
G		Em	Am7	C	D7	Gmaj7

Don't forget to bring along any of the "baggage" with you. For example, since the ii chord is really ii7, you want Am7, not just Am.

Concentrate on the Roots

The main point to remember when transposing is to concentrate on the root notes and to consider anything else—the minors, sevenths, diminished, sharp nines, and what have you—as baggage. Songs often contain chords that are *not* diatonic, and as long as you focus on the roots of the chords, you'll be okay. Take the following chord progression in the key of C:

C   B♭   F   A♭   C   G7   C

Both B♭ and A♭ are not diatonic chords in the key of C, but that doesn't mean you can't transpose them. Think of B♭ as VII♭ and A♭ as VI♭ (notice the uppercase, since they're both major chords), and go with the generic equivalents. Transposing this last progression into the key of A looks like this:

Key of C:		C	B♭	F	A♭	C	G7	C
Generic:		I	VII♭	IV	VI♭	I	V7	I
Key of A:		A	G	D	F	A	E7	A

In the A major scale, G♯ is the seventh degree and F♯ is the sixth. So G, which is a half-step lower than G♯, is the flatted seventh and F (a half-step lower than F♯) is the flatted sixth. You make each of those chords major because the B♭ and A♭ chords in the original progression are major.

Playing with a Capo

Transposing is quite often only the first step. In your first transposing example, you took a chord progression in the key of A♭ and lowered each chord a half-step so that they were all in the key of G. That certainly made the progression easier to play, but what if you were playing with someone who wanted to play the progression in A♭ nonetheless? Would all your transposing work have been wasted?

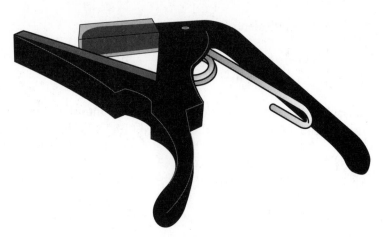

A guitar capo.

No, you'd simply use a capo to solve this situation. A capo is essentially a clamp that you place on the fingerboard of your guitar at any fret. It forms a solid barre across all six strings, much as your index finger does when making barre chords. But with a capo, you still get to use all your fingers instead of having the index finger committed to making the barre. Plus, the capo gives you the sound of ringing open strings (as opposed to the "fretted by fingers" sound) no matter where on the neck you place it.

There are many different types of capos, but they all work the same way. You place the hard bar of the capo on the strings, lining up the capo parallel and close to the fret at the desired spot on the neck, and then you clamp it into place.

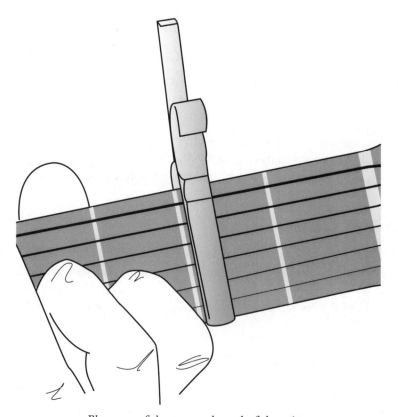

Placement of the capo on the neck of the guitar.

Just as your finger does, the capo raises the pitch of any string to the note at the fret where it's placed. If you place a capo on the first fret of your guitar, the open strings, normally (low to high) E, A, D, G, B, and E, are one half-step higher: F, B♭, E♭, A♭, C, and F.

Raising the Chords

Similarly, any chord you might play is also raised up a half-step because the capo covers all the open strings. Put a capo on the first fret of your neck and play a D chord. While your fingers are placed two and three frets higher than the capo, they are on the third and fourth frets of the guitar. The index finger is at the third fret of the G string, your middle finger is at the third fret of the high E string, and your ring finger is at the fourth fret of the B string.

> **KEEP SHARP!**
>
> Think of the capo as the new "nut" of your guitar. Any fretting you do will be on the body side of the capo. Placing a finger on the frets between the capo and the headstock won't do anything.

Because all the notes of this chord, whether fretted or open, are one half-step higher, the entire D chord is also one half-step higher, making it either a D♯ or an E♭, depending on what you want to call it.

Applying the Math

Going back to the original example, the progression of chords in the key of A♭, you first transposed all the chords of the progression down a half-step so that they were all in the key of G. That part was easy.

To get them all in the key of A♭ again, *and* to make them guitar-friendly, place your capo on the first fret. Even though you're playing a G chord, the capo at the first fret raises it to an A♭ chord. Likewise, the Em you play is actually an Fm, because you raised each note of the chord a half-step by placing the capo on the first fret.

Doublespeak

Initially, using a capo can be confusing because you're essentially playing one chord in terms of fingering, but playing a different chord in terms of actual pitch. Playing G with the capo on the first fret, as you just worked out, is really playing an A♭ chord. It's like you're using two sets of chords at once—one for your fingers and one for the rest of the world.

In fact, if you look at the music for songs where capos are used (whether in chord charts or tablature), either you'll see two sets of chords (one for the guitar with the capo and the other for the rest of the world) or the capo will act as the "0" fret of the tablature and the rest of the tablature numbering will be done relative to the capo.

Next is a chart that can help you know what chords you're really playing when you have a capo on any given fret of your guitar.

Capo on Fret:	1	2	3	4	5	6	7	8	9
Open Chord:									
A becomes	B♭	B	C	C♯	D	E♭	E	F	F♯
C becomes	C♯	D	E♭	E	F	F♯	G	G♯	A
D becomes	E♭	E	F	F♯	G	G♯	A	B♭	B
E becomes	F	F♯	G	G♯	A	B♭	B	C	C♯
F becomes	F♯	G	G♯	A	B♭	B	C	C♯	D
G becomes	G♯	A	B♭	B	C	C♯	D	E♭	E

Capo Considerations

Using a capo, along with a bit of transposing, to make songs with hard chords easier for guitarists to play is just the beginning. Suppose you've learned a song, chords and all, only to find that you can't sing it because the melody isn't in your vocal range. Try the capo at different points along the neck to find a key that you can sing in without scaring off your audience!

A capo also allows you to play with open-position chord voicings farther up the neck. This can give a song a very different sound. Playing with a capo between the fifth and ninth frets brings out the brighter tones of the guitar, giving it a quality much like a mandolin.

"Make Me a Pallet"

Having the option of using a capo is especially cool when you're playing with other guitarists. One guitar can be playing in open position while a second guitar is playing transposed chords up the neck with the aid of the capo.

For example, here's a cool song in the key of G:

 Track 49

Chapter 16, Example 1.

You shouldn't have too much trouble with this song, since it's in the key of G and you're familiar with most of the chords.

Making a Second "Pallet"

Now here's the same song, still in the key of G, but using a capo on the seventh fret. This means that the "fingering" chords are in the key of C:

Track 50

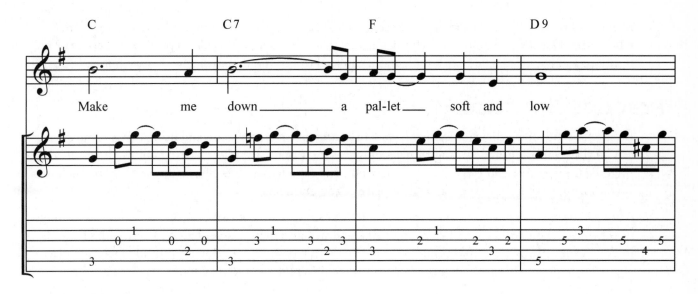

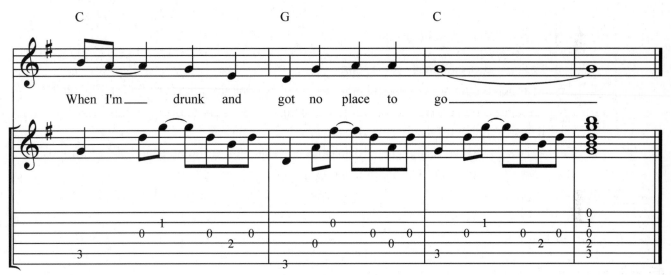

Chapter 16, Example 2.

You can hear how playing the same song using transposed chords and a capo on the seventh fret to put the transposed song back into the key of G gives it a different flavor. In the next track, both versions are played at the same time:

Track 51

This is a great example of how two guitarists can create a lot of depth to a song, even if they're playing basic chords and using very simple picking or strumming.

LISTENING LIBRARY

Jim Croce and Maury Muehleisen used capos to arrange Croce's songs for their two-guitar performances. On "I Have to Say 'I Love You' in a Song," Muehleisen's guitar has a capo on the seventh fret, and he uses the capo on the fifth fret on "Time in a Bottle"; Croce plays without a capo for both songs.

Some guitarists look at the capo as a "cheating" device, feeling that one can use barre chords to the same effect. But the capo allows for chord voicings that are often impossible to play, barre chords or no. It's more a guitar technique than a tool, and it can lead to very imaginative and creative music.

Practice, Practice

Be sure to write down the chords during your first attempts at transposing and using capos. Transposing can be very confusing, and writing things out makes it clearer. Likewise, charting out the notes on a fingerboard map can help you understand just how the capo works, as well as tell you what "real" chords you're forming when you have the capo in place at any given fret.

After some time and practice, you'll want to start transposing simple two-, three-, and four-chord songs in your head. This will be easier than you think and will also help you get better at thinking of chords in their generic form (I, ii, iii, IV, and so on). The more you work at both transposition and capo placement, the more you'll start seeing the possibilities of different ways to play songs.

The Least You Need to Know

- Transposing is changing the key of a song.
- Placing a capo on the neck of the guitar raises the pitch of all six strings one half-step per fret.
- You can transpose a song to a lower key to make the chords easier to play, and then use a capo to raise it back to the original key.
- Capos allow you to create higher chord voicings and still get the ringing sound of open strings.
- Using a capo can instantly add depth to a two-guitar song arrangement.

Beyond Standard Tuning

In This Chapter

- Lowered tunings
- Drop D tuning
- Open tunings
- How to find chords in new tunings
- Alternate tunings in songs

There are all sorts of ways to tune the guitar, and each different tuning, or *alternate tuning*, gives the guitar a different sound. Some alternate tunings are very subtle, and knowing where the new notes and chords are doesn't require much adjustment. Others can be quite exotic, making the guitar sound even more expressive than it normally does.

As a beginner, you might think you don't want to bother "re-learning" how to tune or play the same chords with different fingerings, but exploring alternate tunings can enrich your playing and add to your understanding of how chords are created. A lot of it will be very easy, I promise!

Standards Within Standard

Depending on your point of view, you can break down all tunings into three or four categories. Going with three, they are *standard tuning*, *open tuning*, and *alternate tuning*. Standard is, obviously, the standard tuning that you already know (low to high): E, A, D, G, B, and E.

Open tunings are tunings in which all the strings of the guitar are tuned to a specific chord—when you strum all six open strings of your guitar, you get a recognizable chord. If you tune your guitar so that the strings (low to high) are tuned to the notes C, G, C, G, C, E, you are in *open C tuning*, as each string is tuned to a note of the C major chord. You can argue that every combination of notes is *some* type of chord, so open tunings try to be in very basic major or minor chords. You occasionally also find open tunings of sixth and seventh chords.

Alternate tunings covers everything that is neither standard nor open. Tunings don't usually get formal names (although you'll soon read that there are a few), but are rather identified by the new tuning of the six strings, from low to high. For instance, if you tuned your G string down a whole step to F, the alternate tuning would be called "EADFBE."

Lowering One's Standards

Some guitarists, especially those who play rock, punk, and heavy metal (usually on electric guitars), use *lowered* tunings to make their guitars sound lower and, well, heavier. In a lowered tuning, all six strings are lowered by the same number of steps or half-steps, so the intervals between all the strings are the same as they are in standard tuning. Here are the tunings for the most common lowered tunings:

Standard tuning:	E	A	D	G	B	E
E♭ standard:	E♭	A♭	D♭	G♭	B♭	E♭
D standard:	D	G	C	F	A	D
C♯ standard:	C♯	F♯	B	E	G♯	C♯
C standard:	C	F	B♭	E♭	G	C

KEEP SHARP!

Alternate tunings are used on all types of guitars, whether acoustic, electric, or classical, but you should *not* use alternate tunings if you have an electric guitar with a floating tremolo system (a whammy bar that both lowers and raises the pitch of the strings). Unless you can lock the tremolo system into place, you'll find it almost impossible to keep your guitar in tune if you try any tuning other than standard.

The obvious positive of lowered standard tunings is that all your chord forms are unchanged. You simply have to transpose each chord down the appropriate number of steps and half-steps to figure out what the new chord is. Playing an open-position E chord in E♭ standard gives you an E♭ chord. Playing the same chord in C standard gives you C.

Heavy Flopping

Just to give you an idea of how this works, here's a simple chord progression—E, A, D, A, and E—played entirely with open-position chords in each of the previously listed tunings:

Track 52

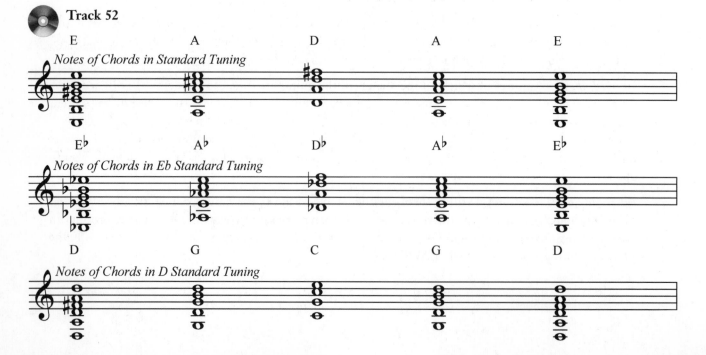

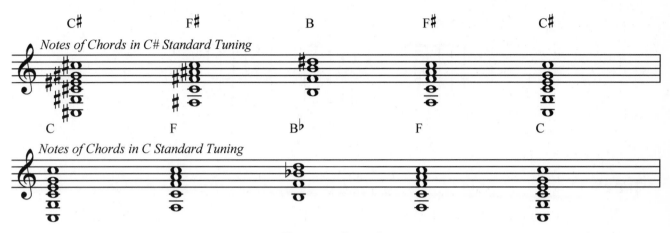

Chapter 17, Example 1.

Lowering the strings more than a step and a half means they're very slack and can get very floppy sounding. But having looser strings usually translates to easier string bending, which is a big plus for guitarists who love to pepper their solos with lots of bends.

Drop D

In general, you want to try to tune *down* for most alternate tunings, which loosens the tension on the strings. Tuning up raises the tension, and if you're tuning up a number of strings, particularly the low ones, you're adding considerable stress to your guitar.

The most common alternate tuning is very simple and is used in almost all musical genres, from rock to folk, to country, to classical. It's called *drop D tuning*, and you'll be surprised by how much different it is, even though all you do is change the tuning of a single string. To get your guitar into drop D tuning, lower the low-E string a full step, down to D.

Standard tuning:	E	A	D	G	B	E
Drop D tuning:	D	A	D	G	G	E

After getting your guitar into drop D, strum a regular open-position D chord, but strum across *all six strings* of the guitar instead of starting your strum on the D string (fourth string), as you usually do. You can hear that you've given your guitar some more "oomph" in the bass with this tuning.

LISTENING LIBRARY

Drop D tuning is used in all kinds of music. You can hear it in Neil Young's "Harvest Moon," John Denver's "Rocky Mountain High," the Beatles' "Dear Prudence," and many of the songs by Fallout Boy.

Since only the low-E string has been changed, you have to worry about different chord fingerings only when the chord you want normally uses that low-E string. So open-position D, Em, and G chords, for example, look like this in drop D:

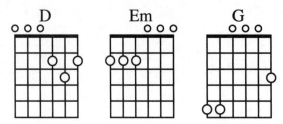

The D, Em, and G chords in drop D tuning.

"Tanz"

Here's a nice, simple classical piece in drop D:

Track 53

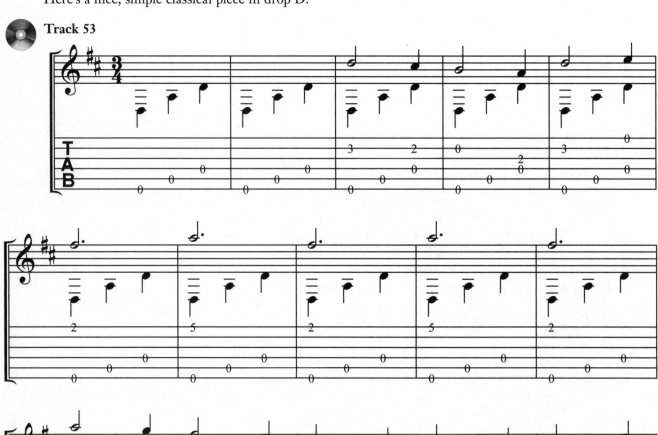

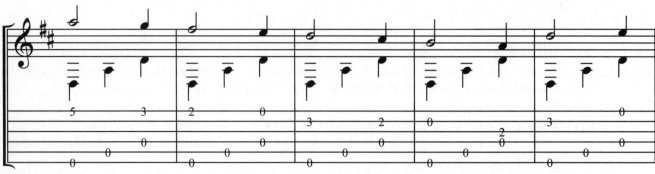

Chapter 17, Example 2.

This short song is also great practice for finger picking. Play the bass notes throughout with your thumb on the three lowest strings (D, A, and D) while pinching the melody notes with your fingers.

Rock On

Rock, punk, and metal players find drop D tuning a favorite because the three lowest strings (D, A, and D) are a ready-made power chord, D5. This means that just sliding a finger to barre across the three low strings at any fret gives them a fast and easy power chord all over the neck.

This is why many lowered tunings also have drop tuning equivalents, where the lowest string is tuned down an additional step in order to be an octave lower than the note of the fourth string. To play drop C tuning, for instance, you start out in D standard tuning (DGCFAD) and then lower the sixth string down to C to get CGCFAD.

Open Season

The most common open tunings are open G, open D, open A, and open E:

Standard tuning:	E	A	D	G	B	E
Open G tuning:	D	G	D	G	B	D
Open D tuning:	D	A	D	F#	A	D
Open A tuning:	E	A	E	A	C#	E
Open E tuning:	E	B	E	G#	B	E

As you see, in each tuning, the guitar's six strings are tuned to notes of the chord of the tuning. To set your guitar in open G, you tune both the high- and low-E strings down a whole step to D and also tune the A string down a whole step to G. You get to open D from standard tuning by tuning both E strings down a whole step to D, tuning the B string down a whole step to A, and tuning the G string one half-step down to F#.

This is also a good time to remember your capo from the last chapter. Instead of tuning three strings up for open A (the D, G, and B strings are all raised one whole step), you can tune to open G and place the capo on the second fret to get open A. Similarly, placing the capo at the second fret after you've tuned to open D tuning gives you open E, which beats raising the A and D strings a whole step and raising the G string a half-step.

Finding Oneself in Uncharted Territory

As you saw with drop D tuning, getting your instrument into the new tuning is just the first step. You then need to figure out where the chords are. It's definitely a good idea to draw out a fingerboard map for the new tuning, just as you did in Chapter 1, but this time the notes will be very different. Take a look at the fingerboard map of open G tuning:

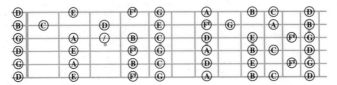

Finding the notes on the fingerboard in open G tuning.

Using your brain certainly helps, too! You know that strumming all six strings gives you a G major chord, so it makes perfect sense that barring across all six strings at any fret gives you the chord with its root note on the fifth string:

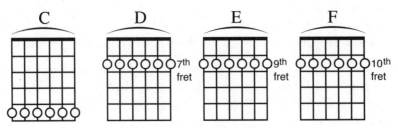

Various major chords in open G tuning.

But the true allure of most open tunings is the enchanting, embellished chords you can create by using a few open strings with the chords you create, especially when you use various finger-picking patterns. Some of the arpeggios you can come up with are quite mesmerizing. Here are some examples in open G:

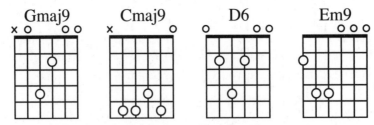

Various embellished chords in open G tuning.

You want to take some time to explore the numerous possibilities any open or alternate tuning has to offer. Again, be sure to map out the fingerboard and make chord diagrams to help you. Create a small notebook for each tuning, if you'd like. You may find some tunings friendlier than others in terms of fingerings for easy chords. And you may like some so much that you end up keeping a spare guitar in that tuning all the time!

The Keith Richards Sound

Open G is part of Keith Richards's signature sound. He uses it in many of the songs the Rolling Stones have recorded, using an open-position Am7 shape to create all sorts of cool, rocking riffs:

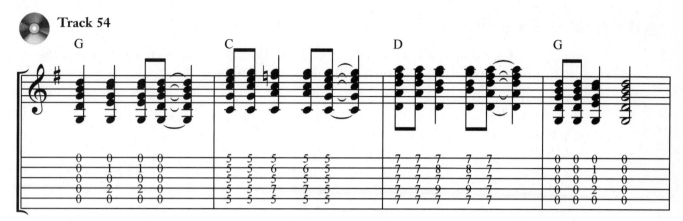

Chapter 17, Example 3.

Not only are many of Richards's guitars tuned to open G, but he also has the sixth string removed so that he always has the root note in the bass when playing the typical barres of major chords in open G.

But Wait! There's More!

Obviously, your knowledge of how chords are made pays off when it comes to open tunings. If you start with open G, tuning the B string down a half-step to B♭, for example, gives you DGDGB♭D, which changes the open G tuning to open Gm. Similarly, again starting with open G, tuning the G note down a half-step to F♯ gives you open Gmaj7 tuning, DGDF♯BD.

But besides creating open tunings for major or minor chords, as well as sevenths and minor sevenths and more, you can create variations for many of these chords as well, which can be quite striking in their differences. For instance, in addition to the "usual" version of open G tuning, many dobro, or resonator guitar, players like to use this variation of open G:

Typical open G tuning: D   G   D   G   B   D

Dobro open G tuning: G   B   D   G   B   D

In this version of open G, the low-E string is raised a step and a half to G and the A string is raised a full step to B. Quite often, different gauges of strings are used to prevent too much stress on the guitar. You can usually find these string sets at your local music store.

This may seem obvious, but where the different elements of a chord are placed in a tuning is a big part of how tuning ultimately sounds. For instance, in open C tuning, you can place the third of the C chord, which is E, on the high-E string, where it really stands out when strummed, or you can "bury it" in the middle strings, giving the tuning more of an open D sound:

Open C tuning #1 (third high):   C   G   C   G   C   E

Open C tuning #2 (third "buried"):   C   G   C   E   G   C

There are obviously a lot of options to explore! But it's a lot of fun exploring, and you can come up with many interesting chord choices and picking patterns.

Alternate Reality

When simply changing the note of any one string creates an alternate tuning, it's truly an understatement to say that there are many possible alternate tunings. Here are a few:

> EADGBD
> EADEAD
> EADF♯BE
> DADGBD
> DADGAD
> DGDGAD
> CGDGBE
> CGDGCD
> CFCGCE

DADGAD is one of the few tunings that can be pronounced as a word. It's also called D modal or Dsus4 tuning. It's a favorite of many fingerstyle guitarists and is found in a lot of arrangements of Celtic music.

> **LISTENING LIBRARY**
>
> DADGBD is sometimes called "double drop D" because both E strings are tuned down a whole step to D. It's another tuning that Neil Young uses quite a bit ("Ohio," "Cinnamon Girl," and "No More"), and you can also hear it in Fleetwood Mac's "The Chain."

Both CGDGBE and CFCGCE are found quite a bit in Hawaiian music. CGDGBE is also called "C-wahine" tuning. You can also think of it as Cmaj9, since it has all the notes of the Cmaj9 chord. CFCGCE is also known as "F-wahine" tuning. Wahine (*wa-hee-nee*), by the way, is Hawaiian for "girl" or "young woman."

This list of alternate tunings doesn't even take into account that you can tune some strings to the same note. The tuning used in "Suite: Judy Blue Eyes," by Crosby, Stills and Nash, is EEEEBE. The A string is tuned down two and a half steps so that it matches the low-E string. The D string is tuned up a whole step to E, while the G string is tuned down a step and a half to the same note of E. Quite a tuning, isn't it? Their song "Carry On" uses the same tuning, but each string is lowered an additional half-step.

"The Lakes of Pontchartrain"

You've read a lot about the many tuning choices open to you as a guitarist, so it makes sense to try the song for this chapter, "The Lakes of Pontchartrain," with two different alternate tunings. First, here it is in DADGAD:

Track 55

NOTE: Guitar in DADGAD tuning

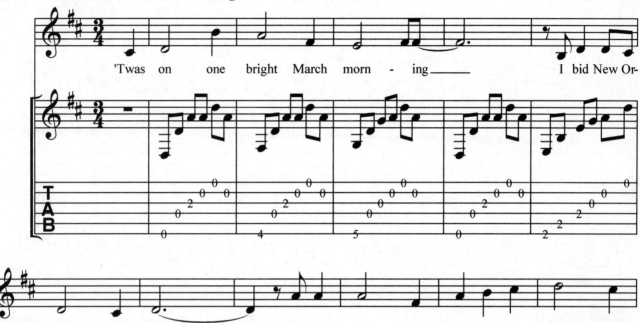

'Twas on one bright March morn - ing_____ I bid New Or-

leans a - dieu_____ And I took the road - to Jack - son

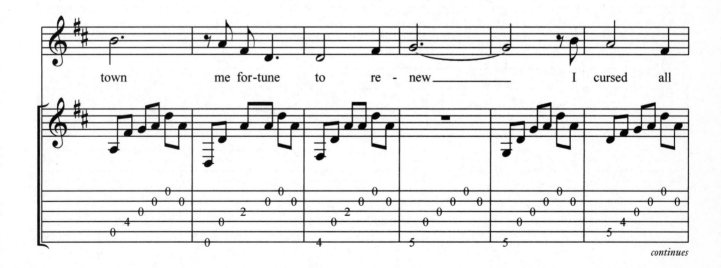

town me for-tune to re - new_____ I cursed all

continues

continued

Chapter 17, Example 4.

And here it is again, but this time not only is it in open G, it also uses a capo on the fifth fret, putting the song in the key of C:

Track 56

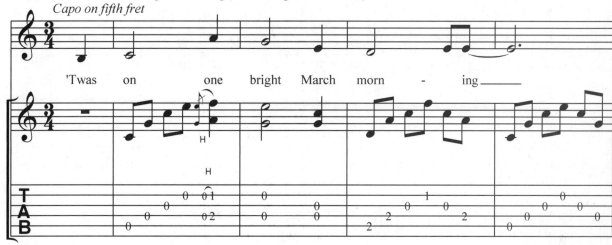

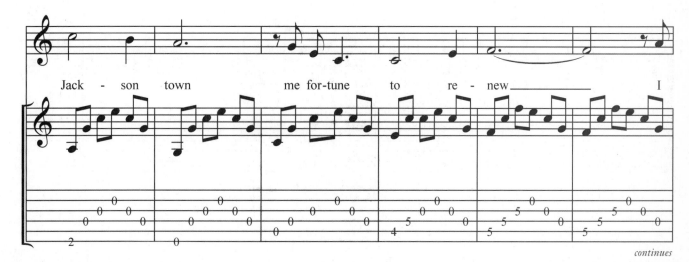

continued

Chapter 17, Example 5.

These arrangements are purposely on the simple side, using very easy arpeggios and basslines so you can navigate these new tunings relatively easily. Notice that the first and fourth lines of the song are the same in terms of the guitar arrangement, as are the second and third lines. That also helps make playing both arrangements a bit easier.

Practice, Practice

Practicing open and alternate tunings can be both confusing and frustrating if you let them be so. Narrow your focus to just one tuning for a period of time. You also need to make notes, preferably written ones, so that the next time you use that tuning, you won't be starting from scratch.

Start with a tuning that you know is used for a song you know and like well enough to learn. You can easily look up more than enough examples of songs on the Internet. Don't worry about specific tablature, although you can probably find that, too, without looking too hard. Instead, focus first on exploring how the chord changes work and what kind of picking or strumming creates the sound you want for the song. And keep making written notes!

The Least You Need to Know

- The four types of tuning are standard, lowered standard, open, and alternate.
- Lowered tunings are used a lot in rock and metal music.
- Drop D is one of the more common tunings.
- Playing major chords in major open tunings involves a single barre across all six strings.
- Alternate tunings can create exotic-sounding music.

Filling In the Blanks

In This Chapter

- Discovering fills
- Using chords to build fills
- The pentatonic scale
- The open-position E minor pentatonic scale
- Blue notes
- Combining major and minor scales to make fills

A guitarist's hands are always busy. The right hand is either strumming the strings with a pick or playing the strings with the fingers, while the left hand is busy changing chords. This division of labor can leave the left hand relatively idle at times, though, especially if a song stays on one particular chord for any length of time.

But the left hand can certainly be doing more than just fingering chords. You've already used techniques like hammer-ons, pull-offs, and other slurs, usually in conjunction with chords, to spice up the left hand's work from time to time. You've also added walking basslines to give the left hand extra duty.

Getting more out of your left hand is important to the solo guitarist. When you play any song, you are your whole band. Not only do you provide the rhythm and chords, but any other fun stuff, like bass notes or short melodic fills, has to come from you. Adding fills to your playing probably seems like (another) huge step forward, but basically it's just expanding on techniques you already know how to do. If you think of your various slurs—hammer-ons, pull-offs, slides, and bends—as words, then fills are just short phrases you can use to make your playing sound even better.

Fills and Riffs

Fills are short musical phrases that usually, like the name says, fill spaces in music or break up what might otherwise be repetitive strumming or picking. *Riffs* are essentially fills, but a riff is usually the center of a song and gets played exactly the same way each time it occurs. Think of the guitar part at the beginning of "Secret Agent Man" or "Margaritaville," or the first guitar part that starts Pink Floyd's "Wish You Were Here." Those are riffs.

DEFINITION

Riffs and **fills** are short musical phrases. Generally speaking, riffs are used as a musical "hook," catching the listener's ear as they're repeated throughout a song. Fills are more like clever one-liners tossed out every now and then to add a bit of musical flash to the ordinary strumming or picking.

Fills are typically more organic and can be played differently each time. The second guitar part in the introduction of "Wish You Were Here" adds fills to the spaces created by the riffs of the first guitar part.

Gather 'Round the Chord

Riffs and fills may sound complicated, but they're usually pretty easy to play. At their simplest, fills are just ways of fooling around with the chords of a song while you're strumming them.

Suppose you had eight beats of a D chord. You could simply strum the chord for all eight beats, or you could get a little fancier by throwing in a bit of Dsus4 and Dsus2 as well, like this:

 Track 57 (0:00)

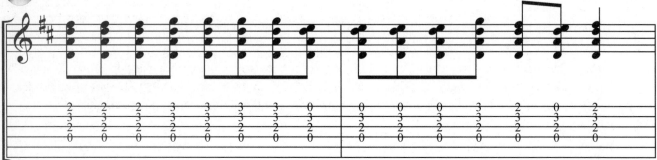

Chapter 18, Example 1.

Anticipation

In this last example, you may have noticed that the chord changes were on the off-beats, on the eighth notes between the "one, two, three, four" count. Coming in ahead of the beat like this is called *anticipation*. Anticipations are commonly used in strumming and single-note playing. They give the impression that the music is picking up speed even though the beat is staying steady.

SOUND ADVICE

Playing anticipations initially requires some concentrated practice. Pick just two chords, such as Em and A, and play a measure of each in eighth notes, strumming down and up for each eighth note. Then try changing between the chords on the upstroke of the second half of the fourth beat of each measure. Do this slowly and deliberately until you get both the timing and the sound of the anticipation clearly set in your head. Then slowly increase the tempo.

The trick with anticipations is to not get fooled into thinking that the beat has changed and lose your sense of tempo and rhythm. Be sure to count it out. Because the changes occur between the beats, you're going to be hitting the new chords on the upstroke, as indicated in the notation on the last example. Take your time to get used to playing this correctly.

Playing Around Some More

Going back to your first fill, try keeping your D chord in place as much as you can. Obviously, you'll need to remove your middle finger from the E string at various points, but keep the index and ring fingers on their respective notes.

Keeping your fingers close to the chord means you can shift from full chord to single notes with minimal effort. The next fill still focuses on the D chord but uses a string of single notes instead of full chord strumming:

Track 57 (0:10)

Chapter 18, Example 2.

If you're keeping as much of your D chord intact as possible, you should find yourself using your pinky for any notes on the fourth fret. That's going to be a stretch at first, especially if you've been shying away from using your pinky much up until now. Try to get in the habit of employing your little finger. You're going to find it more and more helpful as you progress as a guitar player.

Where to Fill and What to Use

As you work on fills, listen for places where you might play one. Take cues from the song itself. Anyplace where the vocal part rests can be a potential spot for a fill. Many blues songs, for example, are played in what's called a *call and response* style. The vocalist, who sometimes is also the guitarist, sings over two measures of the song, then the guitar gets two measures where a fill can easily be played.

Think about what notes you can easily reach from any chord position. Remember the exercise in Chapter 12 (Example 6) where you played notes of the G and C major scales while strumming the rest of the chord? Think along those lines, using notes in the key of the song while hanging on to the chord at hand. "Easy" has to be the key here, especially if you're singing, too!

The Pentatonic Scale

One thing a guitarist can do to make playing fills easier is to scale back on the major scale. Instead of using a full major scale for fills, many guitarists find the *pentatonic scales* more to their liking. Pentatonic scales have five different notes instead of seven, and each note is usually within easy reach of any given chord.

DEFINITION

Major pentatonic scales are built from the root, second, third, fifth, and sixth of the major scale. **Minor pentatonic scales,** when described in terms of the major scale, are the root, minor third, fourth, fifth, and flatted seventh.

Any pentatonic scale is made with the root, second, third, fifth, and sixth notes of its major scale. Making the pentatonic of the G major scale looks like this:

G major scale: G   A   B   C   D   E   F♯   G

G major pentatonic: G   A   B   D   E   G

Mapping out the G major pentatonic in open position, you can find your notes at the following frets:

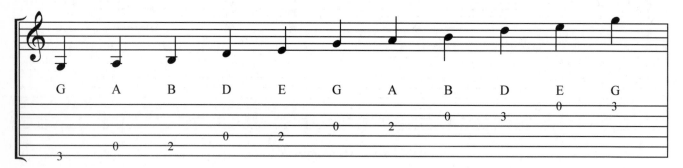

The notes of the G major pentatonic scale.

The "Easy Fill" Solution

Back in Chapter 15, you learned that every major scale has a relative minor, which is made using the same notes of the major scale but starts with the note at the sixth position. Major pentatonic scales also share the same relative minors, so since Em is the relative minor of G major, the Em pentatonic scale is the relative minor of the G major pentatonic scale:

G major pentatonic: G   A   B   D   E   G

E minor pentatonic: E   G   A   B   D   E

Regardless of what you decide to call it, the open-position G major/E minor pentatonic scale is probably the best friend any guitar player could ask for when it comes to adding fills. All the notes are within the first three frets of the fingerboard, and they're all quite easily accessible from the open-position chords you know.

Here are some simple fills for the open-position C, G, D, A, and E chords, all using additional notes from the open-position Em pentatonic scale:

Track 58 (0:00)

continues

continued

Chapter 18, Example 3.

Fitting In

Because music is about rhythm as much as it is about notes, learning one fill can give you dozens of fills at your fingertips. If you vary the rhythmic value of the notes in the first fill from the last example, you can come up with the following variations:

Track 58 (0:40)

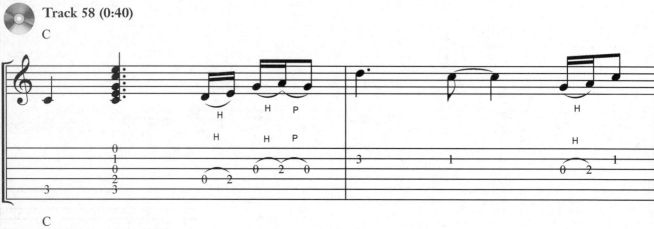

Chapter 18, Example 4.

Revisiting the Blues

Since the blues offers lots of opportunities to practice fills, let's do a second take of "The Complete Idiot's Blues" from Chapter 6 and add some fills to it:

Track 59

Chapter 18, Example 5.

As you can hear on the CD, this example is played relatively slowly so that you can get a feel for the timing of each fill. Be sure to count aloud if you're not getting into the blues groove.

You should also come up with your own fills to play for this song. Don't worry about them being too simple. Quite often the simplest fills sound spot-on and totally fit with a song. As you get more confident with your timing and technique, your fills will get much fancier. But regardless of how flashy you can be, you still want each fill to fit the mood of the song.

Moving Minors About

Knowing the fingerboard pattern of any scale allows you to move it around anywhere on the neck. You can use the open-position Em pentatonic scale pattern for any minor pentatonic scale as long as you start on that scale's root note on the low-E string. For instance, the root note of the Gm pentatonic scale, G, is at the third fret of the low-E string, so the Gm pentatonic scale looks like this:

The G minor pentatonic scale (Root 6 position).

Just as with your full six-string barre chords, this scale can be called Root 6 position because it starts with the root note on the low-E string. Since it's simple enough to find root notes on the sixth string, and because the fingering for the minor pentatonic scale is very easy in Root 6 position, many guitarists favor this scale, regardless of their experience and skill level. A great many riffs and fills, not to mention countless guitar solos, are based on the minor pentatonic scale.

Blue Notes and the Blues

Part of the reason for this popularity is the versatility of the minor pentatonic scale, particularly when it comes to blues music. Much of the tonal quality associated with blues music comes from the interplay of *blue notes* and the notes of the major scale. Blue notes typically are the minor third, flat seventh, and diminished fifth of the major scale.

DEFINITION

Blue notes—the minor third, flat seventh, and diminished fifth—give blues music a lot of its flavor. The interplay of these three blue notes with the notes of the major scale creates many opportunities for tension and resolution of harmonies.

Much of music is all about tension and resolution. Tension comes about when notes aren't in harmony with one another. If you play the B note of the open B string at the same time you play the C note at the fifth fret of the G string, it will make you cringe. Resolution comes about when harmony is restored. Slide that C note on the G string up a whole step to the D note (at the seventh fret), and the tension you heard earlier is resolved.

The tension created when the blue note is played or sung over a major chord is palpable. Go back to the "Complete Idiot's Blues" from earlier in this chapter and listen to the first fill. It starts on a G (third fret of the high E) and then quickly resolves to the open high-E string. This blues song is in the key of E major, but the G note is part of the Em chord. The interplay between major and minor tones gives the fill a very bluesy feel.

The chord progressions of most songs involve tension and resolution on some level. The amount of tension can vary from mild to dramatic. For instance, a lot of jazz music, as you will read in Chapter 28, uses chords that bring out very drastic moments of tension.

"Midnight Special"

This bluesy feel is a strong part of many songs in other genres as well. Country, folk, and especially rock music all have songs that benefit from the tug-of-war between the blue notes and the major chords.

Your second song for this chapter, "Midnight Special," uses fills from both the G major and G minor pentatonic scales, sometimes combining notes from both scales in the same fill:

Track 60

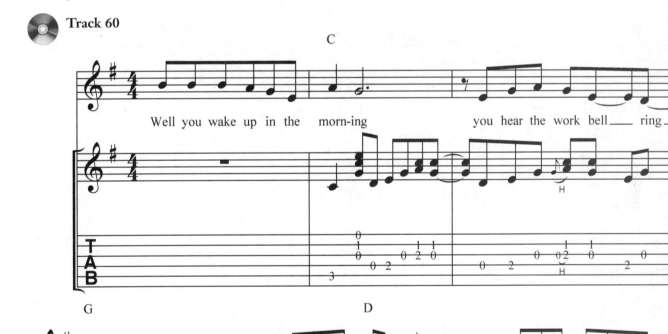

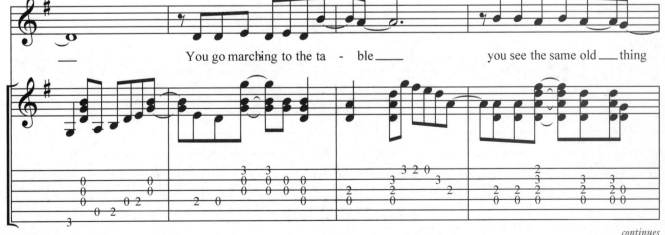

continues

continues

continued

Chapter 18, Example 6.

Although this arrangement is very short, there are fills in practically every other measure, so you'll have quite a bit of material to work with. And while you'll hopefully have some fun playing the fills of this arrangement, the real object is to come up with some of your own. Experiment, play around, and see what you come up with. And be sure to write down the ones you like!

Practice, Practice

Fills are musical phrases that you'll want to use when you play. Obviously, you're going to spend time practicing the various fills you picked up in this chapter as well as those you've come up with on your own. But the real challenge for you is to start working up a "fills phrasebook," a collection of fills large enough to keep you occupied for ages. Where will all these fills come from?

Actually, collecting fills is pretty easy. Just about every song you can name has one or two little fills in it. Track down the sheet music or tablature of songs you like, and learn to play the fills.

SOUND ADVICE

Fills are usually fairly short and often are played very close to the chords being strummed, so try to pick out the notes of a fill by ear. It's great practice for you! Even if you don't get the notes of the fill exactly correct, you'll still end up with a fill you can use.

Pay special attention to how a fill plays out within the context of the song's chords. Is the fill played over a single chord or a progression of chords? Can you work out a transposition of both chords and the fill? The more keys you can play a fill in, the more useful the fill will be.

Likewise, remember to play around with the timing of all the fills you learn. This literally can turn a single fill into dozens you can use to spice up your guitar playing.

And remember that fills in songs may not necessarily be played on the guitar. Don't hesitate to copy a fill played by another instrument, such as a piano, flute, or saxophone. Each instrument has its own nuances when it comes to phrasing, and learning to copy from other instruments will enhance your own style.

The Least You Need to Know

- Fills are short musical phrases used to spice up a song.
- Fills are usually based around chords or scales.
- The open-position E minor pentatonic scale contributes to many guitar fills.
- Blue notes usually are the minor third, flat seventh, and diminished fifth.
- The tension and resolution between blue notes and the notes of the major scale are part of the overall blues sound.

Bringing Melody and Chords Together

In This Chapter

- The musical makeup of a song
- Chord-melody arrangements
- Strumming chord melodies
- Pinch-picking chord melody
- Two-note harmonies
- A chord-melody arrangement of "Beautiful Dreamer"

Without someone singing the melody, a song may sound like just a bunch of chords being strummed. Fortunately for anyone who can't (or won't) sing, your guitar *can*—and beautifully, too! Just as you've learned to use single notes for walking basslines and fills, you can play the single notes of any song's melody. Better yet, you can add chords, either strummed or as arpeggios, for harmony and even bass notes. That's pretty much a whole band!

Anatomy of a Song

Scholars and everyday folks may argue forever and a day over what, exactly, a "song" is. But most agree that any song is made up of three essential components: melody, harmony, and rhythm.

The *melody* is the part that is sung, hummed, or even whistled. It is a line of single notes in a particular rhythm, which is just as important as the note, as you might remember from hearing the difference between a backward scale and "Joy to the World" back in Chapter 4. The *harmony*, simply put, is the chords that accompany the melody. They can be strummed or picked as individual notes, or can even be a single note that is played or sung along with the melody note to give it tonal definition. *Rhythm*, again in the simplest terms, is the pattern of pulses given to a song.

Of these three components, the melody of a song is usually the one that is most readily identifiable— and the one that sticks in your head. Harmonies can be tweaked here and there with subtle chord substitutions, and rhythms can be—and often are—altered and arranged in many, many ways. But a song's melody is usually constant.

If you have a song's melody and know its basic chord structure, you can create what's known as a *chord-melody* arrangement of that song. Creating a chord melody is playing a song so that the melody is clearly heard, as when played by individual notes, and also providing the chords, or parts of chords and even basslines, to provide the song's harmony.

> **DEFINITION**
>
> **Chord melodies** are single-guitar arrangements in which the melody of the song is usually played on the high strings, accompanied by chords (that can be either strummed or played as arpeggios) on the lower strings. The term *chord melody* is most often associated with jazz, but chord melodies can be of songs from almost any musical genre.

Chord melodies can come in many styles. Some can be very simple, using just one or two notes to bring harmony to the melody line, much in the style of "Blackbird" by the Beatles or Paul Simon's "Bookends." Others can use chords of different voicings all over the fingerboard or employ an alternate tuning to allow for lower bass notes or easier fingerings of open-position chords.

Typically, the melody of a song is played on the higher strings of the guitar (the high-E, B, and G strings) so that it can ring out loud and clear when played. Bass notes are usually played on the low strings (D, A, and low E), and the chords are played using whatever strings happen to be free at the time.

A "Twinkle" in One's Eye

Having a familiar melody is the best way to start learning about chord-melody arrangements. A familiar melody that doesn't involve too much work to play allows you to explore the different accompaniment choices you have.

So how about starting with a melody you can probably play in your sleep?

Melody of "Twinkle, Twinkle Little Star."

You probably immediately recognized "Twinkle, Twinkle Little Star" (you might also think of it as "Baa, Baa, Black Sheep" or "The Alphabet Song"). Take a few minutes and practice playing this melody, using these specific notes on these specific strings for now. Notice that all the melody notes occur on the first three strings, which is what you ideally want for a chord-melody arrangement.

Now that you have a melody, you need some chords. You hopefully already figured out from the three sharps in the key signature that this arrangement is in the key of A. And you already know, having read Chapter 15, that the three chords you're most likely to run into in this key are A, D, and E:

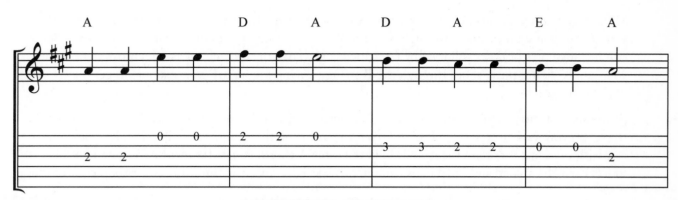

Chords for "Twinkle, Twinkle Little Star."

The Basic Model

Having both melody and chords at your disposal, you are now ready to play your first chord-melody arrangement:

 Track 61 (0:00)

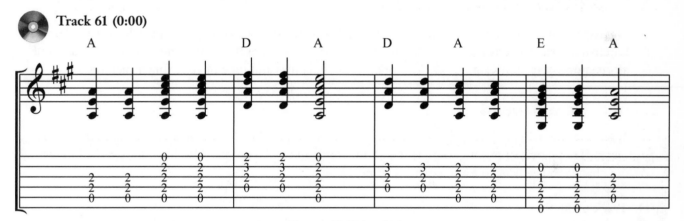

Chapter 19, Example 1.

The first thing you want to do is forget about the tablature and think instead about making the correct chords. Get your A chord in place and strum just the A, D, and G strings with a downstroke. The melody note (the A at the second fret of the G string) is the last note you strike and should ring out cleanly and clearly. Play this twice and then, keeping the A chord in place, strum from the A string in the bass all the way through the high-E string, which is your new melody note. Play this entire A chord through to the high-E string twice as well. Congratulations! You've made it through the first measure.

You change to a D chord to start the second measure. At this point in the song, the melody note is the F♯ at the second fret of the high-E string, so you want to strum all four strings of the D chord. Play this twice and then go back to the full A chord to finish this measure.

💡 **KEEP SHARP!**

Strumming chord melodies requires you to be very accurate in which strings to strum. If the melody note is on the B string, you don't want to hit the high-E string with your picking stroke. Be sure to use short, economical pick movement. Catching the melody note and a few of the chord notes on an upstroke also works nicely.

Measure 3 starts with another D chord, but this time the melody note is the D at the third fret of the B string, so you want to strum through only the B string, leaving the high-E string untouched. These two melody notes of D are followed by C♯, which is played with the A chord as accompaniment. Again, you want to strum the A chord through the B string (leaving the high-E string alone) to get the C♯ note of the melody.

At the start of the fourth measure, the chord changes to E and the melody note is the B of the open B string. So you want to strum the E chord from the low E on through the B string. Finally, you come to rest with the same A note in the melody (and the same A chord) you started with. You should be able to work out the second and third lines from here, especially since the third line is a carbon copy of the first!

This chord-melody arrangement is about as basic as it gets. You can strum it with a pick or with your thumb, all in downstrokes; just be careful to end the strum on the string that has the melody note.

You could do a modified "pinch" or "sweep" as well to play it. To modify the pinch to pick up a few notes of the chord, strike the bass note with a downward motion of your thumb while plucking upward on the melody note with a finger, making a short sweep of the lower adjacent strings as you do so. The melody note should ring loudest, and you will catch a few notes of the accompanying chord as well.

You can also use two or three fingers to pinch two or three strings while playing the bass note. This requires a little concerted practice because you want to make sure the melody note rings the loudest of all the notes played. It's a great way to work on the dynamics and tone of your finger picking.

Second Time Around

Now it's time to apply more of your finger-picking technique. The following arrangement relies heavily on the Travis style of picking, complete with pinching and pedal points. Also look out for the interesting change in the bass notes in measures 4 and 12:

Track 61 (0:20)

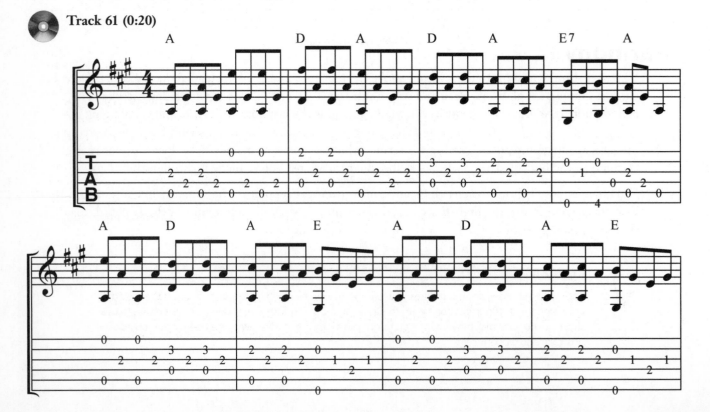

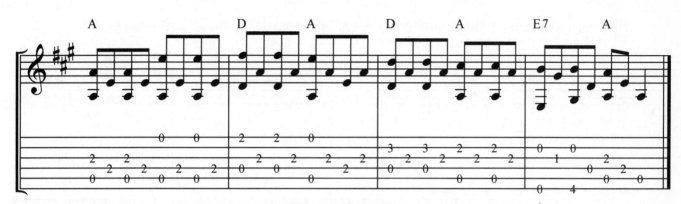

Chapter 19, Example 2.

If you take this arrangement very slowly at first, you shouldn't find anything here that you can't handle. It's all even eighth notes in terms of timing. Keep the beat steady and smooth.

SOUND ADVICE

All finger picking involves a good sense of touch to control the tone, dynamic, and expressive quality of any given note. Practice dynamics and expression in your finger picking by deliberately trying to bring out the melody one time, then the bass notes another, and then the chord accompaniment on another pass. Listen carefully to your playing and record yourself, if you can, to study and improve your sound.

You need your pinky to get the G♯ at the fourth fret of the low-E string in measures 4 and 12, but it's a good stretch for you to work on. Remember, the only other notes you're playing at this point are the open B string in the melody and the E (second fret of the D string) that you're using as a pedal point for the E chord, so you don't have to fret the whole E chord if it makes the stretch to the G♯ easier for you. Just be careful to *not* hit the open G string if you leave it unfretted.

Harmony in Pairs

This second chord-melody arrangement also serves as a great example of how you can imply melody through two notes instead of having to play an entire chord. At the start of the second measure, you pinch the open D string in the bass along with the F♯ at the second fret of the high-E string. Even though you're not playing a full D chord until you get the A (second fret of the G string) into the mix, it certainly sounds like you are.

In standard tuning, your guitar offers many opportunities for this kind of harmony, particularly when you're finger picking the strings. Pinch the open high-E and G strings together and then do the same with the open B and D strings. If you think of the lower string as the root note, these pairs are the interval of a major sixth apart.

KEEP SHARP!

Any two notes can be a part of many different chords. For example, F♯ and A are part of the D chord as well as part of F♯m (and its sevenths and extensions), A6, and even Gmaj9. Keeping track of the different possible chords notes belong to will help you use these "harmony pairs" very creatively.

Here are a few examples of the harmonies you can find using these pairings of the strings:

Harmony pairs in key of C

Harmony pairs in key of G

More harmony pairs in key of G

Examples of implied harmony.

When playing these examples, you'll find it easier (and ultimately faster) if you use your middle finger as an anchor on the lower string of any pair. Any time your fingers are supposed to be on the same fret, use your ring finger on the higher string. Any time your fingers are one fret apart, use your index finger on the lower string.

"Beautiful Dreamer"

You can, and should, use all the techniques and knowledge you've picked up when putting together chord-melody arrangements. This next song, Stephen Foster's "Beautiful Dreamer," combines the basic idea of chord melody with the "harmony in pairs" concept you just read about, and mixes in some new takes on old chord voicings. And just to make things even more interesting, it's in drop D tuning:

Track 62

Chapter 19, Example 3.

You'll also find a lot of half-barre chords, starting with the first one. It's basically the open-position A chord moved up to the seventh fret to serve as D. This allows you to use the open D string as well as the D of the sixth string (the low E is now D because of the drop D tuning). Barring the three high strings at the seventh fret lets you play the D of the melody (tenth fret of the high-E string) with your pinky. You'll also find some interesting half-barre versions of E6, E9, and A7 in the second half of the song.

Practice, Practice

Finding the raw material for chord-melody arrangements is as easy as picking up a book. You don't even need a book specifically for the guitar. Any songbook will have the melody of the songs written out for you. Most will also have the chords that accompany the melody. *Fake books* are especially useful, as they often have hundreds of songs in them, all with melodies and chords.

> **DEFINITION**
>
> A **fake book** is a book of songs in which the melody lines, lyrics, and chords of each song are written out for the musician. They are intended to be a "framework" for musicians, allowing them to create their own arrangements.

More than most of the techniques and ideas you've picked up so far, chord melody takes a fair share of planning. First, you need to decide what key to play the melody in, as well as where on the fingerboard to play it. If the music is in the key of E♭, for example, you probably want to transpose both the melody and the chords to a friendlier key.

You want the melody notes to be the highest notes of their accompanying chord—that is, if they're normally a part of that chord. If the melody note isn't a part of the accompanying chord, then it has to be close enough to be accessible to the chord voicing you choose.

> **LISTENING LIBRARY**
>
> Single-guitar song arrangements in chord-melody style are usually associated with classical and jazz guitar. To hear just how intricate these arrangements can be, give a listen to Joe Pass, Ted Greene, or Tal Farlow.
>
> Because of the ease of digital recording (both audio and visual), you'll find no end to chord-melody guitar arrangements at all levels of playing, especially on sites like YouTube, where you can also find free lessons by instructors from all over the world.

The Least You Need to Know

- The three main musical components of songs are melody, harmony, and rhythm.
- In chord-melody arrangements, your guitar plays the melody and chord accompaniment at the same time, like a small band.
- Chord-melody arrangements can be as simple or as complex as you'd like.
- Two notes can infer a harmony, even when a full chord isn't being played.
- Chord-melody arrangements take planning and use almost all the skills you have as a guitarist.

Making a Solo

In This Chapter

- The elements of soloing
- Phrasing
- Using scales, chords, and slurs when soloing
- The five positions of the pentatonic scale
- Building a solo
- The "technique vs. emotion" trap

When you hear someone talk about making a guitar "sing," you probably first think of soloing, not chord-melody arrangements. But now you can ask yourself, "What does one actually *sing?*" and you'll know that any singing, whether it's a person or a guitar or any instrument, has to be a melody.

It's easy to think of solos as being little more than dizzy, lightning-quick burst of notes, coming out of the guitar so fast that you can't tell whether they're played or poured. But speed is only one aspect of a solo, and it's definitely not the one you'd consider first. Think of the solos you best remember; they're likely ones you can sing along with. In other words, they have melodies. Good solos are like songs within a song—they have a beginning, a middle, and an ending. They can sit on a single note for ages or make mad dashes up and down the fingerboard, usually as a flashy way of getting from one note to another.

You learn slurs and scales and chord shapes in order to move along the neck of your guitar. You use these techniques when playing fills so that you can add interest to the normal strumming or picking of a song. You use these techniques in soloing to enhance a melody. More often than not, a solo without a melody sounds like someone practicing scales, and not much more.

Of course, the best way to learn about soloing is just to dive right in! So get ready to create one on your own very soon!

The Creation Process

When you hear the words *guitar solo*, you probably have an image of someone with an electric guitar playing very loud and very fast to an arena of screaming fans. But guitar solos come in many forms and lengths. They can be as simple as repeating two notes over and over again, or they can seem to use every note on the fingerboard. Good soloists also have a knack for making their solos fit the style and mood of any particular song.

Traditionally, guitarists have learned to solo in one of two ways. The first is to copy solos from songs they know. Not all that long ago, people did this by ear, listening to the solos and trying them out on their guitars. This was good, in that it developed their listening skills and they often learned a lot about music in regard to playing in different keys and styles. Nowadays guitarists get the tablature or the music notation and don't rely so much on listening skills. Plus, they often don't even think that the skills they're learning in one solo will help them with other solos or even rhythm skills.

KEEP SHARP!

Remember that most of the guitar solos you hear on recordings are *not* improvised, but are created and arranged for the song being recorded. Many solos start out as improvisations, and the improvisations serve as a "basic model" that gets tweaked and refined each time it's played.

The second way is to "noodle around" with scales and chords, much as one can with fills. Many solos are created by stringing a bunch of fills in a row. This can involve a lot of trial and error, and if the guitarist only noodles in one particular scale, many of his solos will sound the same.

You might not know it, but you already have the tools to create a good guitar solo. You know scales and chords in different voicings all over the neck; you can play slurs such as hammer-ons, pull-offs, and bends; you've learned how to come up with short fills; and you're developing a sense of melody. Why not use your brain as well as your ear to combine all these elements and make a solo?

Phrases and Phrasing

First, it's important to understand that there's a reason many guitarists obsess with speed when it comes to solos. A great saxophone player, just to pick an example, can certainly play very fast, but eventually he or she has to stop to take a breath. A guitar player doesn't have to stop until his fingers fall off.

Since melodies are sung, they also depend on breath. This is why melodies are usually in phrases, with each phrase having a long note or rest at the end to give the singer a chance to catch his or her breath.

SOUND ADVICE

The melody of a song is always the best place to start when looking for ideas for a solo. It gives you guidelines for phrasing and helps you understand the mood of the song.

Here's a very simple melody, taken from the chorus of the song "Wabash Cannonball." You'll use this chorus as a basis for your soloing in this chapter, so take a little time to get it fixed in your brain.

This chorus uses four phrases, each about four measures long. Melodies often use repeated phrases, and you can hear that the first and third phrases are identical, while the fourth is a slight variation of the second. Also notice how the second phrase mirrors the first and third in terms of the rhythmic value of each note. Even though the notes of the second phrase are different, the rhythm is almost identical to the other phrases, giving the melody a strong sense of unity.

In addition to the song's structure and chords, you want to pay attention to its mood and style. "Wabash Cannonball" is a bouncy, happy tune, and you want your solo to reflect that. The solo you'll work on in this chapter is a mix of country and bluegrass styles, and it can be played on any type of guitar.

Track 63

Chapter 20, Example 1.

Rhythmic Templates

If you played this melody as it stands while other musicians backed you up with strumming chords, a bassline, and drums, you'd have a very nice guitar solo, just like the one you just heard on the CD. This is why knowing a melody or having a strong ear for what might be an alternate melody of a song is a good first step to soloing.

Looking at the makeup of "Wabash Cannonball," you can tell that it's in the key of G and uses only three chords: G, C, and D. You can then "noodle around" with either the G major scale or the G major pentatonic scale to come up with a solo, which is how most guitarists start learning to solo. But a scale is only notes; in and of itself, it has no rhythm or phrasing.

(By the way, go back to Chapter 18 and review the open-position G major/E minor pentatonic scale. You want to be familiar with it when you work on a solo for "Wabash Cannonball.")

SOUND ADVICE

For your first attempts at soloing, try to think of these four *s* words: simple, short, slow, and sing-able (as a melody can be sung).

When you practice scales, you usually do so by playing the notes as even quarter notes or eighth notes (or sixteenth notes, if you're truly obsessed with speed). And this is why many beginning (and quite a few professional) guitarists' solos sound like scales. All the rhythmic values of the notes of the solo are even, just as they are in scale practice. There's no sense of phrasing.

Do yourself a favor and don't worry about notes just yet. Pick one or two or three notes and try to come up with a nice bit of rhythmic phrasing to start. You don't even have to do anything that outrageous—just mix up your quarter and eighth notes. Here's a simple example of this, using just the first four measures of "Wabash Cannonball" as a guide:

Track 64

Chapter 20, Example 2.

You can hear that this rhythm has stops and starts, just like a melody does. This is how you start developing a sense of phrasing.

Adding the Guitar's Voice

Part of what makes a melody into a guitar solo is playing it on guitar. The techniques that are part of a guitar's sound, such as hammer-ons, pull-offs, slides, and bends, should contribute to your solo as much as the notes and rhythms do.

Keeping that in mind, following is a possible lead line for the first phrase of "Wabash Cannonball."

For the most part, it uses notes from the G major pentatonic scale, although it does borrow the initial B♭ (first fret of the A string) from the G minor. Since this song should have a bit of a country or bluegrass feel to it, combining both the major and minor pentatonic scales, as you learned to do in Chapter 18, gives the solo a bit of bite right from the start.

Notice, too, the use of the B at the fourth fret of the G string at the start of the second measure. You could just play a quarter note of the open B string, but using two eighth notes of the same note, played on different strings, creates a very tiny change of dynamic, almost like a stutter. You'll hear this technique used quite a bit in bluegrass and also Celtic music.

Make sure to use your ring finger for the slide from A to B on the G string. This puts your index finger in position to get the D at the third fret of the B string that ends the second measure. And that puts you in perfect position to play the pull-offs in the third measure.

Track 65

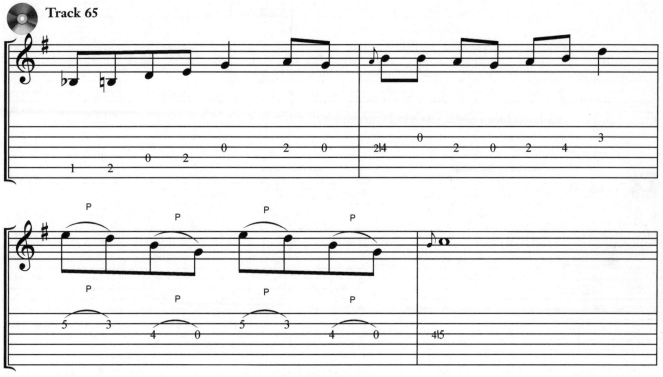

Chapter 20, Example 3.

A New Addition to Bends

Since you've used hammer-ons, pull-offs, and slides as part of your "Wabash Cannonball" solo so far, why not add a bend or two as well? This second phrase begins with a half-step (one fret) bend on the fifth fret of the B string. Actually, it's more of a "three quarter bend," putting the note kind of between a half-step and full-step higher than the original note. You can use either a half-step or a full-step bend if you'd prefer. Whatever your choice, make the bend with your ring finger and hold on to the bent note while you play the A note (fifth fret of the high-E string) with your pinky. Then release the bend after you play that A note. It will sound like the following.

Track 66

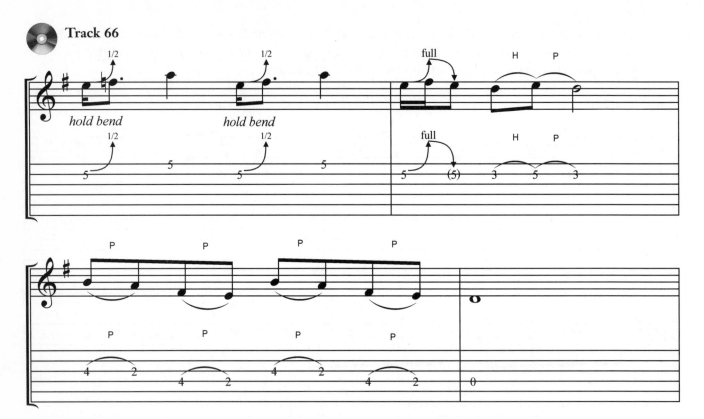

Chapter 20, Example 4.

This little "bend and hold" technique is used in many musical styles, especially with an electric guitar in rock music. It also echoes the sort of fill that a pedal-steel or slide guitar might add to a song.

Speaking of echoing, the end of the second phrase copies the end of the first phrase not only rhythmically, but in its use of pull-offs as well.

Scaling the Fingerboard

Playing fills, you want to minimize moving your fretting hand. Part of the speed comes from keeping your hand close to the chords you're playing, or keeping it close to the notes of the open-position Em pentatonic scale. Much of the speed of soloing also comes from having the fretting hand stay in one place on the fingerboard, when possible.

But you've probably seen guitarists moving their fretting hand all over the neck. They can't possibly be using a single scale to play those solos, can they? Yes, more often than not, they are using the same scale, but they're using a different scale *position* of the same scale.

Taking a Position

Positions, to scales, are much like voicings are to chords. You can find notes all over the fingerboard, so there's obviously more than one way to play any scale. The trick is to find the most logical way to do so, one that doesn't involve your fingers performing impossible contortions along the neck of your guitar.

KEEP SHARP!

Even though there are five different positions for the pentatonic scale, many of them overlap quite a bit. Instead of trying to learn all five at once, go with two or three positions until you have them down cold. The first, third, and fifth positions, for example, cover all the notes of positions two and four, so if you learn those three, you'll be in good shape.

Since you're primarily using the G major/E minor pentatonic scale in this chapter, it's probably best to use it to demonstrate how positions work. Start with the open position you know:

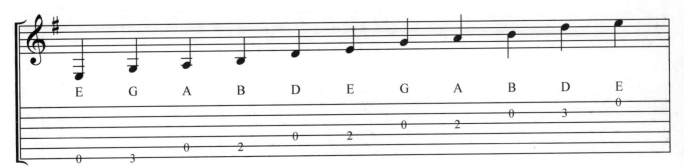

The open-position Em pentatonic scale.

Starting with the note of the open low-E string, these are all the notes you can easily reach without shifting your hand. To give you more of a visual aid, look at how these notes appear on your fingerboard:

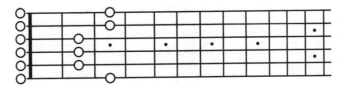

The open-position Em pentatonic scale as fingerboard diagram.

As you know, this scale has five notes: E, G, A, B, and D. Suppose you wanted to start this scale on the G note of the low-E string. You could do so and then continue using the open-position notes. You could also use your middle finger on that starting note of G and play it this way:

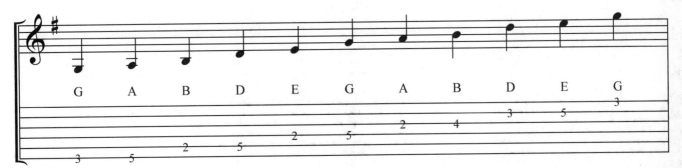

The Em pentatonic scale in second position.

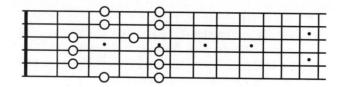

Likewise, you could also start on the A, B, or D of the low-E string and find the following positions:

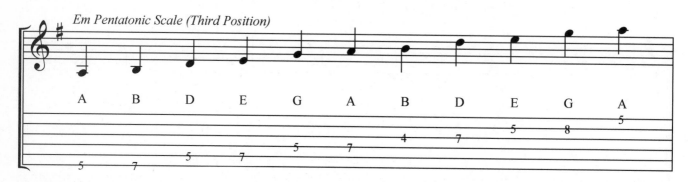

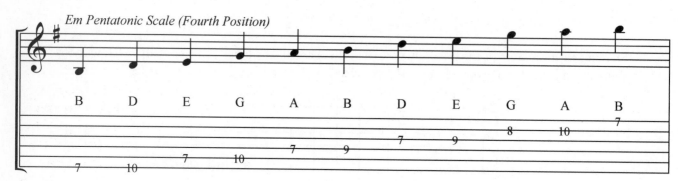

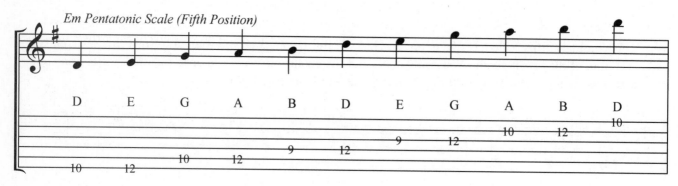

The Em pentatonic scale in Positions 3 through 5.

Position 3

Position 4

Position 5

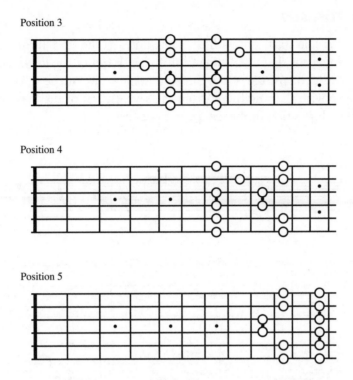

Getting Shifty

Each of these positions, excluding the first (open) position, is a *closed* scale. This means that you can use them in other keys all over the neck, provided that you have a reference note to start with. For instance, if you know that the Bm pentatonic scale is made up of the notes B, D, E, F♯, and A, then the five possible positions of the Bm pentatonic scale start on the seventh fret of the low-E string for the first position, the tenth fret (D) for the second position, the twelfth fret (E) for the third position, the second fret (F♯) for the fourth, and the fifth fret (A) for the fifth.

Notice, too, that all five positions share notes with other positions along the neck. By choosing where and when to shift notes, you can play a single scale pretty much up and down the length of the fingerboard, like this:

Shifting along pentatonic scale positions.

There are no hard-and-fast rules for moving between positions. If you choose, you can skip from open position right to the fifth position if that's where the note you want happens to be.

Third and Fourth Phrases

The third phrase of this solo starts out with the same notes as the first phrase, played farther up the neck. Use your ring finger for the initial slide from B♭ (sixth fret of the low-E string) to B (seventh fret). This sets you up in the third position of the Em pentatonic scale. At the start of the second measure, you're going to slide up with the ring finger from the seventh fret of the D string to the ninth fret, putting you in the fourth position of the Em pentatonic scale:

Track 67

Chapter 20, Example 5.

There are more bends like those in the first phrase in the third measure. Use your ring finger to play the bend at the tenth fret of the B string, and your pinky to hang on to the note at the tenth fret of the high-E string.

The fourth phrase uses some of the "harmony pairs" you encountered in Chapter 19, but these are played as individual strings rather than at the same time, as they were in "Beautiful Dreamer." These pairs are based on the E-shaped D and C partial barre chords (like those in "John Barleycorn" from Chapter 15) and the Em-shaped Bm and Am partial barre chords. Remember to use your middle finger for the notes on the G string during these descending pairs. When the note of the high-E string is on the same fret as the note of the G string, play the high-E string with the ring finger. When it is one fret lower, play the E string note with the index finger.

Now that you've managed to work through each section of this solo, put the pieces together and play the whole thing. On the recording, it's played very slowly the first time and then faster the second:

 Track 68

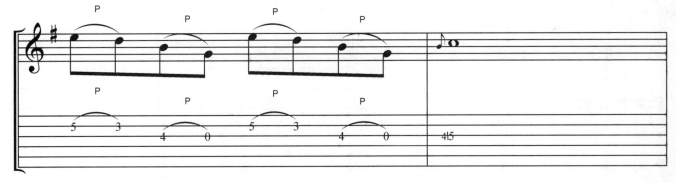

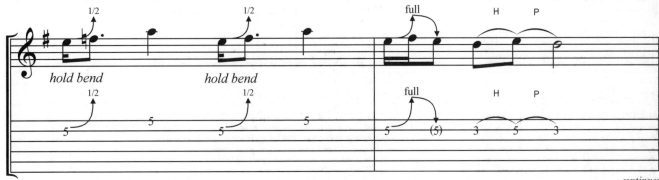

continues

continued

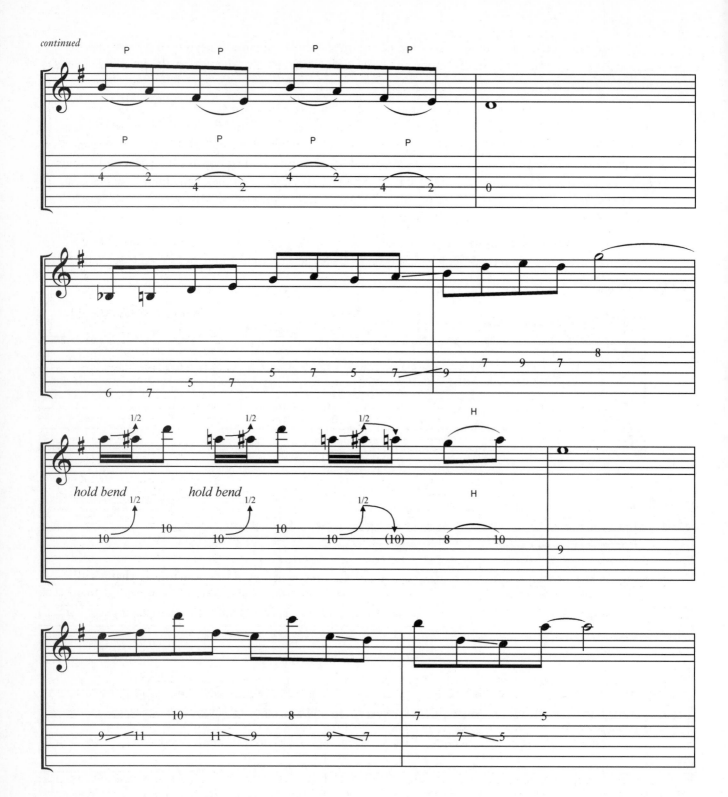

Chapter 20, Example 6.

This isn't too bad of a solo for your first time, especially since it incorporates a lot of what you learned in the earlier chapters of this book. But try to look beyond the technique to see and hear how the solo takes its cues from the original melody in terms of phrasing and the general rise and fall of notes.

It goes without saying that you can come up with many, many solos besides this one. And you should try to! Depending on what you feel more comfortable with, you may want to start with scales in open position or fills based on both open-position or barre-chord shapes. Don't worry about filling every possible space with notes, and keep in mind the whole idea of the solo being, first and foremost, a melody.

Thinking and Feeling

As you gain confidence in your abilities, your soloing will evolve and become more complex, mirroring your abilities. Your sense of phrasing will become better as you listen to more music with an ear for picking out phrases. As you gain speed and dexterity with your fingers, your picking and your slurs will gain speed. All your progress will undoubtedly find its way into your soloing.

Some guitarists, against all better judgment, look at solos as either being "technical" or "emotional" and, worse, rank one as being better than the other. They don't understand that speed—even a lack of speed—is just a tool, part of a guitarist's vocabulary. Playing something fast doesn't mean that it's all technique and no emotion. It just means that someone can play fast. Using long, drawn-out bending to make a single note wail is also technique, and not necessarily a reflection of emotional playing.

LISTENING LIBRARY

The two guitar solos in Pink Floyd's "Comfortably Numb" provide an excellent example of how one guitarist can change the mood of a song. The first solo is captivatingly melodic and follows the phrasing of the song's chorus, while the closing solo is almost blistering with its violent bursts of frenzied notes. Guitarist David Gilmour has an uncanny ability to create almost any mood, and his work with Pink Floyd, as a solo artist, and as a backing guitarist for many musicians is well worth studying.

But it's vital to remember that the song should be the deciding factor when it comes to what tools and techniques to use. Matching the mood of a song—or deliberately playing against the mood of a song—is part of the guitarist's art when it comes to soloing. Use all the tools you have—technique, speed, and brain power—to make an emotional statement. Emotion and technique are part of a whole picture, not separate from one another.

Practice, Practice

Practicing scales isn't the same as practicing soloing. Practicing scales helps you build speed and also helps you know where your notes are on the fingerboard (provided that you want to learn that—otherwise, you'll only learn scale patterns), but they won't help you with phrasing or other elements of soloing unless you incorporate those elements into your practice. Instead of practicing scales from one end to the other, vary the timing as well as the order of the notes. If you're practicing the C major scale, for instance, set your notes in a series of three, going C, D, E, D, E, F, E, F, G, and so on. Play in swing eighths or triplets, or play the first note as a quarter note and the next two as eighth notes. You can come up with hundreds of combinations.

But as much as you might practice scales like they're solos, you're still practicing scales. One good way to practice soloing is to improvise over chord changes. You can either record yourself playing a chord progression and practice over the recording, or you can find "backing tracks" (either online or sold on CDs at music stores) to use when practicing.

Improvising is good, in that it helps you develop a sense of phrasing, but take the extra step and actually arrange a full solo. Write it down so you can play it later without trying to remember what you did. Writing down solos will help you in many ways, one of the most important being that you'll see whether you have a tendency to repeat the same ideas in your solos. If your solos are sounding the same, you can take steps to change that.

The Least You Need to Know

- Guitar solos come in many styles, moods, and speeds.
- Phrasing, dynamics, and rhythm are vital to good soloing.
- You can play the pentatonic scale in five different positions along the fingerboard.
- Try to make your solo fit the mood and style of a song, using all the tools and techniques that help you do so.
- Practice making solos; it's not the same as practicing scales.

Picking Up Speed

In This Chapter

- The convenience of economy picking
- Gaining speed with alternate picking
- "The Temperance Reel"
- Crosspicking and hybrid picking
- Fingerpicks and thumbpicks

Sometimes *how* you play a song makes all the difference in the world. By strumming a song with a pick instead of playing a finger-picking pattern, you're setting part of the mood of that song and, whether they know it or not, setting up your audience's expectations. When you're used to hearing slow, steady strumming on a folk ballad, for instance, you subconsciously expect to hear a folk ballad when the guitarist starts out with a slow, steady strum.

Every new technique you pick up, each bit of music knowledge, gives you more creative freedom. They give you the tools to play songs in completely different styles. And the cool thing is that you can spend your whole life learning more.

This is especially true with picking and strumming. You can pick any single song in many, many ways. You can lazily strum full chords, or you can play so many notes in a measure that it sounds like you have three guitars! And your strumming choices will make a big difference in the overall tone and feel of the song.

Some people never play their guitars with picks, while others use picks to the exclusion of using their fingers to pluck the strings. You may lean one way or the other, but it's good to understand how each style can give your playing a different texture. And since you spent some time on finger picking earlier in Chapter 11, it's only fair to explore the "pick picking" side of things.

Flat-Out Flatpicking

Technically, anytime you play your guitar with a pick, you're "flatpicking." According to the dictionary, the pick should be flat—but that, pardon the pun, is nitpicking. When guitarists talk about "flatpicking," they usually have a specific type of picking in mind, one most often associated with bluegrass or "old timey" music.

Regardless of musical stylings, the actual picking of the guitar can be as regimented or as natural as you like. As with finger picking, it's rare for experienced guitarists to think consciously about playing a pattern. Instead, they go for a feel or a mood and pick accordingly. Whatever "pattern" emerges is simply the result of a lot of time spent playing, not a conscious decision to "first hit the low-E string, then the D, then the G, then the B," and so on.

SOUND ADVICE

Because picks are made of different materials and different thickness, you can get different tonal qualities depending on the pick you choose to use. Some guitarists use the same pick all the time; others change picks depending on what they want to do with a specific song. Try out different kinds of picks—see how they feel and listen to what they do for you.

Experienced players agree that, to have the best control over your picking, you want to use a relatively stiff pick and choke up on it so that there's no more than a quarter-inch of the pick projecting beyond your finger and thumb. You also want your picking motion to be as perpendicular to the strings as possible. The pick itself does not have to be perpendicular. In fact, changing the pick's angle changes the tone. Having the pick push in on the strings (toward the body of the guitar) or flicking outward on the strings (away from the body of the guitar) can give you a cool twang. But as far as building up speed is concerned, it also wastes too much motion and slows you down, putting your hand too far away from the strings.

More Finger Picking

It's also impossible to develop any kind of appreciable picking speed if you use only downstrokes in your picking. If you think about this, it certainly makes sense. For any single downstroke you make, no matter what the speed, you can make two hits on the string using both a downstroke and an upstroke. But although that's simple enough to understand, many beginners (most of whom have no problems making upstrokes when strumming chords) have difficulty picking in both downward and upward directions.

KEEP SHARP!

It's a good idea to work on alternate picking as early in your guitar studies as possible. Although it's not hard to pick up playing this way, it seems to take some guitarists a while to get a handle on it, especially when they haven't attempted it before.

Some guitarists, especially those who like finger picking, find it helpful to use a technique much like finger picking. They play downstrokes on the three low strings (the low E, A, and D) and use upstrokes on the three high ones (the high E, B, and G).

A good way to get used to this style of picking is to play an Em chord and pick the three low strings with downstrokes, starting with the low E and then the A and then the D, and then jump to the high E and play the three high strings in succession with upstrokes.

When you're comfortable with this very basic picking, switch to another chord (try Am or C, for starters) and then just pick single strings as eighth notes in 4/4 timing, like the following.

The object is not to develop a pattern, but just to get used to the idea of making upstrokes with the pick and getting you comfortable with changing directions.

Getting started with basic picking.

Alternate Picking

Changing pick directions with ease is what ultimately gives you speed when picking. In *alternate picking* you change pick direction after each strike of a string. The easiest way to start with alternate picking is to play a scale, hitting each note of the scale twice, first with a downstroke and then with an upstroke, like this:

Getting started with alternate picking.

After warming up with this last exercise, play the scale one note at a time. This involves changing pick directions while changing strings, so take your time and pay close attention to alternating your pick motion on each stroke.

Alternate picking while changing strings.

"The Temperance Reel"

Of course, it's one thing to use alternate picking as an exercise with a simple scale. But when is the last time you heard someone at a concert or an open mic performing just a major scale as a song?

Here's the first part of a traditional Celtic reel (a "reel" is a lively dance) that you can use as a practical example of alternate picking.

Notice that you want to use downstrokes for the first two G notes (the open G string) at the start of the fifth measure. Since the first note is a quarter note in duration, this repeated use of downstrokes helps you keep the "down/up" feel of each beat. Also be sure to notice that this piece is done with swing eighths.

 Track 69

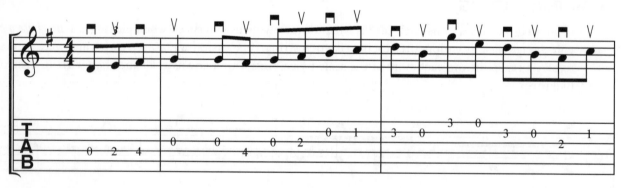

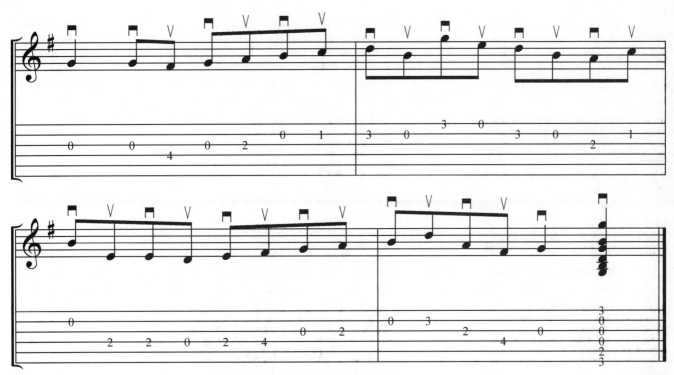

Chapter 21, Example 1.

Picking Up Clues from Tablature

As with so many other aspects of playing the guitar, picking is often a matter of individual style, taste, and comfort. Some guitarists choose to use only alternate picking, and some are exclusively economy pickers, but most players use a combination of the two forms and rarely even think about it. Often the picking is determined by what you're playing (single notes versus chords or partial chords) and what kind of rhythm is involved.

Tablature—and notation, for that matter—rarely gives you specific directions in terms of downstrokes and upstrokes. In fact, if you're a stickler for playing things from "note by note" transcriptions, you're bound to drive yourself crazy trying to follow tablature exactly. For instance, when you see something like this …

An example of strumming in tablature.

... you can't be thinking that the guitarist spent multiple takes in the studio, trying to pick these exact strings in this exact order. He or she was simply strumming a G chord for eight beats in his or her own way.

When you look at tablature, try to read it in measures, as opposed to one number at a time. Doing so helps you to pick out chord shapes, which show you how to best place your fingers to play it. And recognizing whole chords will lead you to knowing when the tablature is saying "just strum the chord however you'd like."

KEEP SHARP!

You can work on developing the ability to read tablature or notation with an eye to chord shapes almost anytime. You don't even need your guitar. Try to always have a bit of music or tablature that you're working on (keep some in your briefcase or backpack or car) so you can study it in your spare time.

Here are a few basic strums, written out only in tablature, which should give you an idea of what to look for in terms of "chord clues." The object here isn't to play the tablature, but to identify the chords you would play:

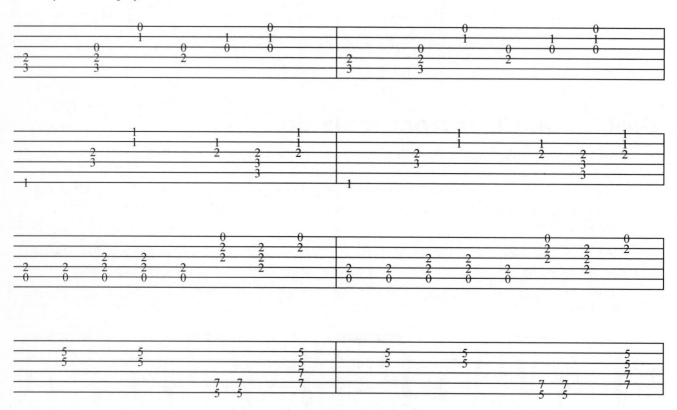

An exercise for identifying chords in tablature.

And here are the answers: The first two measures are C, measures 3 and 4 are F, measures 5 and 6 are A, and the last two measures are an Am barre chord (Em shaped) at the fifth fret.

Crosspicking

Don't get hung up on copying any picking directly from the tablature because you're afraid to make mistakes. This happens to everyone, from beginners just picking up a guitar to performers who have been playing their whole lives. In fact, the only proven way to not make mistakes is to not play. And that's not even worth thinking about.

Your chances of making mistakes in picking increase as you pick up speed. That's a given. But the real danger in making mistakes isn't the mistake itself (unless you draw attention to it, chances are good that practically no one listening will even notice)—it's that you'll let the mistake derail the timing. Then *everyone* will notice. You want to practice playing through whatever mistakes you make.

This is especially true when it comes to *crosspicking*. Crosspicking is a guitar technique that uses a near-constant stream of picked notes to fill up space, much like a bluegrass-style banjo. You can use it to really liven up chord-melody playing (the melody notes are accented heavier than the picking of the accompanying single notes of the chord) or strictly as an accompaniment for a soloing instrument or vocal.

 DEFINITION

Crosspicking involves playing single notes in rapid succession. Usually, but not always, each successive note is played on different strings and is usually struck with different pick strokes (alternating between down or up).

Usually a crosspicking pattern uses three strings, two strings serving as repeated notes while the bass or melody (or both) is played on the third. However, you can find so many exceptions to this that it's best not to worry about it.

 Track 70

continues

continued

Chapter 21, Example 2.

Here you will hear both the pattern, played very slowly to give you a taste of what you want to strive for, and then the "reality" of what happens when you get playing at any appreciable speed. Unless you have a written copy of the intended pattern in your hands, you'd never even know that the second take on Track 70 has any mistakes.

Crosspicking is another technique primarily associated with bluegrass music, but you can use it to great effect in folk, country, and rock songs.

Hybrid Picking

Some guitarists use a technique called *hybrid picking* to combine aspects of both flatpicking and finger picking. In hybrid picking, the guitarist uses a pick held with the thumb and index finger to pick the low three strings, and uses the middle, ring, and pinky fingers to pick the three high strings.

This technique requires quite a bit of practice and patience, but it gives the guitarist a very different voice when it comes to the initial attack of the notes being played. Hybrid picking is mostly associated with country music and early rock 'n' roll, but you will find it used by bluegrass artists such as John Butler, rockers like John Frusciante of the Red Hot Chili Peppers, and guitarists like Richard Thompson who play so many different styles it's hard to label them.

Picking with Fingerpicks

You can also get fingerpicks and thumbpicks to use on individual fingers. These are made of either metal or plastic (guitarists tend to use plastic thumbpicks since metal ones can produce a harsh sound on the thick strings) and are worn on the digits like this:

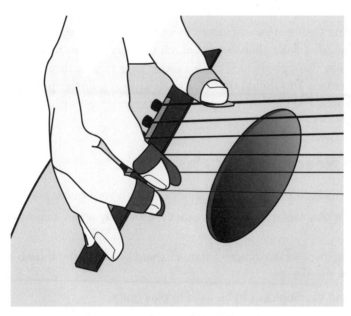

How to wear a thumbpick and fingerpicks.

It's not that hard to get used to playing with a thumbpick. In fact, many finger-picking players use one to give their bass notes more definition and volume.

LISTENING LIBRARY

James Burton, who has played with Elvis Presley, Merle Haggard, Johnny Cash, Emmylou Harris, Ricky Nelson, John Denver, Joni Mitchell, Elvis Costello, Brad Paisley, and many, many others, is probably one of the most influential hybrid pickers in the history of recorded music. His style comes from using a pick, like a hybrid picker, and also using a fingerpick on his middle finger.

Fingerpicks can take longer to get used to than thumbpicks. Guitarists who are used to feeling the flesh of their fingers against the strings find that it takes time to adjust to not feeling the strings. But those who stick with fingerpicks enjoy the crisp attack they provide, especially when playing resonator guitars.

Practice, Practice

Beginning guitarists get tired of hearing it, but almost everything they have trouble doing, from changing chords and making good slurs to playing barre chords and playing at fast tempos, is mostly a matter of practice. There's no magic pill that makes playing the guitar come faster or easier—there's only a million little pills called "practice," to be taken whenever you find yourself with five minutes to an hour with nothing to do!

To learn to play quickly, you need to first be able to play cleanly at a slow speed. It doesn't have to be "tectonic-plate movement" slow, but you should start at a tempo less than your target speed. When you can play a phrase of single notes or a picking pattern (with a pick or with your fingers) cleanly and without mistakes at a slow speed, gradually increase your tempo. Note your mistakes, but play through them. If you make the same mistake at the same place more than twice in a row, practice that section again at a slower speed until you have it right.

As you work on playing your phrase or pattern at an increased speed, take a moment to rest and relax. Then try playing at a speed *faster* than your goal. Don't worry about making mistakes; just note them and do your best to play through them. Try this faster pace two or three times, then rest again before trying at the target tempo. You should find that practicing at a faster speed got you ready to play at the target speed—and maybe even helped you play at the target speed with few, if any, mistakes.

The Least You Need to Know

- Learning alternate picking helps you gain speed with your guitar playing.
- It's okay to not play tablature patterns exactly, especially when it comes to crosspicking at high speeds.
- Hybrid picking involves using both a flatpick (held between the thumb and index finger) and fingers to pick the strings.
- Fingerpicks and thumbpicks can be used to play guitar.
- You have to practice playing cleanly at slow speeds in order to play fast.

Cool Places to Visit

An ever-evolving, ever-expanding universe filled with music awaits you. In this part, you make some short stops to visit a handful of musical genres that welcome guitarists with open arms. Consider it a small taste of what awaits you!

Because there are so many possible places to explore, and because no single book can possibly hope to explain everything about any one genre, you'll be getting more of an overview than anything else. But whether you're into classical, country, folk, blues, rock, Celtic music, or jazz, you'll find plenty to learn from. You'll also see how all musical styles can cross-pollinate and contribute to one another, making them more interesting than before.

A Little Country

"Four Nights Drunk"

Your first country-style song is a quick one, much like you might hear at the local hootenanny. It's also very simple, in that it uses only four chords—primarily G, C, and D—with the occasional A7 thrown in once a verse.

Here's what it looks like:

 Track 71

continues

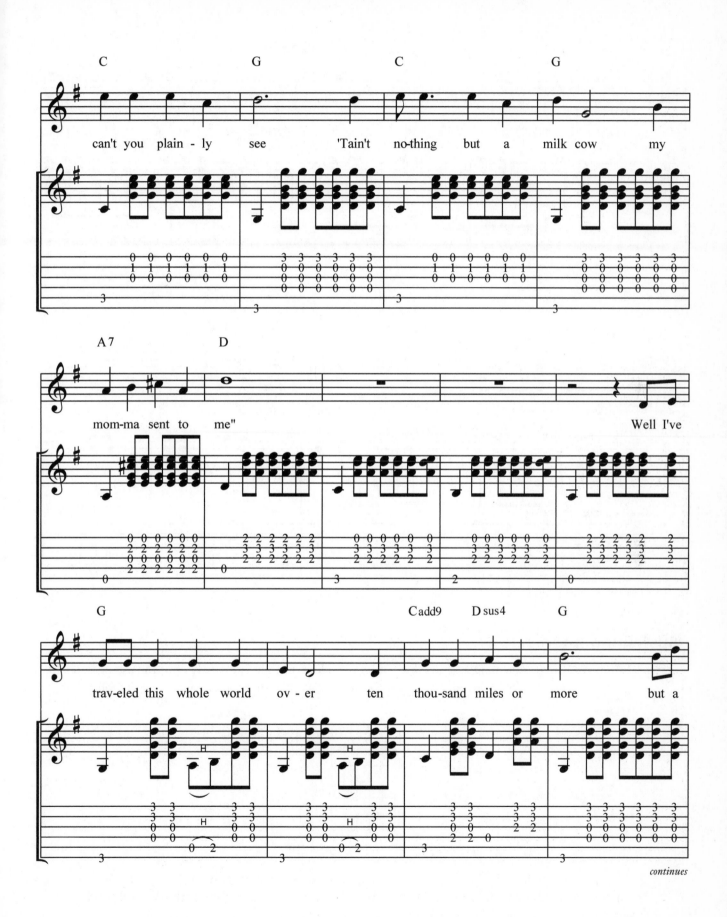

continues

continued

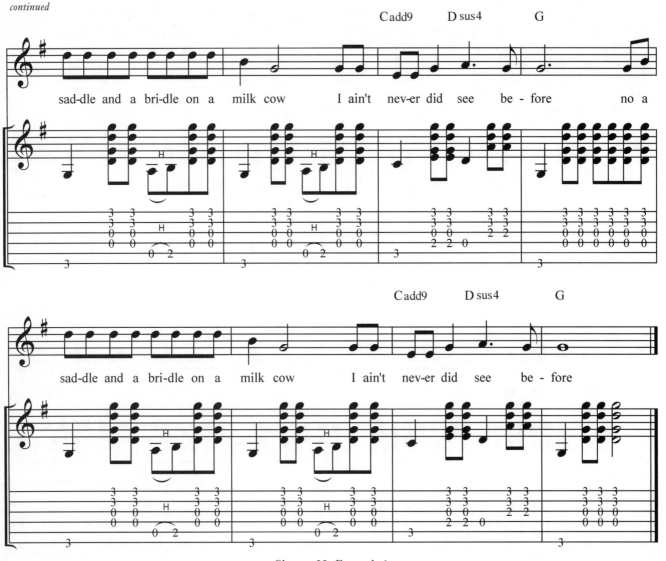

Chapter 22, Example 1.

Sustaining Interest

What makes this arrangement a little more interesting than it might ordinarily be is the use of *sustained notes*, notes that are held over from one chord to the next. Notice that the G chord uses the following voicing:

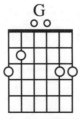

G chord with D note on the B string.

To play this, use your pinky for the G note at the third fret of the high-E string and your ring finger on the D note at the third fret of the B string. Your index finger (second fret of the A string) and middle finger (third fret of the low E) are the same as you usually play the G chord.

But instead of switching from this G to a normal open-position C chord, you keep the ring finger and pinky in place and simply shift your index and middle fingers to the next-higher string. Your index finger is on the second fret of the D string, and your middle finger is on the third fret of the A string. This chord is Cadd9.

Likewise, when you change from C to D, you keep the ring finger and pinky in place and just shift your index finger to the second fret of the G string. This gives you the Dsus4 chord:

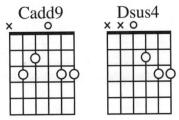

Cadd9 and Dsus4 chords.

A Long Walk

You get a G-to-C walking bassline at the second measure of the song's fifth line, to break up the rhythm a little. There's also a long stretch of D (16 beats!) that occurs immediately after the A7 chord. This is a great place to throw in a slow-moving, descending walking bassline, as shown here:

Track 72

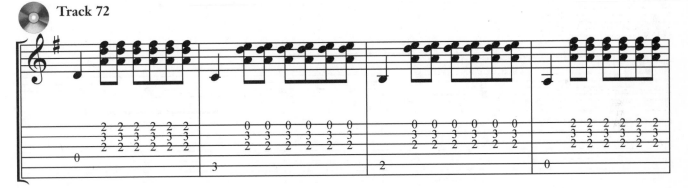

Chapter 22, Example 2.

You need to do a bit of finger shifting. Start with the D chord for the first measure. At the start of the second measure, move your middle finger from the second fret of the high-E string to the C at the third fret of the A string. Keep your index finger at the second fret of the G string.

In the third measure, you move both your middle and index fingers. The middle finger takes the index finger's place at the second fret of the G string, and your index finger goes on the second fret of the A string. The last measure goes back to the normal open-position D chord, but you'll be playing the note of the open A string as your bass note.

A Little Western with Your Country

You get a second country-style song this chapter, "Home on the Range," which you probably know well. The song is in 3/4 time, and it also uses swing eighths. You can use strums like Examples 2 and 3 in Chapter 9 or perhaps one like the following.

Track 73 (0:00)

Chapter 22, Example 3.

At this moderately slow speed, the swing rhythm evokes the clip-clopping of a horse lazily moving across the plains. And that's precisely what you want to convey with your playing.

A7 to D in Harmony Pairs

In the sixth measure, you have an A7 chord. This is the first of three "harmony pairs" (from Chapter 19) that you'll be playing, but you'll also be playing the open G string.

Track 73 (0:12)

Chapter 22, Example 4.

Be sure to have your middle finger on the second fret of the D string and your ring finger on the second fret of the B string when you get to this A7. This allows you to slide your middle finger along the D string to its proper note at each pairs position. You use your index finger for the D (third fret of the B string) and your ring finger again for the E (fifth fret of the B string).

This technique of picking the B, G, and D strings in succession is much like the "banjo roll" technique used by banjo players.

Use the middle finger of your right hand to pick the B string, your index finger to pick the G, and your thumb to strike the D.

This banjo roll is followed up by two measures of D, technically one of D and one of D9. That sounds harder than it actually is. You simply shift your fingers down from the seventh fret of the B and G string to the fifth fret of the same string, like this:

Track 73 (0:22)

Chapter 22, Example 5.

This little fill tries to imitate the sort of fill a pedal-steel guitar player might do in this spot. It's short and uses two notes to make a very dynamic change of chord.

"Home on the Range"

Both the banjo roll and pedal-steel fill make repeat appearances in the chorus of the song. There is also a barre chord, Cm, in the last line of the chorus, just to give you more practice with barres. Making the switch from the open-position C to the Am-shaped barre chord of Cm requires a little practice, so take it slowly the first few times. Have fun!

Track 74

continues

Chapter 22, Example 6.

Note, too, that the D7 (the next-to-last chord in both the verse and the chorus) is played like the open-position C7 chord, slid up two frets on the fingerboard.

LISTENING LIBRARY

You can find many wonderful versions of "Home on the Range," especially from the "singing cowboys" of the 1930s, such as Roy Rogers, Gene Autry, and Fred Kirby. And there are nice covers by the likes of Marty Robbins, too. But if you search around, you can also turn up a haunting version by Tori Amos and an icy-cool a cappella rendition by Neil Young, which he opens and closes with a solo on a single electric guitar.

Rock Solid

When playing rock or any other music without the benefit of a band to back you up, you have to come up with a single guitar arrangement that best suits the song, your guitar, and yourself.

Driving a Song

Rock is about energy and drive. Whether a song has the frenetic punk pace of the Ramones' "I Wanna Be Sedated" or the loping swing of the Rolling Stones' "Midnight Rambler," the music carries you along with its energy. When you're playing rock music, fast or slow, it's important to keep a strong and steady pulse.

You can drive a song in many ways, from using straight eighth notes (all played with downstrokes) to strumming with strong accents, as in the following examples:

Track 75

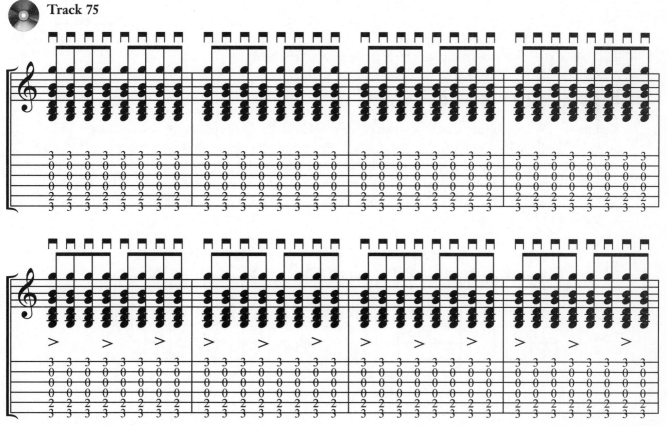

continues

continued

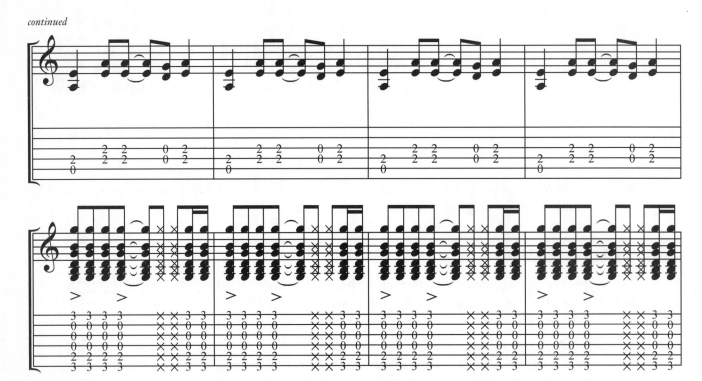

Chapter 23, Example 1.

Notice that the third example doesn't even use full chords, but instead relies on partial chords and double stops to provide a rocking rhythm. And the fourth example uses a pair of sixteenth notes in the last half of the fourth beat to give a little more push to the beat.

Giving Punch to Power Chords

Contrary to what you may think, you can play *power chords* (or 5 chords, as you learned to call them back in Chapter 13) on any type of guitar. They certainly sound different depending on whether you play them with an electric, classical, or acoustic guitar. On an acoustic guitar, you can often use power chords played across five or six strings instead of the two- and three-string versions many electric guitarists use. It's all a matter of figuring out where the notes you need are and what strings you can easily mute.

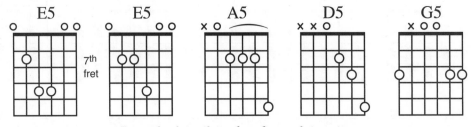

Power chords involving four, five, and six strings.

"Whiskey in the Jar"

The first song of this chapter, "Whiskey in the Jar," starts with an exchange of two chords—G and Em. This arrangement (based a little on Metallica's version, as well as the Thin Lizzy cover that inspired it) employs a simple repeated melody line that you can easily play over both chords:

 Track 76

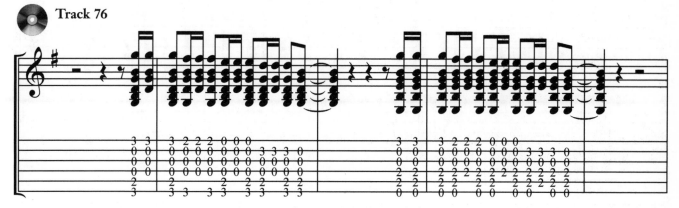

Chapter 23, Example 2.

The trick to playing this is to not worry about hitting every single note of the chord, even though they are written out in the notation. Strum as naturally as possible and do your best to get the melody note to ring out. You'll miss a few notes here and there at first, but it will sound less mechanical. You'll also develop more of a sense of what strings to hit when you strum.

Track 77

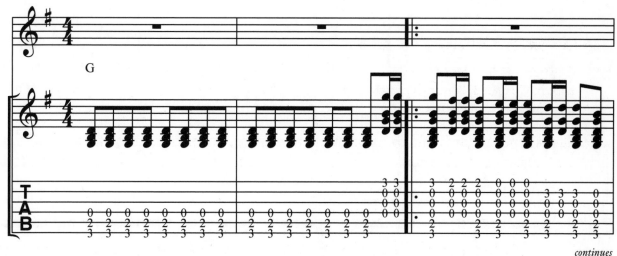

continues

continued

As   I   was   go - ing   o - ver_____   the
first   pro - duced   my   pis - tol_____

Cork   and   Ker - ry____   mount - ains
then   pro - duced   my____   rap - ier

I   saw   Cap - tain   Far - rell
I   said   "Stand   and   de - liv -

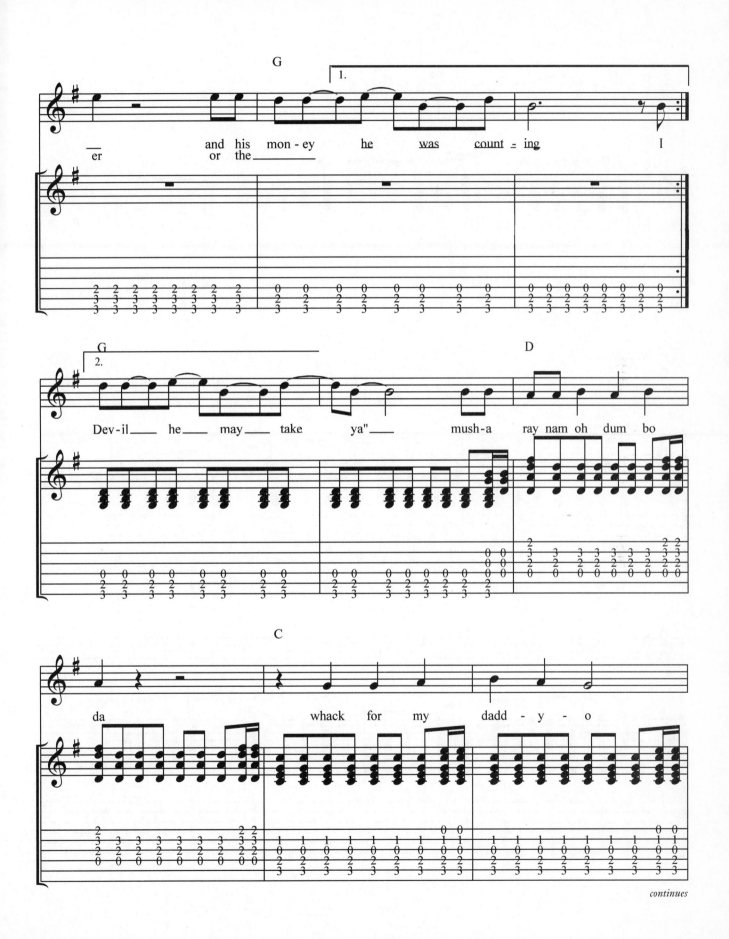

continues

Chapter 23, Example 3.

Another way to create cool rocking rhythms is to put a strong accent on an off-beat, like this:

Track 78 (0:00)

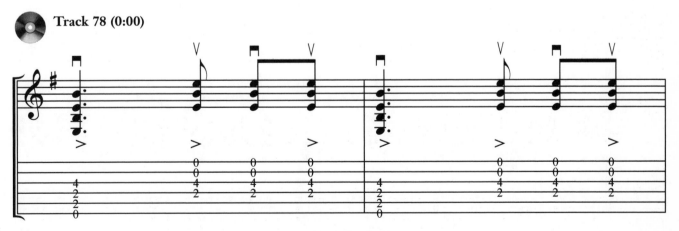

Chapter 23, Example 4.

Playing accents like this isn't hard if you remember all you've learned about keeping the beat steady. You can accent on an upstroke instead of trying to do it on a downstroke and messing up your strumming. Remember that, when in doubt, count out the timing!

"In the Pines"

Using lowered standard tunings, as discussed back in Chapter 17, can also give you a bit more of a rock feel, especially for slow, moody songs. You'll be using E♭ standard in your second song of this chapter, "In the Pines," a traditional tune sometimes called "Where Did You Sleep Last Night?"

In addition to the lowered tuning, "In the Pines" uses some of the different chord voicings discussed earlier and a short moving bassline:

Short descending bassline from "In the Pines."

It gives you a chance to move your fingers from the Bsus4 to the E5 chord when you play the open low E at the end of the riff.

 Track 78 (0:13)

Guitar in recording is tuned in Eb Standard
(Eb, Ab, Db, Gb, Bb, Eb) All strings are one half-step lower
so music (both guitar and voice) will sound a half-step lower
than this notation.

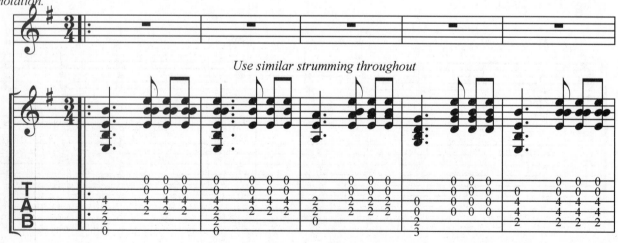

continues

continued

Chapter 23, Example 5.

Blues in the Night

Being a "parent" of rock 'n' roll, country, and jazz, the blues can give any musician a wealth of material that can be played in many musical genres. Blues song structures are found in virtually every musical style, and its rhythms and scales are likewise a thread that runs throughout the entire tapestry of twentieth-century song.

Typical Blues Song Structure

Historically, the blues has many forms and styles. But when you talk about the blues, most musicians automatically think of what's known as the 12-bar blues. In this structure, the verse of a song is 12 measures long (remember that measures are also called "bars"), and every 4 lines is usually 1 line of lyric. More often than not, 12-bar blues songs follow a specific chord structure.

Knowing this structure means that you can play the blues in any major key, provided that you can play the I, IV, and V chords in that key. For instance, if you wanted to play a typical 12-bar blues song in the key of A, the chords would be this:

Measure	1	2	3	4
Chord	A	A	A	A
Measure	5	6	7	8
Chord	D	D	A	A
Measure	9	10	11	12
Chord	E	D	A	A (or turnaround)

A turnaround is a short series of chord changes that usually ends on the V chord of a given key. This ending on the V chord sets you up to start the song again on the I chord, turning the song around to the beginning, if you will. Many blues turnarounds have practically become musical clichés. If you had ended the last measure of the second Chapter 6 song, "The Complete Idiot's Blues (Take 2)," on a B or B7 chord instead of an E, that would have been a classic turnaround.

A lot of the earliest recordings of blues music involved a single guitarist who also sang. Many guitarists still prefer to play single-guitar arrangements to this day. Some don't even sing, but instead create chord-melody-style arrangements, like those you read about in Chapter 19.

Playing a 12-bar blues song in A, for example, your I, IV, and V chords are A, D, and E, all of which are easy open-position chords. And it's also very helpful that the root notes of these chords are notes of the three lowest open strings.

As with any song from any musical genre, keeping the rhythm smooth and steady is vital. The easiest way to do this involves repeatedly playing a chord's root note in the bass strings. For instance, you can play either of these rhythms for an E chord—and remember to use swing eighths when playing blues songs:

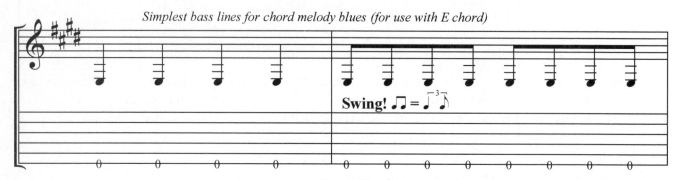

Simplest bass lines for chord melody blues (for use with E chord)

Examples of single-note blues bass rhythms.

When you have the rhythm down, you can then add melody lines and fills. As always, start simply (and slowly!) so that you can establish a good, steady beat:

Track 79

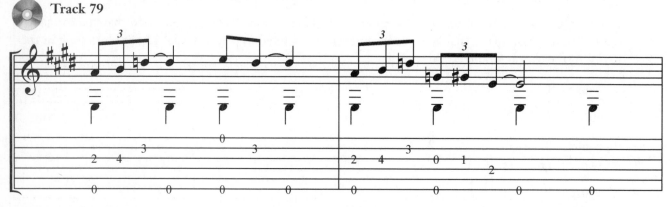

Chapter 24, Example 1.

One way to make the longer notes more interesting is to add a bit of *vibrato* to them. Vibrato is a quick, repeated changing of a note's pitch up and down, like a voice trying to stay on a single note and not quite holding on to it.

Vibrato is produced in much the same manner as bending a string, but instead of just pushing the string up to the desired pitch, you push and pull the string back and forth perpendicular to the neck, as shown here:

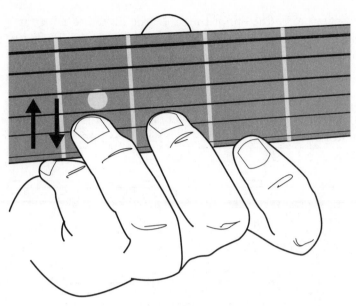

Applying vibrato to a note.

In printed music, vibrato is indicated by a heavy wavy line placed over or under a note (or a tablature number), like this:

Track 80

Chapter 24, Example 2.

Blue Notes, Blues Scales

Blue notes, remember, are the minor third, flatted seventh, and diminished fifth of the major scale. This is why using the minor pentatonic scale of a song (in a major key) produces solos that sound very bluesy. Not the relative minor, but the actual minor: for a blues song in E major, you want to use the Em pentatonic scale, not the C♯m pentatonic, which is the relative minor of E major.

Here are the notes of the Em pentatonic scale, as well as the notes of the E, A, and B chords, which are the I, IV, and V chords in the key of E major:

Em pentatonic scale:	E	G	A	B	D
E major chord:	E	G♯	B		
A major chord:	A	C♯	E		
B major chord:	B	D♯	F♯		

The blue notes of E major are G (the minor third), D (the flatted seventh), and B♭ (the diminished fifth), and two of these notes are part of the Em pentatonic scale. This same scale contains one blue note of the A chord (G, which is the flatted seventh of A) and two blue notes of the B chord (D, which is the minor third, and A, the flatted seventh), so with one scale, you have a whole handful of blue notes at your disposal.

The blues scale has the same notes as the minor pentatonic but also adds the note of the diminished fifth. Here are the notes of the E blues scale:

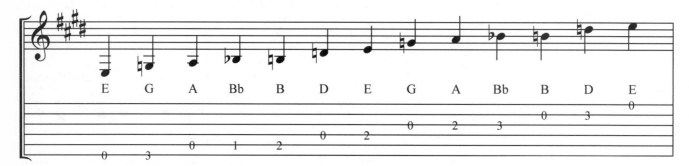

Notes of the E blues scale.

If you've learned the pattern of the minor pentatonic scale, it's a relatively small (and easy) step to add one more note to turn it into the blues scale. And with one easy step, you've given yourself more notes for fills and solos.

"Complete Idiot's Blues" (Take 4)

Now it's time to take your newfound knowledge of vibrato and the blues scale and put them to use with a single-guitar arrangement of an original blues song:

 Track 81

Chapter 24, Example 3.

The best way to go about this is to break the song into phrases of either four or two measures in length. To make this as easy as possible, the bass notes are all quarter notes. Count out the measures if you have to, and remember to use a triplet count of "one and ah, two and ah, three and ah, four and ah" to make certain you play the swing eighths with the proper timing.

"Saint James Infirmary"

"Saint James Infirmary," your second song in this chapter, is a blues song that doesn't follow the typical format of 12 bars. For starters, it's 16 measures long, and it's in a minor key.

The fills are very short and spare, sometimes involving as little as a quick slide, as in measure 4. You want to approach this just as you did the "Complete Idiot's Blues" you just played, learning the song in two- or four-measure phrases and then putting the phrases together to make the whole song.

The final fill in this song is a great example of how a bit of interesting rhythm, combined with a simple skipping of a note or change of direction, is all it takes to make a scale sound more like a polished solo.

 Track 82

continues

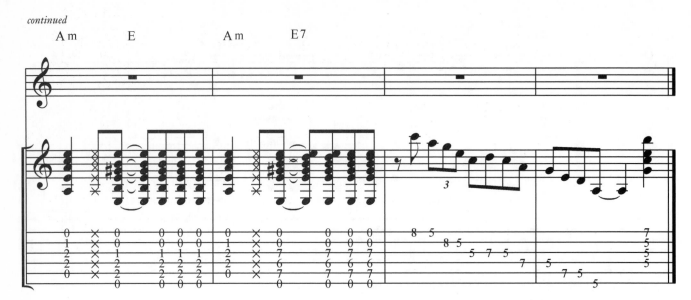

Chapter 24, Example 4.

The Classical Touch

Like other genres of guitar music, classical guitar music covers a wide variety of styles and songs, from medieval ballads that were originally played on the lute; to the romantic, opera-inspired pieces of Mauro Giuliani; to Mason Williams' "Classical Gas," which may be one of the most requested guitar songs in history.

Studying the Studies

Most of the early masters of classical guitar were also guitar teachers, and much of the teaching material they wrote for their students is still available to any guitarist today.

Many of these short studies, especially those by Matteo Carcassi, Mauro Giuliani, and Fernando Sor, are so melodic that they can easily be thought of as songs instead of exercises. Each study usually addresses one or two particular guitar techniques for a student to focus on.

Your first "song" in this chapter is actually a study, written by Mauro Giuliani. It targets finger picking in the key of A minor and also works in short walking basslines while finger picking.

When a classical study focuses on picking, it tells you which right-hand finger to use by means of small letters, written into the notation of the music. If there's a question concerning the use of the left hand on the fingerboard, numbers tell you which finger of the left hand to use on a particular note.

The letters used for the right hand (picking hand) are:

> *P* = Thumb
>
> *i* = Index finger
>
> *m* = Middle finger
>
> *a* = Ring finger
>
> *c* = Pinky finger

The numbers of the left hand (fretting hand) are:

> 1 = Index finger
>
> 2 = Middle finger
>
> 3 = Ring finger
>
> 4 = Pinky finger

Some classical guitar music also uses a zero (0) to indicate that a note is played on an open string.

To demonstrate this system in action, here's the first measure of the study you'll be playing:

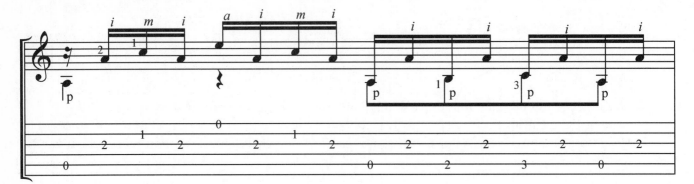

The use of numbering and letters in classical guitar music.

Start with the first two beats. The first note is a half note, the A of the open A string, played with the thumb, which is indicated by the "p" placed beside that note in the notation. This note is to ring out while the fingers play the rest of the notes during these two beats.

The "2" next to the second A note means that they suggest you use your middle finger to fret that note on the fingerboard. The "1" beside the following C note indicates that your index finger should be fretting that particular note.

After you've picked the first note with your thumb, the other letters—i, m, and a—tell you which right hand fingers to use to pick the rest of the notes of this measure. You'll pick the A (second fret of the G string) with your index finger, then the C (first fret of the B string) with your middle finger, and then the A on the G string again with the index finger. Then you pick the open high-E string with the ring finger (indicated by the "a" sitting atop the note) and then use the index finger, middle finger, and index finger again on the appropriate notes and strings.

These fingering directions are typically used once to describe a pattern. It's assumed that you'll recognize the pattern of notes (or strings) should it occur later and that you won't need the pattern written out for you again. That may not seem totally helpful, but it does force you to pay attention and it also keeps the music from being totally cluttered up with directions. Plus, you'll know that anytime more fingering directions appear, some new pattern has come into play.

You might have figured out that all the notes in the first two beats make up an Am chord (and good for you, if so!), but you may wonder why the fingering suggests using the middle finger on the A at the second fret of the G string instead of the ring finger you usually play an Am chord with.

The answer comes in the last half of the measure, where all the notes are either on the low-A string (picked by the thumb) or the A on the second fret of the G string (picked by the index finger). Giuliani suggests that you use your index finger to get the B at the second fret of the A string and then use your ring finger for the C at the third fret of the A string. This may seem awkward on paper, but it actually works quite well in practice.

"Study by Giuliani"

Track 83

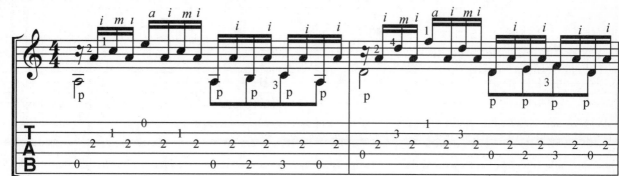

continues

continued

Chapter 25, Example 1.

Each arpeggio in this piece is based on one of four chords. Before you launch into this study, take a few moments to look it over:

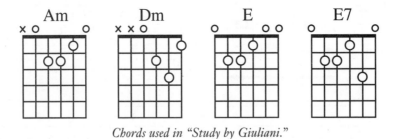

Chords used in "Study by Giuliani."

Three of these chords—Am, Dm, and E—you already know. This voicing of E7 is new, so take a few moments to get used to it, first by playing it by itself and then by switching between it and Am, which is the chord you'll be switching to and from in the study.

You hopefully remember this second voicing of E7 from Chapter 6. Once you reacquaint yourself with it, try the study very slowly. Notice that the written instructions for picking the first measure are never repeated, which means that you can use that pattern until you're told otherwise, which is in measure 9. From that measure onward, you want to pick the first note in the bass with your thumb and then use your index, middle, and ring fingers to pick the G, B, and high-E strings in succession.

Bach in a "Minuet"

Your second song for this chapter is a "Minuet" that is often attributed to Johann Sebastian Bach but that was probably written by Christian Petzold, a friend of the Bach family. You'll recognize it in two measures, tops!

Track 84

continues

continued

Chapter 25, Example 2.

Pay particular attention to the B (second fret of the A string) and D (third fret of the B string) harmony pair at the start of the second measure. You will run into this pair of notes a lot when finger picking. Think about a typical G-to-C bass run and then think of adding harmony notes to it, like this:

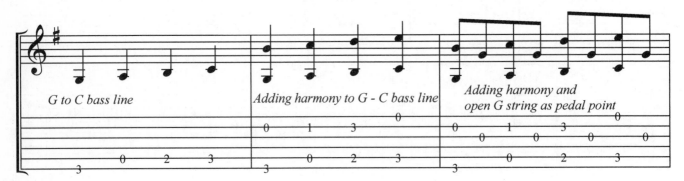

G-to-C bass run with added harmony.

Some Folks Say ...

The term *folk music* is often used to describe songs with no known authors—traditional music that has been passed down through generations. Historically speaking, however, the term itself is fairly new. And in the past 100 years, folk music has been more a term of musical style than of musical definition.

Finger picking and folk music seem to go hand in hand. You can certainly strum most folk songs, but playing them with some Travis-style finger picking seems to give them a bit more flair.

Remember that you don't have to play a single finger-picking pattern throughout a song; in fact, it sounds a lot more natural if you don't. Get a pattern to use as a fallback and don't worry if you miss or add a note here and there. For instance, if you start out with a picking pattern like this …

A basic folk finger-picking pattern.

… you'll probably find yourself doing something like the following at some point:

continues

continued

Variations on a basic folk finger-picking pattern.

Many beginners may think that they have to stay with one picking pattern throughout a song, but doing so is not only hard, it's boring and makes the guitarist sound robotic. Music is organic, and there will always be little "glitches," if you will, with picking and strumming. Your job is to play through them like you know what you're doing. As long as you keep the beat steady, you'll be fine.

"Greenland Whale Fisheries"

Your first song for this chapter is "Greenland Whale Fisheries," and it gives you a lesson on the historical glitches found in folk music right from the first line. The song clearly states the date as June 13, 1853; however, there are other versions of this song with different dates—one was even published as a ballad back in the first quarter of the 1700s!

Musically, you can play this song with all open-position chords, but it's also nice to add some more interesting open-position chord voicings, particularly with the Am and D. Here are two that work well in this song:

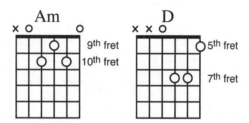

Possible alternate voicings for Am and D.

These voicings also work well with your basic picking pattern, and that's certainly helpful!

 Track 85

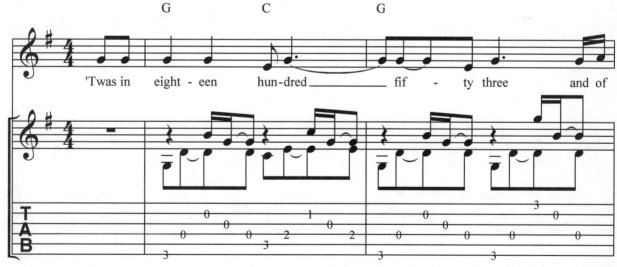

continues

Chapter 26, Example 1.

Since this is a very straightforward arrangement, the different chord voicings add a bit more interest to it. You can also throw in a fill here and there, like this one in measure 7:

Track 86

Chapter 26, Example 2.

This fill follows the four notes of the melody line, from C to B to A to G, by means of some double-stop hammer-ons and pull-offs. If you keep your fingers in the open-position Am shape, the fill is very simple to execute, although it will initially take a bit of practice.

"Scarborough Fair"

Your second song is, in some ways, a little easier. It's an arrangement of the traditional ballad "Scarborough Fair," a song that has been traced back to the late 1600s. This arrangement is very spare and not as intricate as the one English guitarist Martin Carthy taught Paul Simon back in 1965. But it gives you a chance to work on basic arpeggios and simple moving basslines, and it treats you to a few new chord voicings:

Track 87

continues

Chapter 26, Example 3.

In measure 21, you run into a simple but very interesting variation of the D-chord arpeggio, which you could say is actually a fill, since it bears little resemblance to the D-chord arpeggio in the preceding measure:

Track 88

Chapter 26, Example 4.

Even though this seems simple enough on paper, it's a little tricky when you try it out on the guitar. When you get to the note of the open B string, raise all your fingers off the strings and then use either your pinky or your ring finger for the F♯ at the fourth fret of the D string.

This arrangement of "Scarborough Fair" ends with a reprise of the first phrase of the song's melody played by means of *harmonics*. Harmonics are clear, almost bell-like tones that can be played with one of several two-handed techniques. Depending on how harmonics are played, they are either *natural* or *artificial*.

Natural harmonics are easy to play once you know where to find them on your fingerboard. Place a finger on the twelfth fret of your high-E (first) string, like this:

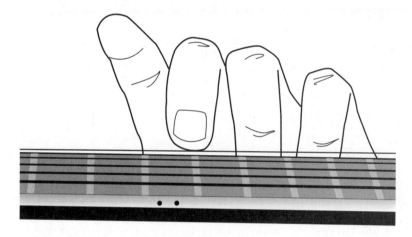

Playing natural harmonics.

Track 89

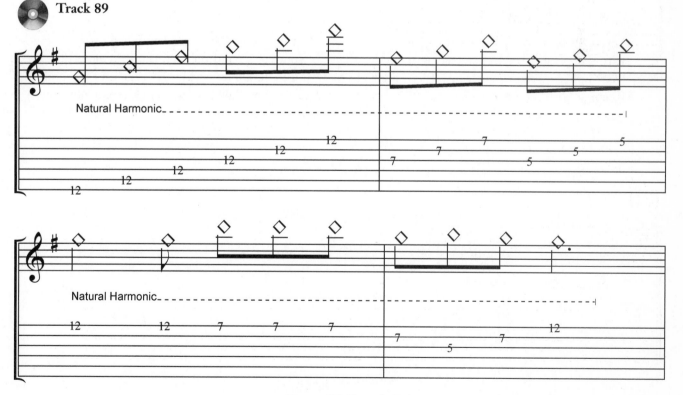

Chapter 26, Example 5.

You want your finger to touch the string at the point directly over the twelfth fret, not in the space between the frets; that would be the metal fret that's closer to the body of the guitar. Be as light as you can be on the string, making the barest contact with the pad of your finger. Some people find they get a better-sounding harmonic by pulling the fretting finger away from the string the instant they pluck the string with the right hand. When you pick the high-E string, you should hear a clean, clear, crystalline tone, such as the one on Track 89.

You find natural harmonics at specific points along the fingerboard of the guitar. The easiest ones to produce are at the twelfth, seventh, and fifth frets. Playing a harmonic at the twelfth fret produces the same note you would get by playing the fretted note in a regular manner. The twelfth-fret harmonic of E is the same E—it's just that you have the harmonic of it, a specific overtone that is part of the regular note's "whole sound."

Fret	12th	7th	5th
	E	B	E
	B	F♯	B
Harmonic note: (strings listed high to low)	G	D	G
	D	A	D
	A	E	A
	E	B	E

At the seventh fret, the harmonics are pitched one octave higher than the notes regularly found on that fret. The harmonic at the seventh fret of the high-E string, for example, is the B found at the nineteenth fret of the high-E string. At the fifth fret, the natural harmonics are an octave higher than those found at the twelfth fret.

You can also create harmonics anywhere on the fingerboard by first fretting a note on any string with the left hand, and then placing the index finger of your right hand very lightly at the note 12 frets higher on the same string. Again, the right-hand finger should be on the wire, not on the wood. Keeping both fingers in place, pluck the string with your thumb. This generates a harmonic one octave higher than the note being fingered by your left hand. This is called an *artificial* or *touch harmonic.*

The Wearing of the Green

"Paddy Whack"

A lot of Celtic music was created for dancing, and you can hear and feel it in the rhythms. Many jigs are written in 6/8 time, which, as you learned back in Chapter 9, has a pulse of two beats. Those beats are further broken down into a triplet feel.

Your first Celtic song for this chapter is actually quite a bit like the "Minuet" you played in Chapter 25, in that you never play more than two notes at a time, but there's still a lot of implied harmony.

 Track 90

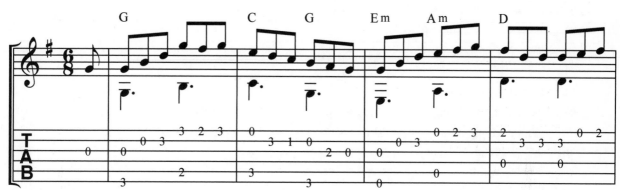

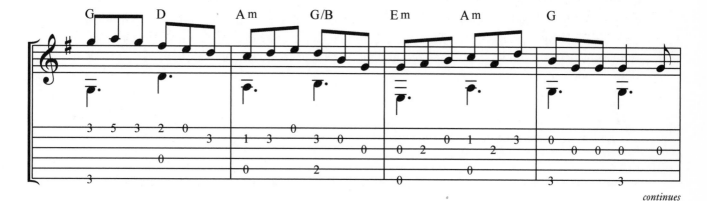

continues

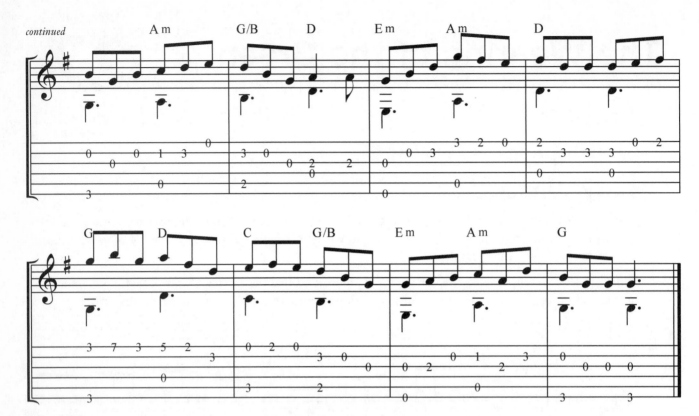

Chapter 27, Example 1.

Notice that the bass notes create the two-pulses-per-measure feeling that you want the music to have. Even when you play it incredibly slow (as you should the first few times!), you can tell this has a very different *feel* from "Minuet."

Hammering Out a Celtic Mood

Hammer-ons and pull-offs recreate the characteristics of pipes and fifes, helping you to dress up your guitar a bit in order to blend in with other traditional Celtic instruments. "Paddy Whack" contains numerous opportunities for hammer-ons and pull-offs in its melody, and it's essential that these be done in correct timing.

Each melody note is one beat (remember that the eighth note designates one beat in 6/8 time), with the exception of a few quarter notes at the end of certain phrases (the third G in measures 8 and 16 and the A close to the end of measure 10). Make sure you don't treat these one-beat hammer-ons and pull-offs as grace notes.

It might help to play just the melody of the song by itself *without* any slurs the first few times so you can get used to what it's supposed to sound like. This is how it's played on Track 90 on the CD. When you're sure you've got it set in your head, add the slurs, keeping the timing nice and even. After you've got all that, go ahead and add the bass notes.

For the most part, you can play "Paddy Whack" in open position and the fingerings will seem fairly obvious. But there are a couple of tricky spots. In measures 5 and 13, use your index finger to barre across all six strings at the third fret.

Measure 13 also involves hitting the B note at the seventh fret of the high-E string. Use your pinky—
it's definitely a big stretch, so don't be disappointed if you don't make it on the first few tries. What will
help more than anything else in this section is to be relaxed and seated using good posture, with the
guitar as perpendicular to the floor as it can possibly be. The more you tip the guitar to watch yourself
play this measure, the harder it will be to play.

"The Irish Washerwoman"

Fifes and pipes also tend to play with a lot of trills. And if you think about bagpipes, you probably first
think of the loud, low drone they make. Your guitar is capable of both of those techniques and more.

Start with just the melody of "The Irish Washerwoman," perhaps one of the best-known traditional
Irish jigs:

 Track 91 (0:00)

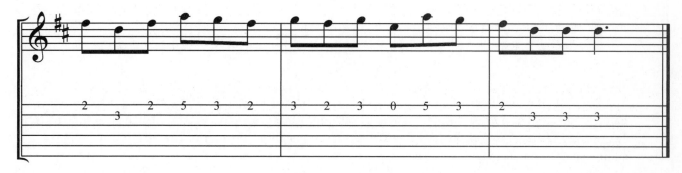

Chapter 27, Example 2.

Since this melody is in the key of D, retune your low-E string down to D, giving you drop D tuning. Remember from Chapter 17 that drop D tuning creates a D5 chord (D, A, and D) on the three low strings, which is a pretty powerful drone. Now you're ready to sound like a bagpipe! Play the melody again, this time brushing your thumb across the three bass strings on the first beat of each measure:

Track 91 (0:24)

Guitar tuned to Drop D tuning–low to high DADGBE

Chapter 27, Example 3.

You can also take advantage of all the D and A notes in the melody, and add to your opportunities to hammer-on from or pull-off to these notes, by retuning your guitar to DADGAD (last seen in Chapter 17). Setting D and A as your highest first two open strings gives you a lot of chances to play around adding slurs to the melody of this song:

Track 92

Guitar tuned to DADGAD tuning–low to high DADGAD

Chapter 27, Example 4.

There's something very cool going on during the last few measures:

Track 93

Chapter 27, Example 5.

You end this song by playing the D note three times, each in a different fashion. First, hammer the open second string at the fifth fret with your middle finger. Then play the open first string. Finally, place your index finger at the fourth fret of the second string (which is C♯) and then bend the note a half-step up to D.

Playing these three notes in a very different way gives the song a wavering feel, much like hearing pipes or even voices that are not quite right in tune. It's not the sort of sound you'd expect from a guitar, and it fits perfectly with the Celtic mood you're trying to create.

Retuning the strings down in pitch (as you do with several strings in DADGAD tuning) gives the strings more slack, allowing you easier bends and more play from your hammer-ons and pull-offs.

LISTENING LIBRARY

To get a sample of great Celtic guitar playing, check out Daithi Sproule, as well as Randall Bays, Donal Clancy, Michael O'Dohmhnail, and Donogh Hennessy, either on CD or on the Internet.

Jazzin' It Up

Jazz, like most genres, is hard to define, mostly because (again like most genres) no one single characteristic makes a piece of music "jazz." A lot of elements—swing rhythms, syncopation, blues notes, and improvisation—go into jazz, but not every element has to be present to call something a jazz number.

Whether you're into traditional songs or blues or rock, if you like to experiment with rhythms and exotic chords or just like adding some swing to your playing, you can find a style of jazz that suits you and your guitar.

Rhythm and swing have a lot to do with jazz, but a lot of your initial focus is going to be on chords. Jazz songs rarely use the basic simple major and minor chords that you're familiar with. Sometimes it will seem that the simplest chords you'll find in jazz songs are sixth and seventh chords.

Jazz gets much of its flavor from its use of extended chords. It's not unusual to find jazz songs riddled with ninth chords, augmented chords (with dominant sevenths added), diminished chords (with either dominant or diminished sevenths added), and eleventh and thirteenth chords. You'll also run into more than your share of altered chords, such as D7♯9.

The idea of learning pages of new, complicated chords probably seems more than a little daunting. Although you may have a lot to learn, you do get some unexpected help. Almost all jazz chords are based on movable barre chords, so you can learn the shape of the chord instead of trying to pick out all the individual notes. And if you notice where the chord's root note is in each shape, you can play these chords anywhere on your guitar's fingerboard.

Here are some of the basic chord shapes you're likely to run into in jazz music. Notice that the root note of each chord is marked with an "R" in the appropriate finger circle.

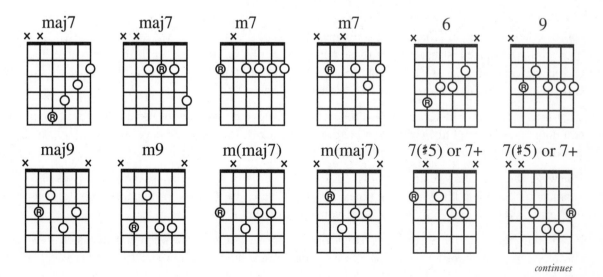

continues

continued

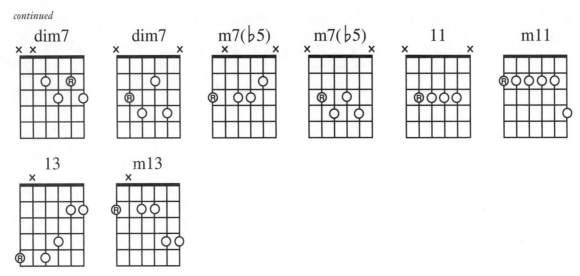

Some typical moveable jazz chords.

You may have noted that many of the chords in the last example involve playing notes on just four strings. That's some more unexpected help. Remember that there are five different notes in ninth chords, eleventh chords have six, and thirteenth chords have seven. Your guitar has only six strings, so you have to drop some notes here and there when you play any extended chord.

Plus, the more notes your chord has, the more likely the chord can perform double duty. For example, the notes of a C6 chord are C, E, G, and A. These are the same notes that make up an Am7 chord. Start with A as your root and work it out—A, C (minor third), E (fifth), and G (flatted seventh).

As long as you remember the four basic chords—major, minor, augmented, and diminished—as well as the different types of seventh chords, you'll always have chords to use as fallback positions.

These four notes are also part of the Fmaj9 chord: A is the third, C the fifth, E the major seventh, and G the ninth. So if you've got a bass player (or someone else) taking care of the root note, you can play Am7 when you see Fmaj9 on a chord sheet and usually get away with it!

As you look into the makeup of chords, you will find all sorts of relationships between them. Learning even just one or two of these shortcuts can keep you from getting overwhelmed by all the new chords.

This is particularly true of both augmented chords and diminished seventh chords. An augmented chord, as you learned in Chapter 13, is made of the root, the third, and the augmented fifth. What you may not have realized is that each of these notes is the interval of a perfect third (two whole steps) from the other. In Caug (C, E, G♯), for instance, E is two whole steps from C and G♯ is two whole steps from E. And guess what note is two steps higher than G♯? Yes, it's C.

That means the notes of Caug are also the notes of Eaug and G♯aug, and instead of knowing one chord, you now know three. This works for all augmented chords, so instead of needing to know 12 of them, you only have to learn 4. That's pretty cool!

Likewise, the four notes of any diminished seventh chord are all equally spaced at intervals of one and a half steps. So if you know that the notes of Cdim7 are C, E♭, G♭, and A, you also know all the notes of E♭dim7, G♭dim7, and Adim7. Try it out yourself and see!

Playing chords on just three or four strings also can make changing between chords easier. Just like chord progressions in other music, jazz chord progressions tend to follow specific patterns. When you're concerned with notes on only three or four strings, you can often find chords very close to each other. You might even move your hands and fingers less than you do playing open-position chords!

Just to give you an example, here's the first line from "Beautiful Dreamer," the song you learned back in Chapter 19:

 Track 94

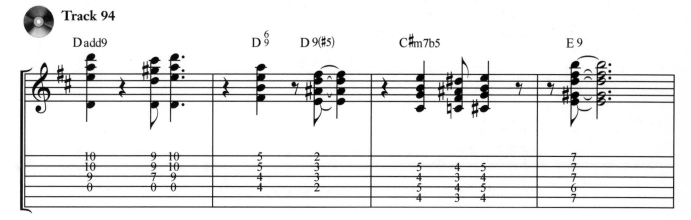

Chapter 28, Example 1.

That's quite a bit different than you remember it, right? For starters, it's in 4/4 time rather than 3/4! It may seem like this should be hard to play, but the chord shapes are all very similar to each other, and some, like the three that go with the "wake unto" lyrics, are simple chromatic shifts of the same chord shape.

Likewise, jazz solos may sound complicated, and they definitely involve playing more than just a simple pentatonic scale, but at heart, they are still based on the ideas you learned in Chapter 20. Here's a relatively simple one for you to work with:

 Track 95

Swing Eighths

Chapter 28, Example 2.

Even though this solo has a lot of short chromatic steps, and even though it sounds like it's playing all over the place, it all takes place between the fourth and eighth frets of the fingerboard. You'll also notice how it uses repeated rhythmic ideas, like the triplets at the start of measures 3 and 4, and that there's a Cdim7 arpeggio in measure 5.

You also can hear how this solo swings. It's obviously played in swing eighths, but there are lots of anticipations as well.

Going Comping

All the ideas of chord melody and soloing in jazz are used in comping, which is accompanying the soloist or vocalist with chords that punctuate the rhythm. Comping differs from strumming, in that strumming is usually very steady rhythmically, while comping can be freer while still maintaining the overall beat.

Jazz guitarists also tend to avoid ringing open strings, as evidenced by how they usually play some sort of closed barre chord, even when it uses only three or four strings. Because of all the notes that make up many jazz chords, you don't want a lot of ringing overtones to clutter up the harmonies. So the comped chords are usually played with short, clean picking strokes, whether you're using a pick or your fingers.

"Take Me Out to the Ballgame"

When you're starting out on jazz guitar, it's a good idea to begin with songs you're very familiar with so you can work out swing rhythms and different chords without also having to learn a new song! Here's an example of comping using a song you probably know very well:

  Track 96

continues

continued

Chapter 28, Example 3.

This arrangement isn't totally in jazz style, as it does have a few basic, simple chords (C, Dm, and F), and it does make use of open strings to create a nice rhythm. But it should give you an idea of what comping is like. Notice how easy it is to move from C to C#dim by using the indicated chord voicing. The only difference between the C chord (C, E, and G) and C#dim (C#, E, and G) is the root note, so if you do your chord voicing with that in mind, it's a breeze to change from one to the other. That's another example of how knowing even a little theory can help you a lot.

There's a cool little chromatic bassline in the fifteenth and sixteenth measures, just to give you a break from playing chords the entire time. And the song ends with a C 6/9 chord, which is a very cool jazz chord that adds both the sixth (A, in this case) and ninth notes (D) to the standard major triad.

Pop

Historically, most musical genres have produced some sort of pop music. Folk, blues, country, jazz, and rock have all had their day dominating—or at least popping up on—the pop music scene. If nothing else, pop music has helped people discover musical genres they might never have listened to otherwise.

Pop music, like jazz, encourages musicians to experiment with arrangements. The song itself is important, but good songs can be arranged in many different styles. Changes in rhythm, tempo, mood, and instrumentation are all welcomed with open arms.

As you know, songs are melodies with harmonies (chords) and rhythm. And you know that you can use your guitar to play any or all of these three elements. When you look at a song, think of two of these elements, the melody and the harmony, as your "book."

"Piano Style" Guitar Playing

Sometimes you can change a lot about how a song sounds by imitating other instruments, as you learned in Chapter 27 on Celtic music. This doesn't always have to be a huge undertaking, either. For instance, one very easy way of getting your guitar to have more of a pop-piano feel is to simply reverse your "boom-chuck" approach. Instead of hitting the root note of a chord first and then the chord, play it the other way around, like this:

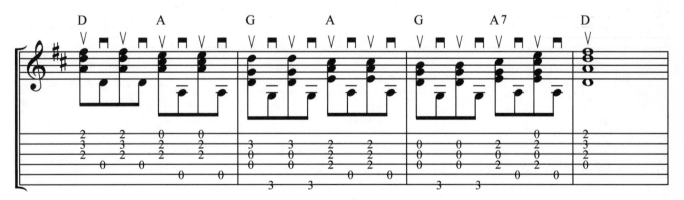

Getting more of a piano quality.

This might not be as easy as it seems, since you want to start your playing on the upstroke. But once you get the hang of it, you'll be surprised how different it makes your guitar sound. Combining this technique with suspended chords and other embellished chords makes things even more interesting.

Playing short, repeated musical phrases, like an arpeggio of the same three notes played over the changing chords, is a basic technique for most musicians. Remember that you are an arranger as well as a guitarist. If you only go "by the book," you'll miss out on the many possible chances to make your playing more interesting.

"The Water Is Wide"

This arrangement of "The Water Is Wide," a beautiful traditional song that has been covered by many artists, uses a similar approach with the repeated D, G, A, and B notes played during the first three measures, while the root note of the accompanying chord shifts from G to C and back to G. Taking advantage of as many ringing strings as possible gives the guitar a harplike quality that fits well with the mood of the song.

 Track 97

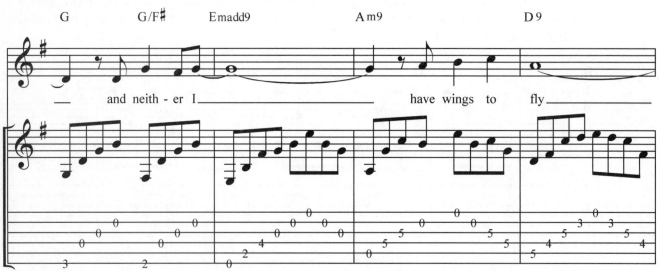

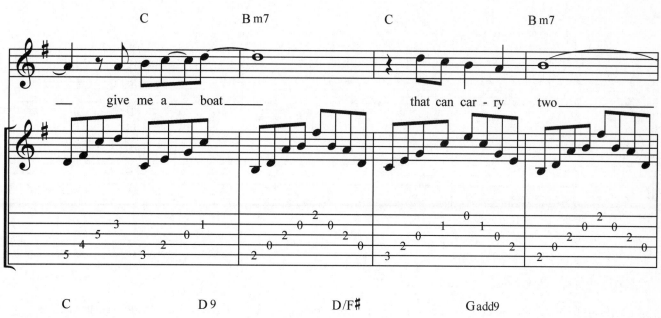

Chapter 29, Example 1.

Now suppose that playing all those ringing strings in "The Water Is Wide" put you in the mood to do some more finger picking. And suppose you want to try to play this progression of C to B♭ to F to C just to see what happens. You might put together some of the theory you've gleaned from Part 3 and hit on the idea of playing a G chord up on the seventh and eighth frets of your guitar to serve as a starting place for your C chord. Using your middle finger to play the C on the eighth fret of the low-E string and your index finger to play the E at the seventh fret of the A string, you could then shift your ring finger off the high-E string (E is a note of the C chord) and place it instead on the G at the eighth fret of the B string. Leaving the D string open gives you Cadd9, which sounds very nice. Playing around with this, you might come up with the following picking.

Track 98 (0:00)

Capo on third fret–tablature and notes shown relative to the capo

Chapter 29, Example 2.

"Julia and John"

From here, it's not a stretch to come up with other chords and to also find more interesting voicings—and before you know it, you might have a song. Please note, though, that this arrangement (as well as the picking in the last illustration) uses a capo on the third fret.

 Track 98 (0:13)

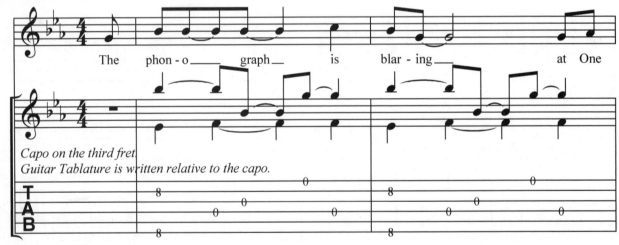

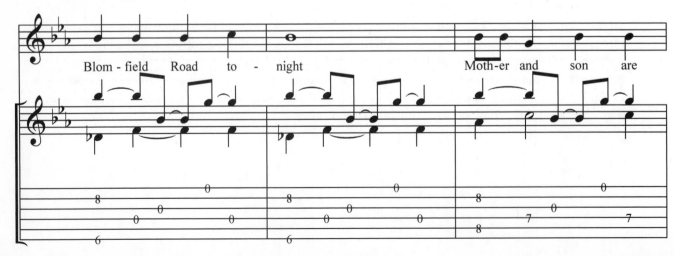

continues

continued

Chapter 29, Example 3.

Now, that may seem like a bit of magic to you, but the truth is that it was just taking what you've learned in this book and putting it to use to create a song. The chords of the chorus use the same open-position G chord shape as the C chord that starts the song, but since the A string doesn't figure into the picking pattern, there's no reason to have a finger on it.

Once you established the picking pattern, the song's melody sprang naturally from it, particularly in the chorus. Knowing that the verse's opening C chord was actually Cadd9 (because of the use of the open D string) led to using a "normal" open-position Cadd9 in the chorus.

I can't say it strongly enough: Coming up with a song like this is not beyond your skills at this point! You've come a long, long way from figuring out how to get your guitar in tune, from trying to get your first Em chord to sound right, and from learning how to strum with proper timing. As you practice and develop as a guitarist and as a musician, you'll hopefully often find yourself in awe of what you can create. And it won't be long before you have the chance to teach others, too! They'll be the ones asking, "How did you do that?"

Directory of CD Tracks

Appendix

A

1. Tuning (Chapter 1)

2. Chapter 2, Example 1 (0:00)
   Chapter 2, Example 2 (0:17)

3. The Simplest Chord Change (Chapter 3)

4. Your First "Official" Song (Chapter 3)

5. Chapter 4, Example 1 (0:00)
   Chapter 4, Example 2 (0:20)

6. Chapter 4, Example 3

7. Chapter 5, Example 1 (0:00)
   Chapter 5, Example 2 (0:13)

8. Chapter 5, Example 3

9. Chapter 5, Example 4

10. Chapter 5, Example 5

11. Chapter 5, Example 6

12. Chapter 5, Example 7

13. Chapter 6, Example 1 (0:00)
    Chapter 6, Example 2 (0:15)
    Chapter 6, Example 3 (0:29)
    Chapter 6, Example 4 (0:40)

14. Chapter 6, Example 5

15. Chapter 6, Example 6

16. Chapter 7, Example 1 (0:00)
    Chapter 7, Example 2 (0:18)

17. Chapter 7, Example 3

18. Chapter 7, Example 4

19. Chapter 8, Example 1 (0:00)
    Chapter 8, Example 2 (0:06)
    Chapter 8, Example 3 (0:13)
    Chapter 8, Example 4 (0:29)

20. Chapter 8, Example 5 (0:00)
    Chapter 8, Example 6 (0:06)
    Chapter 8, Example 7 (0:19)
    Chapter 8, Example 8 (0:30)

21. Chapter 8, Example 9

22. Chapter 8, Example 10

23. Chapter 8, Example 11

24. Chapter 8, Example 12

25. Chapter 9, Example 1 (0:00)
    Chapter 9, Example 2 (0:24)
    Chapter 9, Example 3 (0:36)

26. Chapter 9, Example 4

27. Chapter 9, Example 5 (0:00)
    Chapter 9, Example 6 (0:12)

28. Chapter 9, Example 7

29. Chapter 9, Example 8

30. Chapter 9, Example 9

31. Chapter 10, Example 1 (0:00)
    Chapter 10, Example 2 (0:11)

32. Chapter 10, Example 3

33. Chapter 10, Example 4

34. Chapter 10, Example 5

35. Chapter 10, Example 6 (0:00)
    Chapter 10, Example 7 (0:21)

36. Chapter 10, Example 8

37. Chapter 11, Example 1

38. Chapter 11, Example 2

39. Chapter 11, Example 3 (0:00)
    Chapter 11, Example 4 (0:17)
    Chapter 11, Example 5 (0:32)

40. Chapter 11, Example 6

41. Chapter 11, Example 7

42. Chapter 12, Example 1

43. Chapter 12, Example 2

44. Chapter 13, Example 1 (0:00)
    Chapter 13, Example 2 (0:18)

45. Chapter 14, Example 1

46. Chapter 14, Example 2

47. Chapter 14, Example 3

48. Chapter 15, Example 1

49. Chapter 16, Example 1

50. Chapter 16, Example 2

51. "Make Me a Pallet" played by two guitars
    (Chapter 16)

52. Chapter 17, Example 1

53. Chapter 17, Example 2

54. Chapter 17, Example 3

55. Chapter 17, Example 4

56. Chapter 17, Example 5

57. Chapter 18, Example 1 (0:00)
    Chapter 18, Example 2 (0:10)

58. Chapter 18, Example 3 (0:00)
    Chapter 18, Example 4 (0:40)

59. Chapter 18, Example 5

60. Chapter 18, Example 6

61. Chapter 19, Example 1 (0:00)
    Chapter 19, Example 2 (0:20)

62. Chapter 19, Example 3

63. Chapter 20, Example 1

64. Chapter 20, Example 2

65. Chapter 20, Example 3

66. Chapter 20, Example 4

67. Chapter 20, Example 5

68. Chapter 20, Example 6

69. Chapter 21, Example 1

70. Chapter 21, Example 2

71. Chapter 22, Example 1

72. Chapter 22, Example 2

73. Chapter 22, Example 3 (0:00)
    Chapter 22, Example 4 (0:12)
    Chapter 22, Example 5 (0:22)

74. Chapter 22, Example 6

75. Chapter 23, Example 1

76. Chapter 23, Example 2

77. Chapter 23, Example 3

78. Chapter 23, Example 4 (0:00)
    Chapter 23, Example 5 (0:13)

79. Chapter 24, Example 1

80. Chapter 24, Example 2

81. Chapter 24, Example 3

82. Chapter 24, Example 4

83. Chapter 25, Example 1

84. Chapter 25, Example 2

85. Chapter 26, Example 1

86. Chapter 26, Example 2

87. Chapter 26, Example 3

88. Chapter 26, Example 4

89. Chapter 26, Example 5

90. Chapter 27, Example 1

91. Chapter 27, Example 2 (0:00)
    Chapter 27, Example 3 (0:24)

92. Chapter 27, Example 4

93. Chapter 27, Example 5

94. Chapter 28, Example 1

95. Chapter 28, Example 2

96. Chapter 28, Example 3

97. Chapter 29, Example 1

98. Chapter 29, Example 2 (0:00)
    Chapter 29, Example 3 (0:13)

Chord Charts

Here are chord charts for most of the chords you'll come across when playing guitar. First, the most common open-position chords:

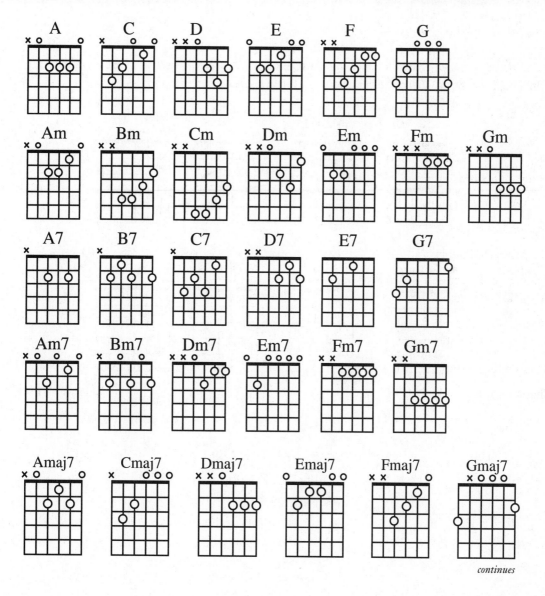

continues

continued

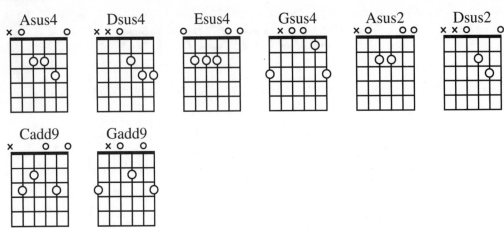

And these are generic charts for making most barre chords you'll find yourself using in songs. The "R" in the chart indicates where the root note is on the sixth or fifth string:

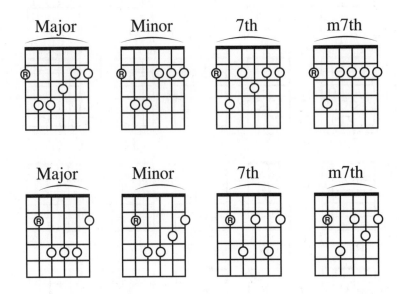

Finally, here are some interesting chords, as well as some different voicings of basic chords that you may enjoy playing:

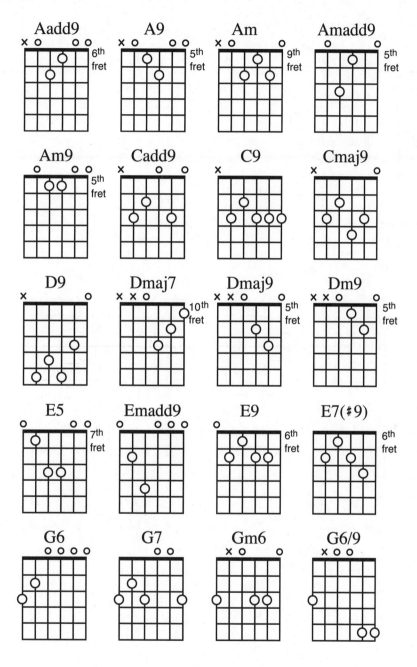

For Further Study

To the guitarist, the term *self-taught* pretty much means "learning without a formal teacher." These days, with books, videos, CD and DVD tutorials, and thousands of tutorial websites on the Internet, any aspiring guitarist has a world of resources from which to learn.

Just as no guitarist is self-taught, no guitarist learns from one single source. *The Complete Idiot's Guide to Guitar* was designed and written to get you started on your musical journey, and it gives you a lot of material to learn and techniques that you'll use for as long as you play guitar. When you have these basics well in hand, you'll want to explore further.

The first thing you'll probably want to do is find material to practice your new skills and to take your playing to the next level. Grab a copy of Hemme Luttjeboer's *The Complete Idiot's Guide to Guitar Exercises* (Alpha, 2010), and you'll have yourself a full workout, from warm-ups and basic technique drills to dexterity- and stamina-building exercises, to single-note scale and chord exercises. There are even exercises for finger picking.

Practicing is an essential part of improving as a guitarist, and you can help yourself raise both your mind and your body to their best by reading *The Musician's Way: A Guide to Practice, Performance and Wellness*, by Gerald Klickstein (Oxford University Press, 2009), and Jamie Andreas's *The Principles of Correct Practice for Guitar* (Jamey World, Inc., 2nd edition, 2005). Both of these books will put you in the proper mindset to make the most of your practice and to become the best guitarist you possibly can.

To learn more about music theory, try Michael Miller's *The Complete Idiot's Guide to Music Theory* (Alpha Books, 2002), and Tom Serb's *Music Theory for Guitarists* (Noteboat, Inc., 2003). By the way, Tom is the founder of the Midwest Music Academy in Plainfield, Illinois—a great place to take lessons if you live in the area.

When it comes to learning the basic guitar techniques, as well as discovering all sorts of ways to put them to practical use, you can't find a much better source than *Acoustic Guitar* magazine. In addition to their monthly publication, they have an exceptional website, a virtual treasure trove of archived tutorial material. And their books, such as *Rhythm Guitar Essentials* (String Letter Publishing, 2009) and *Flatpicking Guitar Basics* (String Letter Publishing, 2010), are usually chock-full of great lessons.

If you can't get enough of finger picking, you'll probably get a lot of help from Mark Hanson's many books, such as *Beyond Basics Fingerstyle Guitar* (Alfred, 1998) or *The Art of Contemporary Travis Picking* (Music Sales America, 1992). In addition to his basic tutorial books, Mark has some great transcription books, like *Paul Simon—Transcribed* (Music Sales America, 1993).

Mark also wrote *The Complete Book of Alternate Tunings* (Music Sales America, 1995), a wonderful introduction to the universe of nonstandard tunings. If you're more the type to explore one alternate tuning at a time, Julie Henigan's *DADGAD Tuning* (Mel Bay, 1999), a collection of 13 Irish songs and dances, might be of particular interest.

Listing the countless books on guitar solos would mean writing another book! Look for note-for-note transcriptions of the guitarists you like. If you can't settle on a single artist or band, try out compilation books like the *Acoustic Guitar Tab White Pages* (Hal Leonard, 2003), which has tablature for over 100 songs.

And when you're done copying solos, read Michael Miller's *The Complete Idiot's Guide to Solos and Improvisation* (Alpha, 2004), and combine both what you learn from him and the techniques you've been honing from copying your idols to make your own guitar solos.

Books focusing on musical genres are as plentiful as books on guitar solos. But when it comes to the music of the classical guitar, no one does better than the great Frederick Noad. His *Solo Guitar Playing, Volume 1* (Hal Leonard, 3rd edition, 1994), is the twentieth century's equivalent to the methods of the masters from the 1800s. And his collections of the best studies from those masters, such as his *100 Graded Classical Guitar Studies* (Music Sales America, 1992), are perfect for developing your classical guitar skills.

To work up some serious speed and bluegrass skills, try Mickey Cochran's *Guitar Crosspicking Technique* (Mel Bay, 2002), as well as Orrin Star's *Hot Licks for Bluegrass Guitar* (Music Sales America, 1992). For blues instruction, try John Ganapes's *Blues You Can Use* (Hal Leonard, 1995), and any of Dave Rubin's "Inside the Blues" tutorial books, like *12-Bar Blues* (Hal Leonard, 1999). Both of these authors are excellent teachers, and you'll learn a lot from them.

Fans of Celtic music will want to check out Glen Weiser's *Celtic Guitar (Acoustic Masters)* (Alfred, 2000), as well as Jeff Jacobson's arrangements of *Celtic Favorites for Open-Tuned Guitar* (Cherry Lane Music, 2001). And if that's not enough to keep you busy, just add *Mel Bay's Complete Celtic Fingerstyle Book*, by Stefan Grossman, Duck Baker, and El McMeen (Mel Bay, 2000) to your list.

If you decide to get serious about jazz, pick up a copy of Jody Fisher's *Beginning Jazz Guitar* (Alfred, 2006), the first of his series of three jazz tutorials. These are good enough to be used by the National Guitar Workshop. Another book worth your time and attention is *Mickey Baker's Complete Course in Jazz Guitar* (Ashley Publications Inc./Lewis Music Publishing Co., 1996). This book, originally written in the 1950s, assumes you can read music and chord charts already (in other words, there's no guitar tablature), but it will teach you more in 64 pages than you would ever think possible.

As good as any books or websites may be, you still probably want to think about getting a teacher. One-on-one instruction will give you instant feedback, and a good teacher is a musical guide and a continual source of encouragement. Finding the right match in an instructor is important. Don't sign up with a teacher before talking with him or her first. Discuss your goals and ask questions of a potential mentor.

Remember that the best guitarist may *not* be the best teacher. A guitar teacher's focus should be on you and your goals. Good teachers will work with you in putting together a lesson plan, setting out practice routines, and making the most of your abilities.

Please feel free to write and ask me any questions, too. My e-mail address is dhodgeguitar@aol.com. You can also reach me at Guitar Noise (www.guitarnoise.com), a wonderful free guitar tutorial website, or contact me through my blog at www.davidhodge.com. I try to answer every e-mail I get, but I do spend my days teaching, so please don't worry if I don't respond immediately.

I look forward to hearing from you!

Glossary

12-bar blues   A standard blues song format involving specific chord changes over the course of 12 measures.

accent   To apply extra stress to a note, usually by striking it harder with the pick.

accidental   A sharp sign (♯), flat sign (♭), or natural sign (♮).

acoustic guitar   A guitar that doesn't use electronic processing or amplification. Nowadays an acoustic guitar is differentiated from a classical guitar by its steel strings (as opposed to the nylon strings used on a classical guitar), but technically a classical guitar is also an acoustic guitar.

alternate picking   Picking single notes using a continual down-and-up pick motion.

alternate tuning   Tuning the strings of the guitar to notes other than those of standard tuning.

alternating bass   Type of strum played like the "boom-chuck," but differing in that the root note is played on the first beat only and another note (usually the fifth of the chord) is played on the third beat.

anticipation   Arriving at your target note or chord before the beat, usually coming in a half a beat earlier.

arpeggio   A chord played one note (usually on separate strings) at a time, usually in an ascending or descending order.

articulation   How a note is played—crisply, long, short, slurred, and so on.

augmented chord   One of the four basic chord types, made up of the root, major third, and augmented fifth degrees of the major scale.

bar   Also called a *measure*. A distinct measurement of beats, dictated by the time signature. The end of a bar is indicated by a vertical line running through the staff or bass guitar tablature lines.

barre chords   Chords that are formed by placing the index finger flat across the strings at a single fret to play some notes while the other fingers fret others higher up on the neck. Fretting across all six strings is called a *full barre*, and fretting between two and five strings is called a *half barre*.

bend   A guitar slur technique of pushing a string along the fingerboard toward the center of the neck to raise its pitch from one note to another.

blue notes   The minor third, diminished fifth, and flat seventh of a key. The tension between the blue notes and the regular notes of the major scale is a key factor in the blues sound.

boom-chuck   Type of strum made by playing the root note of a chord in the bass on the first and third beats, and a strum of the rest of the chord (on the other strings) on the second and fourth beats.

bridge   Part of the body of the guitar, usually a small wedge or support system where the strings are raised above the soundboard. Along with the nut, the bridge is one of the two vibrational endpoints for each string.

capo   A clamp attached to the neck and fingerboard to raise equally the pitch of all six strings.

chord   Three or more different notes played together at the same time.

chord chart   A grid or diagram that shows you where to place your fingers on the guitar to play a specific chord.

chord progression   A sequence of chords played in a song or in a phrase of a song.

chromatic notes   Notes taken from outside a given major scale. *See* diatonic.

chromatic scale   A scale made up of all 12 possible notes, each one a half-step from the other.

circle of fifths   A pattern that can be used to study the relationship of keys to one another; also an excellent tool for practicing scales, riffs, or phrases in all keys.

classical guitar   An acoustic guitar with nylon strings, usually slightly smaller than a steel-string acoustic guitar.

common time   The symbol "C" used as a time signature; another name for 4/4 time.

crosspicking   Method of playing guitar with a pick in which the guitarist uses a steady stream of single notes, usually played across three or four strings.

DADGAD tuning   A popular alternate tuning in which the six strings of the guitar are tuned (low to high) to D, A, D, G, A, and D. This is often used in Celtic music.

diatonic   The notes used in a given major scale, or the chords derived from the triads of that scale.

diminished chord   One of the four basic chord types, made up of the root, minor third, and diminished fifth degrees of the major scale.

dotted note   A dot added to a note to give it more length. A dotted half note is three beats long, a dotted quarter note is one and a half beats long, and so on.

double stops   Simultaneously playing two notes on adjacent strings.

drop D tuning   An alternate tuning in which the low-E string is tuned down a whole step to D.

dynamics   Changes in volume or tempo while playing.

eighth note   A note of half a beat's duration.

eighth-note rest   A rest of half a beat's duration.

electric guitar   A guitar requiring amplification to be heard. Most electric guitars have solid bodies, but there are hollow-body and semihollow-body electric guitars as well.

fill   A short musical phrase that fills a space in the music. It's similar to a riff, except that riffs are usually repeated note by note, while fills usually are different each time.

flat   An accidental sign (♭) indicating lowering a note a half-step.

finger picking   Style of guitar playing that uses the fingers of the right hand (instead of a pick) to strike the strings.

fingerboard The area along the front of the guitar's neck where the player places his fingers to fret notes on the strings.

fret Metal wire on the neck of the guitar. Also the act of placing a finger on the neck of the guitar, which presses the string against a fret, thus changing the pitch of the string.

grace note A note played and then quickly changed to another note within the shortest time possible.

half note A note of two beats' duration.

half rest A rest of two beats' duration.

half-step The difference, between two notes, of one fret of the guitar.

hammer-on A left-hand slurring technique in which a second note is sounded by the addition of a finger after the first note is picked or plucked by the right hand.

harmonics Clear, bell-like tones produced at various points along the fingerboard of the guitar. This is done by lightly touching the string at one of those points, picking the string, and then immediately removing the touching finger. This playing technique suppresses the string's fundamental frequency in favor of harmonics.

harmony Two or more notes played simultaneously.

hybrid picking Style of guitar playing in which the guitarist uses a pick (held with the thumb and index finger) to play notes on the three low strings and uses the middle, ring, and pinky fingers to play notes on the three high strings.

interval The distance, in terms of steps and half-steps, of one note from another.

key The tonal center of a piece of music.

key signature The number of flats or sharps (if any) used in a song, which indicates the key the song is in.

major chord One of the four basic chord types, made up of the root, major third, and perfect fifth degrees of the major scale.

major scale The basic building block of music theory, the major scale begins on any note and uses the following sequence:

> root   whole step   whole step   half-step   whole step   whole step   whole step   half-step (the root again)

measure Also called a *bar*. A distinct measurement of beats, which is dictated by the time signature. The end of a measure is indicated by a vertical line running through the staff or bass-guitar tablature lines.

metronome A device used to audibly count out the tempo of music.

minor chord One of the four basic chord types, made up of the root, minor third, and perfect fifth degrees of the major scale.

modes A scale created by taking a major scale and beginning on a note other than the root and going through the steps of the scale until reaching the starting note again. There are seven modes: Ionian, Dorian, Phrygian, Lydian, Mixolydian, Aeolian, and Locrian.

music notation   A system for reading music using a staff and notes placed upon it. The location of the note on the staff determines its name, and the type of note indicates its duration.

natural sign   An accidental sign ♮ indicating to play a note with neither flats nor sharps.

note   A musical tone of a specific pitch.

nut   Notched strip of hard plastic, bone, or other material located between the neck and the headstock on the guitar's fingerboard. Along with the bridge, the nut is one of the two vibrational endpoints of each string of the guitar.

octave   An interval of eight named notes from the root note, always bearing the same name as the root note.

open tuning   Tuning the strings of the guitar so that they create an easily identifiable chord when strummed without any strings being fretted. For example, strumming the open strings of a guitar tuned to open G tuning sounds a G-major chord.

pick   Also called a plectrum. A hard, flat piece of material (usually plastic) used to strike the strings instead of a finger of the right hand.

pinch   A finger-picking technique in which the right hand plays two strings simultaneously by plucking the lower one with the thumb and the higher one with a finger.

pull-off   A left-hand slurring technique in which a second note is sounded by the removal of a finger.

quarter note   A note of one beat's duration.

quarter rest   A rest of one beat's duration.

riff   A short musical phrase, often repeated during the course of a song.

root note   The note named by a chord; C is the root note of a C-major chord.

saddle   Raised area on the guitar's bridge that supports the string. Saddles are usually made of hard plastic or bone.

sharp   An accidental sign (♯) indicating raising a note a half-step.

shuffle   A rhythm using the first and third of a set of triplets, commonly used in blues, jazz, and swing styles.

sixteenth note   A note of one quarter of a beat's duration.

sixteenth rest   A rest of one quarter of a beat's duration.

slide   A left-hand slurring technique that involves sliding a finger from one fret to another, resulting in a change of notes without picking the second note.

slur   Using a left-hand technique to articulate a note or series of notes without picking.

staff   A set of five lines used in music notation to indicate note names.

standard tuning   How the strings of a guitar are usually tuned—from low to high: E, A, D, G, B, and E.

step   The pitch difference between two notes, equal to two frets on the neck of the guitar.

straight eighths   Eighth notes that are played as even eighth notes—that is, dividing the beat perfectly in half.

swing eighths   Playing eighth notes as the first and last of a set of triplets (as opposed to straight eighths).

syncopation   Accented notes that occur at times other than those normally expected, often on the off-beats.

tablature   A system of reading music that involves six horizontal lines (indicating the strings of the guitar) and numbers (indicating which frets to play in order to sound the notes).

tempo   The speed of a song, usually indicated in beats per measure (BPM).

tie   An arched line connecting two notes of the same pitch, adding the time value of the second note to the first. For example, a whole note tied to a half note lasts for six beats.

time signature   Usually indicated by a ratio at the start of a piece of music. The time signature tells you how many beats each measure receives (the upper number of the ratio) and which type of note is designated as a single beat (the lower number).

transposing   Changing the notes (and chords) of a song from one key to another.

trill   A left-hand technique involving a rapid change from one note to the next-higher (or lower) note.

triplet   A note of a third of a beat's duration.

turnaround   A quick chord progression at the end of a song to prepare the listener for a second verse; usually ends on the V chord.

vibrato   A left-hand technique that adds a quavering quality to a note; usually used with notes of longer duration.

whole note   A note of four beats' duration.

whole note rest   A rest of four beats' duration.

Index

Numbers

3/4 time, 95
   alternate strumming, 97
   basic strumming, 96-97
   music notation, 95-96
   pulses, 99-100
   "The Streets of Laredo," 98-99
5 chords, 146-147
6/8 time, 99-100

A

A major chord, 26-27
A minor chord, 25-27
accents, 99
accidentals
   music notations, 33
   notes, 7
acoustic guitars, guitar body, 6
alternate tuning, 185, 192
alternating bass, G major chord, 69-70
Amos, Tori, 255
anatomy of guitar, 5-7
anticipation, fills, 200
arpeggios, 100-104
   finger picking, 117
   "Scarborough Fair," 288-289
articulated notes, 79-83
augmented chords, 146
augmented intervals, 144
Autry, Gene, 255

B

B7 chords, 49
Bach, Johann Sebastian, 278-280
Badrezbanian, Alan Shavarsh, 3
"The Banana Boat Song," 49
barre chords, 74, 153
   "Down by the Riverside,"
     155-157
   full, 154-155
   half, 153-154
   "Jesse James," 160-162
   "Motherless Children," 158
   moving across strings, 154
   Root 6 barre chord, 155
   slash chords, 160
   translating open-position
     chords, 158
bass, G major chord, 69-70
bass notes, alternating, 38
basslines, walking, 137-138, 251
beats
   rhythm, 29
     counting time, 41-46
     Day-O song, 47-49
     practice, 49-50
     strumming patterns, 47
     time signatures, 29-30
   shuffle rhythms, 55
     double stops, 56-57
     expanding number of notes,
       61-63
     regular eighth notes, 57-58
   sixteenth notes, 105-107
   triplets, 53
     strumming, 54
     swing rhythm, 55
"Beautiful Dreamer," 218-220

Beck, Jeff, 15
Belafonte, Harry, 49
bends, 80
blues
   fills, 204-206
   many forms, 271-272
   "Midnight Special," 207-210
   minor pentatonic scales,
     206-207
   one-man band, 267
     blue scale, 269-270
     "Complete Idiot's Blues," 270
     fills, 268
     vibrato, 268-269
   practice, 63-64
   seventh chords, 58-59
     D and D7, 59
     rhythm template, 60-61
   shuffle rhythms, 55
     double stops, 56-57
     expanding number of notes,
       61-63
     regular eighth notes, 57-58
   song structure, 267
   triplets, 53
     strumming, 54
     swing rhythm, 55
blues shuffle, 55
   double stops, 56-57
   expanding number of notes,
     61-63
   regular eighth notes, 57-58
body, guitar part, 6
"boom-chuck" technique, 36-37
Bream, Julian, 3
bridge, 6
Buckingham, Lindsey, 15
Burton, James, 243

C

C chord, 66-67
  C7 variation, 67-68
  changing between G major
    chord, 70
  walking bassline, 70-73
C7 chord, C chord variation, 67-68
call and response style, 201
capos
  locating good melody vocal
    range, 180-184
  playing, 177-179
    chord double meaning,
      179-180
    raising chords, 179
  transposing, 175-176
    concentrate on root notes,
      177
    secret codes, 176-177
Carcassi, Matteo, 117, 128
Cash, Johnny, 38, 243
Celtic music
  "The Irish Washerwoman," 293
    DADGAD, 294-296
    droning, 294
  timing, 291-292
    fingering, 292-293
    hammer-ons, 292
Celtic reels, 238
chords, 21-22
  A major, 26
  A minor, 25-26
  B7, 49
  barre, 153
    "Down by the Riverside,"
      155-157
    full, 154-155
    half, 153-154
    "Jesse James," 160-162
    "Motherless Children," 158
    moving across strings, 154
    Root 6 barre chord, 155
    slash chords, 160
    translating open-position
      chords, 158

building
  5 chord, 146-147
  adding to chords, 148
  extended chords, 149-150
  intervals, 143-144
  practice, 151-152
  seventh chords, 148-149
  slash chords, 150-151
  triads, 144-146
capos, 179-180
change, 23
  chord #2, 23-24
  chord #3, 24-25
  practice, 25
charts, 22-23
E major, 25
E minor, 23
fills, 200
jazz music, 297
  dropping notes, 298
  progressions, 298-302
  shapes, 297
melodies
  "Beautiful Dreamer," 218-220
  harmony pairs, 217-218
  practice, 220
  song anatomy, 213-214
  "Twinkle, Twinkle Little
    Star," 214-217
playing first song, 26-27
power, rock 'n' roll music, 258
progressions, 65-66
  C chord, 66-67
  C chord and C7 chord
    variation, 67-68
  changing between G major
    chord and C chord, 70
  F chord, 74-76
  G major chord, 68-70
  "Michael Row Your Boat
    Ashore," 76
  practice, 78
  walking bassline, 70-73
scales, 138-139
seventh, blues, 58-61
translating grids, 22-23

chromatic scales, 131-132
  12 notes, 133
  major, 133
  playing, 134
    closed position, 134-135
    moving around fingerboard,
      135-136
    Root 5 major scales, 136-137
  putting into chords, 138-139
  walking basslines, 137-138
cithara, 3
classical music, 275
  Bach, Johann Sebastian, 278-280
  masters teaching materials, 275
    notation, 275-276
    "Study by Giuliani," 278
classical sitting positions, 13
closed scales, 134-135
"Comfortably Numb," 233
comping, jazz music progression,
  300
"Complete Idiot's Blues," 270
Costello, Elvis, 243
counting time, 41-42
  counting by eight, 43
  counting by four, 42-43
  Day-O song, 47-49
  practice, 49-50
  skipping beats, 43-44
    missing downstrokes, 44-45
    practice, 45-46
  strumming patterns, 47
country music
  "Four Nights Drunk," 247-251
    sustained notes, 250-251
    walking basslines, 251
  "Home on the Range," 251
    A7 to D in harmony pairs,
      252
    pedal-steel guitar, 252-255
Croce, Jim, 183
crosspicking, 241-242
"The Cruel War," 126-127

D

D chord, 59
D7 chord, 59
DADGAD, "The Irish
  Washerwoman," 294-296
Darin, Bobby, 78
Day-O song, 47-49
Denver, John, 187, 243
diatonic triads, 164-166
diminished chords, 146
diminished intervals, 144
double stops, 56-57
"Down by the Riverside," 155-157
downstrokes, 42
  practice rhythms, 45-46
  skipping beats, 44-45
droning, "The Irish
  Washerwoman," 294
drop D tuning, 187
  rock music, 189
  "Tanz," 188-189

E

E major chord, 25-27
E minor chord, 21-23
  chord changes, 23
    chord #2, 23-24
    chord #3, 24-25
    practice, 25
  playing first song, 26-27
ear-training intervals, 144
eighth notes, 33
electric guitars
  alternate tunings, 186
  guitar body, 6
embellishments, 169
emotions, guitar solos, 233
extended chords, 149-150

F

F chord, 74
  C to F walking bassline, 76
  F major seventh chord, 75
  half barre, 74
F major seventh chord, 75
fake books, 220
Farlow, Tal, 220
fills, 199-200
  anticipation, 200
  blues music, 204-206, 268
  chord changes, 200
  moving minors, 206
    blues music, 206-207
    "Midnight Special," 207-210
  playing, 201
    pentatonic scale, 201-202
    rhythm variations, 204
  practice, 201, 210
finger picking
  arpeggios, 117
  Celtic music, 292-293
  folk music, 281-283
    following melody, 286
    "Greenland Whale
      Fisheries," 283
  pinching, 118-119
  selecting finger to use, 115-116
  Travis-style, 119
    pinching, 124-125
    variations on contrary
      motion, 120-123
fingerboards
  guitar solos, 226
    positions, 226-228
    shifting positions, 229
    third and fourth phrases,
      230-233
  mapping open tuning, 190
  playing scales, 135-136
fingerpicks, 243
fingers, right hand position, 15
flatpicking, 235-236

alternate picking, 237
Celtic reel, 238
strumming in tablature,
  239-240
up and down strokes, 236
flats, note accidentals, 7
flatted intervals, 144
flatted seventh chords, 149
Fleetwood Mac, 192
floating tremolo systems, 186
folk music
  finger picking, 281-283
    following melody, 286
    "Greenland Whale
      Fisheries," 283
    "Scarborough Fair," 286
      arpeggios, 288-289
      harmonics, 289-290
      natural harmonics, 290
"Four Nights Drunk," 247-251
  sustained notes, 250-251
  walking basslines, 251
fretboards, 6
fretting, notes, 18
full barres, 74, 153-155

G

G clef, 31
G major chord, 68
  alternating bass, 69-70
  changing between C chord, 70
  voicing options, 69
  walking bassline, 70-73
"The Gallows Pole," 111-112
gauge, strings, 7
genres
  blues music, 267
    many forms, 271-272
    one-man band, 267-270
    song structure, 267
  Celtic music
    "The Irish Washerwoman,"
      293-296
    timing, 291-293

classical music, 275
    Bach, Johann Sebastian,
        278-280
    masters teaching materials,
        275-278
country music
    "Four Nights Drunk,"
        247-251
    "Home on the Range,"
        251-255
folk music
    finger picking, 281-283, 286
    "Scarborough Fair," 286-290
jazz music, 297-302
pop music, 303
    changing arrangements, 303
    getting creative, 305-306, 309
    style changes, 303
rock 'n' roll music, 257
    driving song, 257-259
    strumming pace, 264
Gilmour, David, 233
Giuliani, Mauro, 275
*The Golden Age of English Lute
    Music*, 3
grace notes, 82-83
Green Day, 57
Greene, Ted, 220
"Greenland Whale Fisheries," 283
Guiliani, Mauro, 128
guitar solos, 221-222
    combining technique and
        emotions, 233
    phrasing, 222
        bend additions, 225-226
        guitar techniques, 224-225
        rhythm values, 223-224
    practice, 234
    scaling fingerboard, 226
        positions, 226-228
        shifting positions, 229
        third and fourth phrases,
            230-233
guitarra, 3

guitars
    selection, 3-4
        anatomy, 5-7
        left vs. right handed, 4
    tuning, 7
        notes, 7
        piano or keyboard, 10
        practice listening, 11
        relative, 11
        string names, 8
        using tuner, 8-10

H

Haggard, Merle, 243
half barres, 74, 153-154
half notes, 33
half rests, 107
hammer-ons, 80-82
    Celtic music, 292
    grace notes, 82-83
harmonic minor scales, 166-167
harmonics, "Scarborough Fair,"
    289-290
harmonies
    chord-melody note pairs,
        217-218
    pairs, A7 to D, 252
    song anatomy, 213
Harris, Emmylou, 243
headstock, 6
history, guitar, 3
"Home on the Range," 251
    A7 to D in harmony pairs, 252
    pedal-steel guitar, 252-255
"The House of the Rising Son,"
    101-104
hybrid picking, 242

I

"In the Pines," 264-266
instruments, guitar selection, 3-4
    anatomy, 5-7
    left vs. right handed, 4

intervals, 21, 143-144
"The Irish Washerwoman,"
    293-296
    DADGAD, 294-296
    droning, 294

J

Jagger, Mick, 78
jazz music, chords, 297
    dropping notes, 298
    melodies, 214
    progressions, 298-302
    shapes, 297
"Jesse James," 160-162
"John Barleycorn," 169-172
"Julia and John," 306-309

K

keyboards, tuning guitar, 10
keys, 163
    minor, 166
        harmonic, 166-167
        melodic, 167
    twelve signatures, 163-166
Kirby, Fred, 255
Knopfler, Mark, 15

L

"The Lakes of Pontchartrain,"
    192-197
ledger lines, 32
left hands, 16-17
    fretting notes, 18
    gripping guitar, 17-18
    guitar selection, 4
left-hand muting, 108-109
"Life During Wartime," 26
lowered tuning, rock 'n' roll music,
    264
lowered tunings, 186-187
lutes, 3

M

major pentatonic scales, 202
major scales, note intervals, 133, 143-144
major second intervals, 143
major third intervals, 143
"Make Me a Pallet," 180-184
measures, 29-30
melodic minor scales, 167
melodies
    chords
        "Beautiful Dreamer," 218-220
        harmony pairs, 217-218
        practice, 220
        song anatomy, 213-214
        "Twinkle, Twinkle Little Star," 214-217
    folk music, 286
    rock 'n' roll music, 259
metronomes, 30
"Michael Row Your Boat Ashore," 76
"Midnight Special," 207-210
minor intervals, 144
minor keys, 166
    harmonic, 166-167
    melodic, 167
minor pentatonic scales, 202
    fills, 206
        blues music, 206-207
        "Midnight Special," 207-210
minor third intervals, 144
"Minuet," 278-280
"Motherless Children," 158
Muehleisen, Maury, 183
music
    rhythm, 29
        chords in notation, 34
        counting time, 41-46
        Day-O song, 47-49
        music notation, 31-33
        note values, 33
        playing techniques, 36-40
        practice, 40, 49-50
        rhythmic notation, 35-36
        strumming patterns, 47
        tablature, 30-31
        ties, 34-35
        time signatures, 29-30
    tablature, 18-19
        practice, 20
        warming up, 19-20
music genres
    blues music, 267
        many forms, 271-272
        one-man band, 267-270
        song structure, 267
    Celtic music
        "The Irish Washerwoman," 293-296
        timing, 291-293
    classical music, 275
        Bach, Johann Sebastian, 278-280
        masters teaching materials, 275-278
    country music
        "Four Nights Drunk," 247-251
        "Home on the Range," 251-255
    folk music
        finger picking, 281-283, 286
        "Scarborough Fair," 286-290
    jazz music, 297-302
    pop music, 303
        changing arrangements, 303
        getting creative, 305-306, 309
        style changes, 303
    rock 'n' roll music, 257
        driving song, 257-259
        strumming pace, 264
music notations
    3/4 time, 95-96
    chords, 34
    classical music, 275-276
    note values, 33
    rhythm, 31-36, 108
muting, rests as rhythm, 108
    left-hand muting, 108-109
    palm muting, 109-110
    percussive stroke, 110

N

natural harmonics, "Scarborough Fair," 289-290
natural minor scales, 166
neck of guitar, 6
Nelson, Ricky, 243
notations, music
    3/4 time, 95-96
    chords, 34
    classical music, 275-276
    note values, 33
    rhythm, 31-36, 108
notes
    accidentals, music notation, 33
    chords in notation, 34
    intervals, 143-144
    root, 37, 177
    scales, blues music, 269-270
    shuffle rhythms, 55
        double stops, 56-57
        expanding number of notes, 61-63
        regular eighth notes, 57-58
    sixteenth, 105-107
    slurs, 79-83
    sustained, 250-251
    tablature, 18-19
        practice, 20
        warming up, 19-20
    triplets, 53
        strumming, 54
        swing rhythm, 55
    tuning guitars, 7
    twelve signature keys, 163-164
    values, 33

O

octaves, 149
"Oh! Susanna," 139-142
open strings, 21
open tunings, 185, 189
    chord variations, 191
    fingerboard map, 190
    Richards, Keith, 190-191

Oud Masterpieces from Armenia, Turkey and the Middle East, 3
ouds, 3

P

Paisley, Brad, 243
palm muting, 109-110
parts, guitar, 5-7
Pass, Joe, 220
pausing play, 107
  rests as rhythm, 108
    left-hand muting, 108-109
    palm muting, 109-110
    percussive stroke, 110
pedal points, 119
pedal-steel guitar, "Home on the Range," 252-255
pentatonic scales, 201-202
percussive stroke, 110
perfect intervals, 144
Petzold, Christian, 278
phrases, solos, 222
  bend additions, 225-226
  guitar techniques, 224-225
  rhythm values, 223-224
pianos, tuning guitar, 10
picking
  crosspicking, 241-242
  finger
    arpeggios, 117
    folk music, 281-283, 286
    pinching, 118-119
    selecting finger to use, 115-116
    Travis-style, 119-125
  fingerpicks, 243
  flatpicking, 235-236
    alternate picking, 237
    Celtic reel, 238
    strumming in tablature, 239-240
    up and down strokes, 236
  hybrid, 242

picks
  holding, 16
  selection, 15
pinching
  finger picking, 118-119
  Travis-style picking, 124-125
Pink Floyd, 233
playing techniques, rhythm, 36
  alternating bass notes, 38
  "boom-chuck," 36-37
  practical application, 39-40
plectrums, 15
pop music, 303
  changing arrangements, 303
  getting creative
    "Julia and John," 306, 309
    music theory, 305
  style changes
    piano quality, 303
    "The Water Is Wide," 304-305
positions, 13
  guitar solos, 226-229
  left hand, 16-17
    fretting notes, 18
    gripping guitar, 17-18
  right hand, 15
    holding a pick, 16
    pick selection, 15
    thumb and fingers, 15
  sitting, 13-14
  standing, 14
posture, 13
  left hand, 16-17
    fretting notes, 18
    gripping guitar, 17-18
  right hand, 15
    holding a pick, 16
    pick selection, 15
    thumb and fingers, 15
  sitting, 13-14
  standing, 14
power chords, rock 'n' roll music, 258
practice
  "Beautiful Dreamer," 218-220
  blues, 63-64

building chords, 151
  learning sounds, 151
  visual identification, 151-152
chord-melodies, 220
"The Cruel War," 126-127
fills, 210
"The Gallows Pole," 111-112
guitar solos, 234
"Jesse James," 160-162
"John Barleycorn," 169-172
"The Lakes of Pontchartrain," 192-197
"Make Me a Pallet," 180-184
"Michael Row Your Boat Ashore," 78
"Midnight Special," 207-210
"Motherless Children," 158
"Oh! Susanna," 139-142
putting pieces together, 167-168
rhythm, 40
speed, 243-244
strumming, 49-50
"Tanz," 188-189
Presley, Elvis, 243
progressions
  chords, 65-66
    C chord, 66-67
    C chord and C7 chord variation, 67-68
    changing between G major chord and C chord, 70
    F chord, 74-76
    G major chord, 68-70
    "Michael Row Your Boat Ashore," 76
    practice, 78
    walking bassline, 70-73
  jazz music, 298-299
    comping, 300
    solo swing, 299-300
    "Take Me Out to the Ballgame," 300-302
pull-offs, 80
pulses, 3/4 time, 99
  6/8 time, 99-100
  signatures changing, 100

Q–R

quarter notes, 33
Queen, 57

Ramones, 257
relative tuning, 11
rests, 107
    as rhythm, 108
        left-hand muting, 108-109
        palm muting, 109-110
        percussive stroke, 110
rhythm, 29
    chords in notation, 34
    counting time, 41-42
        counting by eight, 43
        counting by four, 42-43
        skipping beats, 43-46
    Day-O song, 47-49
    fills, 204
    guitar solos, 223-224
    music notation, 31-33
    note values, 33
    playing techniques, 36
        alternating bass notes, 38
        "boom-chuck," 36-37
        practical application, 39-40
    practice, 40, 49-50
    rests, 108
        left-hand muting, 108-109
        palm muting, 109-110
        percussive stroke, 110
    rhythmic notation, 35-36
    song anatomy, 213
    strumming patterns, 47
    tablature, 30-31
    ties, 34-35
    time signatures, 29-30
rhythmic notation, 35-36, 108
rhythms
    chord progressions, 65-66
        C chord, 66-67
        C chord and C7 chord
            variation, 67-68
        changing between G major
            chord and C chord, 70

F chord, 74-76
G major chord, 68-70
"Michael Row Your Boat
    Ashore," 76
practice, 78
walking bassline, 70-73
shuffle, 55
    double stops, 56-57
    expanding number of notes,
        61-63
    regular eighth notes, 57-58
swing, 55
Richards, Keith, open tuning,
    190-191
riffs, 199-200
    anticipation, 200
    chord changes, 200
    practice, 201
right hands, 15
    guitar selection, 4
    holding a pick, 16
    pick selection, 15
    thumb and fingers, 15
rock music, drop D tuning, 189
rock 'n' roll music, 257
    driving song, 257-258
        melody, 259
        power chords, 258
        strumming pace, 264
Rogers, Roy, 255
Rolling Stones, 257
Root 5 major scales, 136-137
Root 6 barre chords, 155
Root 6 major scales, 136
root notes, 37, 177

S

saddle, 6
scales, 131-132
    12 notes, 133
    guitar solos, 226
        positions, 226-228
        shifting positions, 229
        third and fourth phrases,
            230-233

harmonic minor, 166-167
major, 133, 143-144
melodic minor, 167
notes, blues music, 269-270
pentatonic, 201-202
playing, 134
    closed position, 134-135
    moving around fingerboard,
        135-136
    Root 5 major scales, 136-137
    putting into chords, 138-139
    walking basslines, 137-138
"Scarborough Fair," 286
    arpeggios, 288-289
    harmonics, 289-290
    natural harmonics, 290
seventh chords, 148-149
    blues, 58-59
        D and D7, 59
        rhythm template, 60-61
sharps, note accidentals, 7
shuffle rhythms, 55
    double stops, 56-57
    expanding number of notes,
        61-63
    regular eighth notes, 57-58
signatures, keys, 164
sitting position, 13-14
sixteenth notes, 105-107
slash chords, 150-151, 160, 172
slides, 80
slurs, 79-83
sock puppet approach, strumming,
    41-42
    counting by eight, 43
    counting by four, 42-43
    skipping beats, 43-46
solos, 221-222
    combining technique and
        emotions, 233
    phrasing, 222
        bend additions, 225-226
        guitar techniques, 224-225
        rhythm values, 223-224
    practice, 234

scaling fingerboard, 226
   positions, 226-228
   shifting positions, 229
   third and fourth phrases,
     230-233
songs
   3/4 time, 95
     alternate strumming, 97
     basic strumming, 96-97
     music notation, 95-96
     pulses, 99-100
     "The Streets of Laredo,"
      98-99
   chord-melodies, 213
     arrangements, 213-214
     "Beautiful Dreamer," 218-220
     harmony pairs, 217-218
     "Twinkle, Twinkle Little
      Star," 214-217
   rhythm, 29
     chords in notation, 34
     counting time, 41-46
     Day-O song, 47-49
     music notation, 31-33
     note values, 33
     playing techniques, 36-40
     practice, 40, 49-50
     rhythmic notation, 35-36
     strumming patterns, 47
     tablature, 30-31
     ties, 34-35
     time signatures, 29-30
   structure, blues music, 267
Sor, Fernando, 128
speed
   crosspicking, 241-242
   fingerpicks, 243
   flatpicking, 235-236
     alternate picking, 237
     Celtic reel, 238
     up and down strokes, 236
   hybrid picking, 242
   practice, 243-244
   strumming in tablature, 239-240
standard tuning, 185. *See also*
  tuning guitars, 7
standing position, 14

stop playing, 107
   rests as rhythm, 108
     left-hand muting, 108-109
     palm muting, 109-110
     percussive stroke, 110
straps, 17
"The Streets of Laredo," 98-99
strings
   barre chords, 154
   gauge, 7
   guitar parts, 6
   naming, 8
   tension, 7
   tuning guitars, 7-8
strumming
   3/4 time, 96-97
   arpeggios, 100-104
   counting time, 41-42
     counting by eight, 43
     counting by four, 42-43
     skipping beats, 43-46
   patterns, 47
   practice, 49-50
   rock 'n' roll music, 264
   sixteenth notes, 105-107
   tablature clues, 239-240
   triplets, 54
"Study by Giuliani," 278
substitutions, 169
suspended chords, 147
sustained notes, 250-251
swing rhythms, 55-57

T

tablature, 18-19
   chords, 34
   practice, 20
   rests, 108
   rhythm, 30-31
   strumming clues, 239-240
   warming up, 19-20
"Take Me Out to the Ballgame,"
  300-302
Talking Heads, "Life During
  Wartime," 26

"Tanz," 188-189
techniques, playing, 36
   alternating bass notes, 38
   "boom-chuck," 36-37
   practical application, 39-40
tempo, 30
tension, strings, 7
thumb, right hand position, 15
ties, rhythm, 34-35
time, strumming, 41-42
   counting by eight, 43
   counting by four, 42-43
   patterns, 47
   skipping beats, 43-46
time signatures, 29-30
timing
   3/4 time, 95
     alternate strumming, 97
     basic strumming, 96-97
     music notation, 95-96
     pulses, 99-100
     "The Streets of Laredo,"
      98-99
   Celtic music, 291-292
     fingering, 292-293
     hammer-ons, 292
transposing, 175-176
   concentrate on root notes, 177
   secret codes, 176-177
Travis, Merle, 119
Travis-style picking, 119
   pinching, 124-125
   variations on contrary motion,
     120-123
treble clef, 31
tremolo systems, 186
triads, building chords, 144-145
   5 chord, 146-147
   four basic, 145-146
triplets, 53
   strumming, 54
   swing rhythm, 55
tuners, 8-10
tuning guitars, 7
   alternates, 185, 192
   drop D, 187
     rock music, 189
     "Tanz," 188-189

"The Lakes of Pontchartrain,"
    192-197
lowered, 186-187, 264
mechanisms, 6
notes, 7
open, 185, 189
    chord variation, 191
    fingerboard map, 190
    Richards, Keith, 190-191
pegs, 6
piano or keyboard, 10
practice listening, 11
relative, 11
standard, 185
string names, 8
using tuner, 8-10
turnarounds, 267
twelve signature keys, 163-166
"Twinkle, Twinkle Little Star,"
    214-217
    chord-melodies, 215-216
    finger-picking technique,
        216-217

U-V

upstrokes, 42

vibrato, blues music, 268-269
vihuela, 3
voicing, 59, 69

W-X-Y-Z

"Wabash Cannonball," 222
walking bassline
    adding D or D7 chord, 72-73
    switching between G and C
        chord, 70-71
walking basslines, 137-138, 251
"The Water Is Wide," 304-305
"Whiskey in the Jar," 259-263
whole notes, 33
whole rests, 107

Williams, Hank, 38
Williams, Mason, 275

Young, Neil, 187, 192, 255

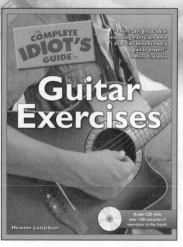

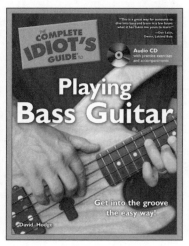
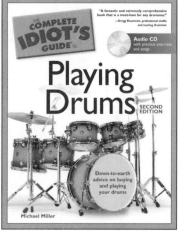
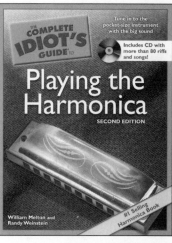
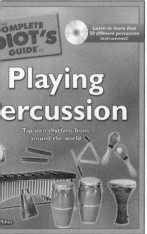
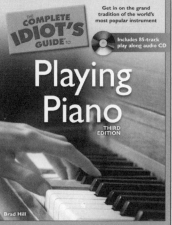